Workbook
LOW INTERMEDIATE

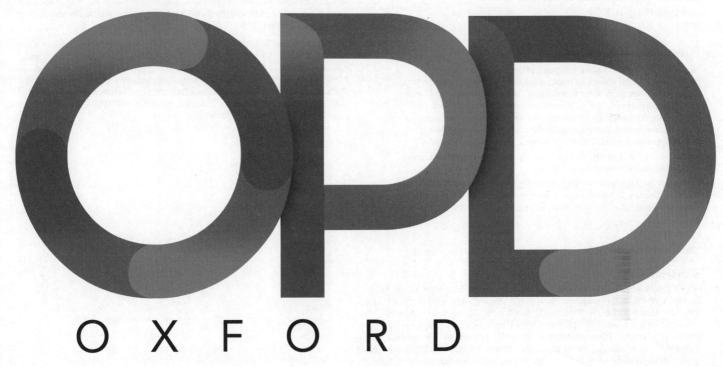

OXFORD

PICTURE

DICTIONARY

Marjorie Fuchs

Margaret Bonner

OXFORD
UNIVERSITY PRESS

198 Madison Avenue
New York, NY 10016 USA

Great Clarendon Street, Oxford, ox2 6DP, United Kingdom

Oxford University Press is a department of the University of Oxford.
It furthers the University's objective of excellence in research, scholarship,
and education by publishing worldwide. Oxford is a registered trade
mark of Oxford University Press in the UK and in certain other countries

ISBN: 978-0-19-4511230

Printed in China

This book is printed on paper from certified and well-managed sources

ACKNOWLEDGMENTS

Illustrations by: Argosy: 206; Barb Bastian: 15, 160; Kenneth Batelman: 13, 46; John
Batten: 3, 88-89; Kathy Baxendale: 32, 108, 120, 207, 247; Annie Bisset: 12, 26, 125,
146, 187; Arlene Boehm: 70, 71; Kevin Brown/Top Dog Studio: 7, 244; Dominic
Bugatto/Three-in-a-Box: 100, 116; Carlos Castellanos: 58, 62, 251; Andrea Champlin:
25, 91, 247; Dominik D'Andrea: 97; Mona Daly/Mendola Art: 90, 106; Jim Delapine:
241; Bill Dickson/Contact Jupiter: 10, 42; Jody Emery: 67, 133, 196, 252; Jim Fanning/
Ravenhill Represents: 66, 81; Mike Gardner: 145, 185; Glenn Gustafson: 76, 126;
Betsy Hayes: 143; Kevin Hopgood: 2, 43, 197; Infomen/Debut Art: 51, 54, 74, 117,
154, 175, 227, 250; Emma Jacob/Lemonade: 33, 94; Janos Jantner/Beehive
Illustration: 79, 152, 177, 195, 223, 262; Ken Joudrey/Munro Campagna: 68; Mike
Kasun/Munro Campagna: 74, 102, 162, 201; Keithley Associates: 157, 254; John
Kurtz: 210; Deb Lofaso: 25, 62, 113, 118, 145, 156, 178; Denis Luzuriaga: 34, 47;
Scott MacNeill: 19, 66, 75, 114, 242; Adrian Mateescu/The Studio: 28, 55, 248; Karen
Minot: 118, 159, 192, 231; Paul Mirocha/The Wiley Group: 217, 222; Terry Pazcko:
47, 53, 83, 221; Pronk&Associates: 4, 5, 6, 8, 9, 11, 14, 16, 17, 18, 19, 20, 21, 27, 28,
29, 33, 35, 36, 37, 38, 40-41, 49, 50, 52, 57, 59, 65, 68, 71, 72-73, 77, 78, 82, 83, 84,
85, 92, 94, 95, 97, 101, 105, 106, 110, 115, 119, 130, 134, 148-149, 157, 158, 164,
165, 169, 183, 185, 193, 197, 204, 205, 208, 216, 221, 225, 229, 233, 241, 245; Mark
Reidy/Munro Campagna: 136 (stamp); Robert Roper/Wilkinson Design Studio:
23, 60; Marcos Schaaf/NB Illustration: 76, 93; Phil Scheuer: 171, 224, 258; Robert
Schuster: 24, 34, 48, 69, 155, 233 (icons), 235; Ben Shannon: 146, 181; Geoffrey Paul
Smith: 194, 239; Sam Tomasello: 63, 186; Samuel Velasco (5W Infographics): 26,
39, 79, 147, 168, 174, 191, 213, 240, 244, 261; Anna Veltfort: 131, 264; Ralph Voltz/
Deborah Wolfe: 158, 243, 255; William Waitzman: 18, 167, 179; Mark Watkinson/
Illustrationweb.com: 173, 234, 240; Simon Williams/Illustrationweb.com: 45;
Graeme Wilson/Graham-Cameron Illustration: 56, 62, 107, 287, 288; Tracey Wood/
Reactor Art: 105.

Chapter icons: Anna Sereda

*The publisher would like to thank the following for their kind permission to reproduce
photographs:* p.8 OUP/Dennis Kitchen Studio, Inc (all); p.26 OUP/Image Source,
OUP/Shutterstock/oliveromg, OUP/Shutterstock/Jack Z Young; p.32 Yuri_Arcurs/
Getty Images; p.40 Leonard McCombe/Life Magazine/The LIFE Images Collection/
Getty Images; p.48 Samuel Borges Photography/Shutterstock; p.49 karamysh/
Shutterstock, romakoma/Shutterstock, Iriana Shiyan/Shutterstock; p.50 Nikola
Spasenoski/Alamy Stock Photo; p.51 UpperCut Images/Alamy Stock Photo, ML
Harris/Getty Images; p.57 Blend Images/Superstock; p.72 g-stockstudio/Shutterstock;
p.80 BJI/Blue Jean Images/Getty Images; p.84 Jeff Greenberg/AGE fotostock; p.108
Rick Gomez/Blend Images/Superstock; p.117 OUP/Photodisc/Jacqueline Veissid, OUP/
Shutterstock/Johan Larson; p.120 Superstock/age fotostock; p.122 Lane Oatey/
Blue Jean Images/Getty Images; p.129 Barry Winiker/Getty Images, Richard I'Anson/
Getty Images; p.135 Andersen Ross/Getty Images; p.138 Rob Lewine/Getty Images;
p.142 Fuse/Getty Images, 1000 Words/Shutterstock, imageBROKER/Superstock,
Robert Nicholas/Getty Images, OUP/Blend Images/David Buffington; p.156 Exotica/
Superstock; p.163 szefei/Shutterstock, Blend Images - Jose Luis Pelaez Inc/Getty
Images; p.172 OUP/Shutterstock/Venus Angel; p.177 PHOVOIR/Alamy Stock Photo;
p.187 Mike Grandmaison/Getty Images; p.192 age fotostock/Superstock; p.193 Peter
Adams/AGE fotostock; p.209 DEA/A. DAGLI ORTI/De Agostini/Getty Images, PRISMA
ARCHIVO/Alamy Stock Photo, Universal History Archive/UIG via Getty Images,
Photos 12/Alamy Stock Photo, Arcaid Images/Alamy Stock Photo; p.214 OUP/Graphi-
Ogre, Robert Harding/Masterfile; p.219 Audrey Snider-Bell/Shutterstock; p.220 Eric
Farrelly/age fotostock/Superstock, Giulio Ercolani/Alamy Stock Photo; p.227 Juice
Images/Alamy Stock Photo, Corbis/Superstock, MBI/Alamy Stock Photo, ZouZou/
Shutterstock, Frank Sanchez/Alamy Stock Photo; p.232 AlaskaStock/Masterfile;
p.237 OUP/Ingram, titov dmitriy/Shutterstock; p.241 Hero Images/Superstock;
p.249 dave stamboulis/Alamy Stock Photo, Eisenstaedt/The LIFE Picture Collection/
Getty Images, Blend Images/Superstock, Asia Images/Masterfile; p.257 Westend61/
Superstock, Rgtimeline/Shutterstock, Blend Images/Superstock, Norman Pogson/
Alamy Stock Photo.

*The publisher would like to thank the following for their permission to reproduce copyrighted
material:* 136–137: USPS Corporate Signature, Priority Mail, Express Mail, Media
Mail, Certified Mail, Ready Post, Airmail, Parcel Post, Letter Carrier Uniform, Postal
Clerk Uniform, Flag and Statue of Liberty, Postmark, Post Office Box, Automated
Postal Center, Parcel Drop Box, Round Top Collection Mailbox are trademarks of
the United States Postal Service and are used with permission. 210: Microsoft icons
reprinted by permission of Microsoft.

Welcome to the Oxford Picture Dictionary Third Edition Workbooks

The *Low Beginning, High Beginning,* and *Low Intermediate Workbooks* that accompany *The Oxford Picture Dictionary* have been designed to provide meaningful and enjoyable practice of the vocabulary that students are learning. These workbooks supply high-interest contexts and real information for enrichment and self-expression.

The Oxford Picture Dictionary Third Edition provides unparalleled support for vocabulary teaching and language development.

- New and expanded topics including job search, career planning, and digital literacy prepare students to meet the requirements of their daily lives.

- Updated activities prepare students for work, academic study, and citizenship.

- Oxford 3000 vocabulary ensures students learn the most useful and important words.

Page-for-page correlation with the Dictionary

The *Workbook* pages conveniently correspond to the pages of the *Picture Dictionary*. For example, if you are working on page 50 in the *Dictionary*, the activities for this topic, Apartments, will be found on page 50 in all three *Picture Dictionary Workbooks*.

Consistent easy-to-use format

All topics in the *Low Intermediate Workbook* follow the same easy-to-use format. Exercise 1 is always a "look in your dictionary" activity where students are asked to complete a task while looking in their *Picture Dictionary*. The tasks include judging statements true or false, correcting false statements, completing charts and forms, categorizing, odd one out, and pronoun reference activities where students replace pronouns with the vocabulary items they refer to.

Following this activity are one or more content-rich contextualized exercises, including multiple choice, quizzes and tests, describing picture differences, and the completion of forms, reports, letters, articles, and stories. These exercises often feature graphs and charts with real data for students to work with as they practice the new vocabulary. Many topics include a personalization exercise that asks "What about you?" where students can use the

new vocabulary to give information about their own lives or to express their opinions.

The final exercise for each topic is a Challenge which can be assigned to students for additional work in class or as homework. Challenge activities provide higher-level speaking and writing practice, and for some topics will require students to interview classmates, conduct surveys, or find information outside of class by looking in the newspaper, for example, or online.

Each of the 12 units ends with Another Look, a review which allows students to practice vocabulary from all the topics of a unit in a game or puzzle-like activity, such as picture comparisons, "What's wrong with this picture?" activities, photo essays, word maps, word searches, and crossword puzzles. These activities are at the back of the *Low Intermediate Workbook* on pages 248–259.

Throughout the *Workbook*, vocabulary is carefully controlled and recycled. Students should, however, be encouraged to use their *Picture Dictionaries* to look up words they do not recall, or, if they are doing topics out of sequence, may not yet have learned. *The Oxford Picture Dictionary Workbooks* can be used in the classroom or at home for self-study.

Acknowledgments

The publisher and author would like to acknowledge the following individuals for their invaluable feedback during the development of this workbook:

Patricia S. Bell, Lake Technical County ESOL, FL; Patricia Castro, Harvest English Institute, NJ; Druci Diaz, CARIBE Program and TBT, FL; Jill Gluck, Hollywood Community Adult School, CA; Frances Hardenbergh, Southside Programs for Adult and Continuing Ed, VA; Mercedes Hern, Tampa, FL; (Katie) Mary C. Hurter, North Harris College, TX; Karen Kipke, Antioch Freshman Academy, TN; Ivanna Mann-Thrower, Charlotte Mecklenburg Schools, NC; Holley Mayville, Charlotte Mecklenburg Schools, NC; Jonetta Myles, Salem High School, GA; Kathleen Reynolds, Albany Park Community Center, IL; Jan Salerno, Kennedy-San Fernando CAS, CA; Jenni Santamaria, ABC Adult School, CA; Geraldyne Scott, Truman College/ Lakeview Learning Center, IL; Sharada Sekar, Antioch Freshman Academy, TN; Terry Shearer, Region IV ESC, TX; Melissa Singler, Cape Fear Community College, NC; Cynthia Wiseman, Wiseman Language Consultants, NY

Table of Contents

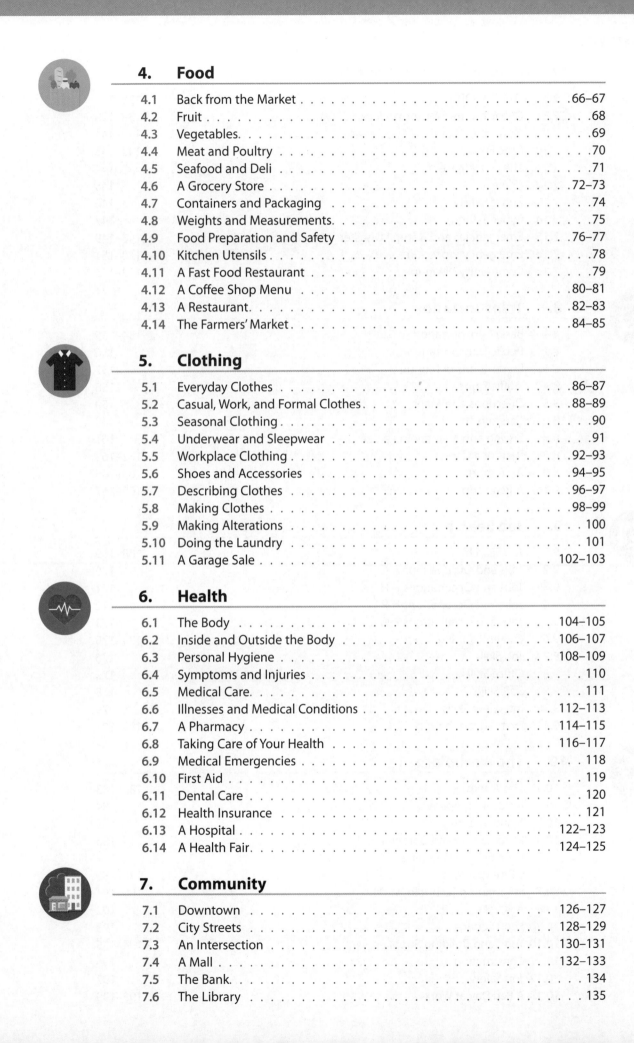

Contents

11. Academic Study

12. Recreation

Meeting and Greeting

1. **Look at pages 2 and 3 in your dictionary. How many people are . . . ? Write the number.**

   _4_ **a.** saying "Hello"

   ___ **b.** hugging

   ___ **c.** smiling

   ___ **d.** waving

   ___ **e.** asking "How are you?"

   ___ **f.** introducing themselves

   ___ **g.** introducing a friend

   ___ **h.** kissing

   ___ **i.** bowing

   ___ **j.** shaking hands

   ___ **k.** saying "Goodbye"

   ___ **l.** greeting people

2. **Look at the pictures. *True* or *False*?**

   a. Picture 1: Eric says "Hello" to Ana. _____false_____

   b. Picture 1: Lisa and Ana smile. _____

   c. Picture 1: Lisa and Ana kiss. _____

   d. Picture 2: Eric introduces himself. _____

   e. Picture 2: Eric smiles. _____

   f. Picture 3: Ana and Eric bow. _____

   g. Picture 4: Eric says "Goodbye." _____

   h. Picture 4: Ana waves goodbye. _____

2

3. **Match. Then write what they are doing. You can use your dictionary for help.**

_4_ **a.** Hi, I'm Mario. **1.** Fine, thanks. _____

____ **b.** Bye. **2.** Goodbye. _____

____ **c.** How are you? **3.** Hi. _____

____ **d.** Carlo, this is Beata. **4.** Hi, I'm Olga. _introducing themselves_

____ **e.** Hello. **5.** Nice to meet you. _____

4. **Circle the words to complete the sentences.**

DIFFERENT GREETINGS
People from different countries (greet) / meet in different ways.
a.

In some countries, people bow / kiss.
b.

In some countries people

wave / shake hands.
c.

In other countries people hug / wave,
d.

and sometimes good friends hug / kiss.
e.

Sometimes people just

smile / wave and say,
f.

"Goodbye" / "Hello."
g.

b.

c.

d.

Hello.

e.

f., g.

5. **What about you? How do you greet people? Check (✓) the columns.**

	Bow	Shake Hands	Kiss	Hug	Say, "Hello"
a good friend (woman)					
a family member (man)					
a classmate (man)					

CHALLENGE Look at Exercise 2. Write the story. Begin: _Eric and Lisa are in school. Lisa sees Ana . . ._

Personal Information

1. **Look at the form in Exercise 2. Match the information with its number on the form. Write the number.**

    a. January 15, 1980 _14_

    b. *John Zakarovsky* ____

    c. 000-22-7982 ____

    d. Zakarovsky ____

    e. 210 Parker Road ____

    f. 94610 ____

2. **Circle four more mistakes on Ann Brown's registration form.**

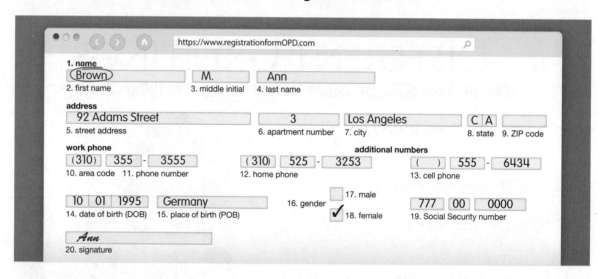

3. **What about you? Fill out the form with your own information.**

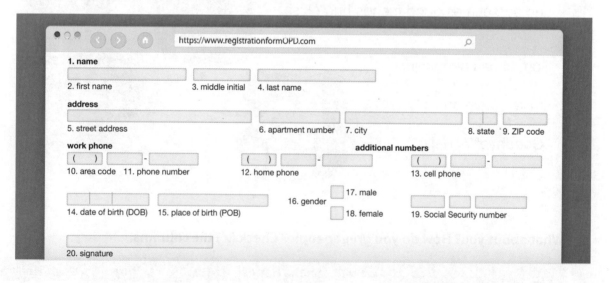

CHALLENGE Describe the mistakes in Exercise 2. **Example:** *In number 2, she wrote her last name in the first name text box.*

1. **Look at page 5 in your dictionary. Complete the notes with the job titles.**

Sunnydale School **NEWSLETTER**

September / October 2018

Sunnydale STAFF NOTES

a. Welcome, all. It's going to be a great year! *Maria Gomez,* _____ *Principal*

b. Seniors—Let's talk about college soon. *Rita Cheng,* _____

c. If you're late, come to the office to sign in. *Miki Kato,* _____

d. Our class will visit historic places near school. *Doug Tran,* _____

e. Meet me at the track for running practice. *Sam Powell,* _____

2. **Look at the list of events. Write the names of the places. Use the words in the box.**

computer lab   ~~library~~   gym   main office   cafeteria   auditorium

DATE	TIME	EVENT	PLACE
a. Sept. 24	2:00 p.m.	Reading Club	*library*
b. Oct. 1	12:00–1:00	Pizza Lunch	
c. Oct. 15	7:00 p.m.	Concert: Sunnydale Chorus	
d. Oct. 23	2:30 p.m.	Learn Internet Safety	
e. Oct. 25	all day	Registration for Senior Class Trip	
f. Oct. 30	4:30 p.m.	Girls Basketball Practice	

3. **Make words with the scrambled letters.**

SCHOOL SCRAMBLE

a. rcakt _t_ _r_ _a_ (c) _k_

b. lacsmoors _____

c. erstmoros _____

d. lalhyaw _____

Make a new word with the circled letters: _____

CHALLENGE Draw a map of your school. Label the places.

1. **Look at page 6 in your dictionary.** *True* **or** *False*? **Correct the** <u>underlined</u> **words in the false sentences.**

        A student

    a. **Picture A:** ~~The teacher~~ is raising his hand.   *false*

    b. **Picture B:** The teacher is listening to <u>the student</u>.   _____

    c. **Picture C:** The student is using <u>headphones</u>.   _____

    d. **Picture G:** The student is opening his <u>dictionary</u>.   _____

    e. **Picture I:** The student is picking up a <u>book</u>.   _____

    f. **Picture J:** The student is <u>picking up</u> a pencil.   _____

2. **Circle the words to complete the instructions.**

Test Instructions

Tomorrow is our first test. Please bring a <u>pen</u> / (pencil) with an eraser.
                                                 a.

When you come into the classroom, please <u>sit down</u> / <u>stand up</u> at your
                                            b.

<u>desks</u> / <u>LCD projectors</u>. <u>Close</u> / <u>Open</u> your test books, <u>pick up</u> / <u>put down</u>
     c.   **d.**   **e.**

your pencils, and begin the test. If you have a question for me,

<u>listen to a recording</u> / <u>raise your hand</u> and ask. Please do not talk to other
                f.

<u>students</u> / <u>teachers</u> during the test. When you are finished,
      g.

<u>pick up</u> / <u>put down</u> your pencils, and bring your tests to me. Good luck!
      h.

3. **Cross out the word that doesn't belong.**

    a. chalk   ~~headphones~~   pen   highlighter

    b. bookcase   chair   clock   desk

    c. dry erase marker   3-ring binder   workbook   spiral notebook

    d. learner's dictionary   picture dictionary   notebook paper   textbook

    e. chalkboard   marker   screen   whiteboard

    f. LCD projector   computer   document camera   bulletin board

4. **Look at the picture. Complete the classroom inventory.**

Classroom Inventory—Room 304

	NUMBER	ITEMS		NUMBER	ITEMS
a.	2	bookcases	**g.**		clocks
b.	0	bulletin boards	**h.**		computers
c.		LCD projector	**i.**	19	
d.	20		**j.**		markers
e.	1		**k.**	3	
f.		chalkboard erasers	**l.**		screen

5. **What about you? Write about items that are in your classroom. Use your own paper.**

Example: *There are four bookcases. There aren't any bulletin boards.*

[CHALLENGE] Describe the ideal classroom. What does it have? How many of each item?

1. **Look at page 8 in your dictionary. What are the students using to . . . ?**
   Check (✓) the correct box or boxes.

	Textbook	Dictionary	Notebook
a. check pronunciation	☐	✓	☐
b. copy a word	☐	☐	☐
c. draw a picture	☐	☐	☐
d. look up a word	☐	☐	☐
e. share a book	☐	☐	☐

2. **Fill in the blanks to complete the instructions for the test. Then take the test.**

Review Test

1. ___Circle___ the words to complete the questions.
   a. (What)/ Who is your name?   b. When / Where do you live?

2. _____ the word that does not belong.
   a. coach   principal   ~~marker~~   teacher
   b. pen   chalk   computer   pencil

3. _____ the words.
   _3_ a. Check   1. a sentence.
   ____ b. Help   2. a classmate.
   ____ c. Dictate   3. the pronunciation.

4. _____ the blanks.
   Put ___away___ your books and _____ a piece of paper.
       a.   b.

5. _____ the words.
   a. n a t r s t a l e ___translate___   b. s c u d s i s _____

6. _____ the pictures.

   a. ___pencil___   b. _____

3. Circle the words to complete the article.

There are many different ways to learn. Here are just a few.

* "Word-smart"	students like to dictate / (read) books and copy / cross out information a. b. in their notebooks.

* "Picture-smart"	students like to check / draw pictures. They also find it helpful to
	                              c.
	ask / copy new words.
	    d.

* "People-smart"	students love to ask / work with a partner or in a group. They like to
	                          e.
	brainstorm / translate solutions. They often help / share their classmates.
	          f. g.

* "Feelings-smart"	students like to discuss / translate problems and put away / share their h. i. feelings with their classmates.

In which ways are you smart? Find your style, and make learning fun!

4. **What about you? What helps you learn? For each activity, check (✓) the column that describes your learning style.**

Activity	Helps me a lot	Helps me some	Helps me a little	Doesn't help me
Looking up words				
Copying words				
Translating words				
Helping classmates				
Asking questions				
Reading definitions				
Discussing problems				
Dictating sentences				
Working in groups				
Drawing pictures				
Other: _____				

CHALLENGE Interview someone about his or her learning style. Use the ideas in the questionnaire.
Write a paragraph about what you learn.

1. **Look at page 10 in your dictionary. *True* or *False*? Correct the <u>underlined</u> words in the false sentences.**

     at home
     a. **Picture D:** The student is studying ~~in school~~.   _____*false*_____

     b. **Picture E and Number 4:** The student's test grade (78%) is <u>C</u>.   _____

     c. **Picture G and Number 4:** The student's test grade (96%) is <u>B</u>.   _____

     d. **Picture J:** The student is working <u>in a group</u>.   _____

2. **Match.**

     _3_   a. set a goal   **1.** "Oh. That's not right. The answer is 4c."

     ___   b. hand in a test   **2.** "Last time I got a C. This time I got a B!"

     ___   c. make progress   **3.** "I want to read the newspaper in English."

     ___   d. correct a mistake   **4.** "Here you are, Mr. Smith."

3. **Complete the paragraph. Use the words in the box.**

requested	bubbled in	checked	corrected	got	handed in
participated	~~passed~~	set	studied	took	

Carlos is a student. He _____*passed*_____ his first test, but his
                                   a.

grade was only a D. Carlos _____ a goal: He wanted
                                   b.

to get better grades. Before his next test, he _____
                                       c.

at home for several days, and he _____ help in
                                d.

class when he didn't understand something. He also

_____ better notes and _____ more
        e.   **f.**

in class discussions. During the test, Carlos carefully _____ the answers with his
                                                       g.

pencil. Then, before he _____ his answer sheet to the teacher,
                              h.

he _____ his answers and _____ one or two mistakes. Yesterday
       i.   **j.**

Carlos got his test back. He _____ a good grade—a B! Carlos was happy.
                               k.

CHALLENGE   Make a list of ways to succeed in school. Compare your list with a classmate's list.

10

1. **Look at page 11 in your dictionary. Answer the questions.**

   a. What time do the students enter the classroom? <u>   6:55   </u>

   b. Who turns on the lights? _____

   c. How many students are taking a break? _____

   d. Which room number does the student deliver the books to? _____

   e. What time do the students leave class? _____

2. **Complete the student's composition. Use the correct form of the words in the box.**

buy	carry	drink	have	go back
leave	~~run~~	take	turn off	walk

My Day at School

I go to school every Tuesday and Thursday after work. Sometimes I

_____<u>run</u>_____ to class. I don't want to come late! When I have more time,
   a.

I _____. I like it better that way because I always _____
   b.   **c.**

a lot of things—my textbook, a dictionary, and a 3-ring binder. Class

meets for two hours, and we always _____ a fifteen-minute break.
                                      d.

I usually _____ a snack in the cafeteria. I also _____ a
            e.   **f.**

cup of coffee while I _____ a conversation with some of my
                        g.

classmates. After the break, we _____ to class. At 8:00 p.m., the
                                  h.

teacher _____ the lights and we all _____ the classroom
          i.   **j.**

and go home.

CHALLENGE   Write about a day at your school.

1. Look at page 12 in your dictionary. Match.

_4_ **a.** start a conversation

____ **b.** explain something

____ **c.** disagree

____ **d.** decline an invitation

____ **e.** check your understanding

____ **f.** refuse an offer

1. "Sorry. I'm busy Friday night."

2. "You're wrong! It's not bad. It's good!"

3. "Then, sign your name here."

4. "Tell me about your class."

5. "No, thanks."

6. "Now?"

2. Read part of a story. Match each numbered sentence with its description below.

"Ouch!" Nikki cried, as something hard fell on her foot. "I'm really sorry. My
<u>   </u>
1.
science book fell out of my locker," said Ben. He picked it up. "That's OK," said Nikki
<u>   </u>
2.
as she looked at the handsome face. "I'm just glad it wasn't that big dictionary!"

"My name's Ben. <u>Are you a new</u>
3.
<u>student here?</u>"

"Yes, I'm Nikki. Nikki Lewis."

"Oh! I heard your piano concert last week. <u>You were great!</u>"
4.
"<u>Oh, thanks!</u> I'm playing again Friday
5.
night. <u>Would you like to come?</u>"
6.
"<u>Sure!</u> Where is it?" Ben asked.
7.
"I'll give you the address," said Nikki.

"Thanks. I'm glad we met, Nikki."

"<u>Me, too.</u> See you soon, Ben!"
8.

a. ____ Ben started a conversation.

b. ____ Ben accepted an invitation.

c. _1_ Ben apologized.

d. ____ Nikki agreed with Ben.

e. ____ Nikki invited Ben.

f. ____ Nikki accepted an apology.

g. ____ Ben complimented Nikki.

h. ____ Nikki thanked Ben.

CHALLENGE Choose an item in your dictionary (for example, _making small talk_). Make a list of ways to do this. Compare your list with a classmate's. **Example:** _What do you think of this weather?_

1. **Look at page 13 in your dictionary. Label the weather symbols.**

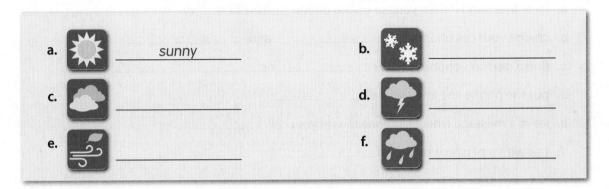

a. _sunny_

b. _____

c. _____

d. _____

e. _____

f. _____

2. **Look at the weather map. Write reports for six cities. Use your own paper.**

Example: *It's windy and very cold in Chicago, with temperatures in the 20s.*

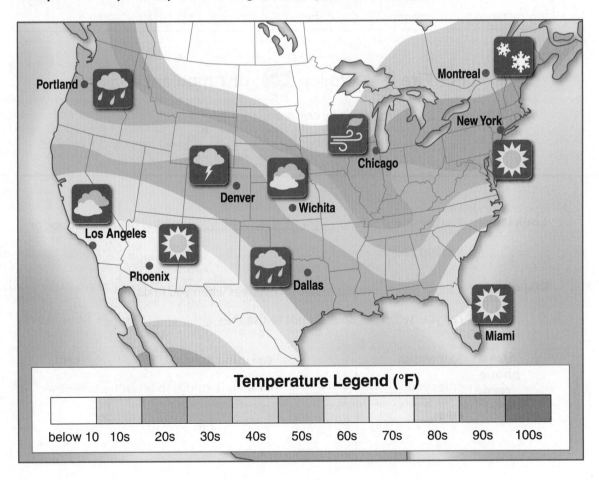

Portland

Montreal

Chicago

New York

Denver

Wichita

Los Angeles

Phoenix

Dallas

Miami

Temperature Legend (°F)

| below 10 | 10s | 20s | 30s | 40s | 50s | 60s | 70s | 80s | 90s | 100s |

3. **What about you? Write today's weather report for your city. Use Exercise 2 as an example.**

[CHALLENGE] Look at page 260 in this book. Follow the instructions.

1. **Look at pages 14 and 15 in your dictionary. What do you need to . . . ?**

   a. have free hands when you are on the phone ___*headset*___ or _____

   b. charge your cell phone _____ and _____

   c. find a person's phone number _____ or _____

   d. put the phone line into the wall _____

   e. leave a message when someone misses your call _____ or _____

   f. talk with a person who is deaf _____

2. **Complete this information from a phone book. Use the words and number in the box.**

access	phone	directory assistance	~~emergency~~	state
give	hang up	international	local	stay
long-distance	operator	code	911	

   For Fire , Police , or Ambulance

   To make an ___emergency___ call, dial: _____ .
   a.   b.
   _____ the emergency, _____ your name, and, if possible,
   c.   d.
   _____ on the line. Don't _____!
   e.   f.

   Look it up! You can avoid calls to _____ by using the phone book or
   g.
   looking online.

   Dial direct. Calling another city or state? It costs less when you make a _____
   h.
   call yourself. If possible, try not to use the _____ .
   i.

   Use a phone card. To make an _____ call using a _____ card,
   j.   k.
   enter your _____ number. Then dial the country code, the
   l.
   area _____, and the _____ number.
   m.   n.

3. **Look at Linda Lopez's phone bill. Answer the questions.**

rtr	**Bill Summary** October 8–November 8, 2018
Customer ID 505-555-6090	Linda Lopez 1212 Marble Lane Roswell, NM 88203

Charges for Oct 8 – Nov 8	$53.00
Other	$7.23
Taxes	$3.41
Total Charges	**$63.64**

a. Who is Linda's carrier?   *rtr*

b. What is the billing period for this bill? _____

c. What are her monthly charges? _____

d. How much will she pay in additional charges? _____

e. What is Linda's phone number? _____

f. What is Linda's area code? _____

4. **What about you? How often did you use the telephone last week? Answer the questions. How many times did you . . . ?**

a. make or receive an international call ____

b. miss a call ____

c. make an Internet phone call ____

d. access data on a smartphone ____

e. leave a voice mail message ____

f. use an automated phone system ____

g. have a weak cell phone signal ____

h. receive a text message ____

CHALLENGE Look at page 260 in this book. Follow the instructions.

1. **Look at the Table of Contents <u>in the beginning</u> of your dictionary. Write the numbers.**

   a. On what page does Unit 1 begin? __2__

   b. On what page does it end? ____

   c. How many pages are in the Table of Contents? ____

   d. The first unit of your dictionary is called *Everyday Language*.
      What is the name of the eleventh unit? _____

   e. How many pages are in the eighth unit? ____

2. **Look at the math test. Circle all the mistakes. Then give the test a percent grade (each question = five points).**

   ┌───┐

   Baker High School

   Grade: _____ %
   Student's Name: _____*Ryan Jones*_____

   1. What's next?

   a. eleven, twelve, thirteen, _____*fourteen*_____

   b. one, three, five, _____*seven*_____

   c. two, four, six, _____(*ten*)_____

   d. ten, twenty, thirty, _____*forty*_____

   e. ten, one hundred, one thousand, __*ten thousand*__

   2. Write the numbers.

   a. XX _____*twenty*_____

   b. IX _____*nine*_____

   c. LI _____*fifty-one*_____

   d. IV _____*six*_____

   e. C _____*one hundred*_____

   3. Match the numbers with the words.

   __1__ a. 12   1. ordinal number

   __3__ b. DL   2. cardinal number

   __2__ c. 2nd   3. Roman numeral

   4. Write the numbers.

   a. zero _____*0*_____

   b. one hundred _____*100*_____

   c. one million _____*1,000,000,000*_____

   d. ten thousand _____*10,000*_____

   e. one hundred thousand _____*100,000*_____

   f. one billion _____*1,000,000*_____

   g. one thousand _____*1,000*_____

   └───┘

CHALLENGE Explain the mistakes on the test in Exercise 2. **Example:** *Question 1c—the next number is eight, not ten.*

1. **Look at page 17 in your dictionary. Cross out the number or word that doesn't belong. Write the category.**

   a. _____Percents_____   20%   70%   ~~80~~   100%

   b. _____   1/3   .5   2/4   1/2

   c. _____   .10   .333   .75   25

   d. _____   inch   height   width   depth

2. **Forty-two percent of the students at Baker High School are female. Which pie chart is correct? Circle the correct letter.**

   a. 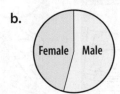   b. 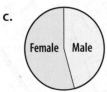   c.

3. **Look at the pie chart. Answer the question.**

   Students who want to go to college in the United States take the SAT.
   The highest math score = 800.
   The lowest math score = 200.

   What percent of students scored between 400 and 600 points?

   a. forty-eight   **b.** fifty-eight   **c.** sixty-eight

   Based on information from: The College Entrance Examination Board, 2015.

   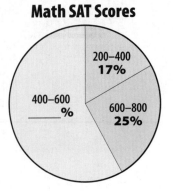

   Math SAT Scores

4. **Look at these math SAT scores. Rank the students.**
   (first = the student with the highest score)

Name	Rank
a. Raz	_____
b. Eva	_____
c. Ito	_____
d. Dan	_____
e. Mai	_____
f. Ali	_first_
g. Luz	_____
h. Ivy	_____

   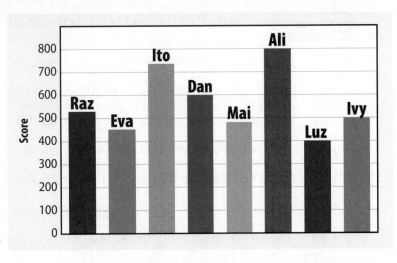

CHALLENGE How many students are in your class? What percent are male? What percent are female? Draw a pie chart like the one in Exercise 3.

1. Look at <u>pages 38 and 39</u> in your dictionary. Write the time of each activity in numbers and words. Use your own paper.

   a. get dressed   **b.** eat breakfast   **c.** clean the house   **d.** go to bed

   Example: *get dressed: 6:30, six-thirty*

2. Look at Ed's time management worksheet. The clocks show the time that he begins each activity. Complete his worksheet.

   a.    **b.**    **c.**    **d.**    **e.**    **f.**

   CLOCKER Inc.

TIME MANAGEMENT WORKSHEET		Ed Tresante		
	ACTIVITY	**TIME BEGAN**	**TIME ENDED**	**TOTAL TIME**
a.	get dressed	7:15 a.m.	8:00 a.m.	45 minutes
b.	brush teeth		8:01 a.m.	
c.	drive to work		9:00 a.m.	
d.	have lunch		1:15 p.m.	
e.	have class		9:15 p.m.	
f.	talk to Ana		11:40 p.m.	

3. Circle the words to complete the report. Use the information in Exercise 2.

   CLOCKER Inc.   TIME MANAGEMENT PROGRAM REPORT

   Before our program, Ed was taking forty-five <u>seconds /(minutes)</u> to get dressed,
           a.
   from a quarter <u>to / after</u> seven until eight <u>p.m. / o'clock</u>. Now it takes him fifteen
         b.   **c.**
   <u>hours / minutes</u>. (He puts his clothes out the night before.) Because he finishes
     d.
   getting dressed by seven-<u>thirty / -fifteen</u>, Ed can eat breakfast, brush for three
                  e.
   minutes, and catch an eight <u>hour / o'clock</u> bus instead of driving. He studies during
                  f.
   his lunch hour, from <u>half past / a quarter after</u> twelve until a quarter <u>to / after</u> one. Ed
             g.   **h.**
   used to talk to his girlfriend until twenty to <u>eleven / twelve</u>. Now he calls her forty
                  i.
   minutes earlier, at <u>twenty to / half past</u> ten, and he gets more sleep.
         j.

4. **Look at the time zone map on page 19 of your dictionary. Ed is planning several business trips. Complete the online flight information.**

www.flightpicker_reservation_schedule.us

PICK YOUR FLIGHT

	FLIGHT NUMBER	FLIGHT	DEPARTURE TIME	ARRIVAL TIME	TOTAL TRAVEL TIME
a. Select	20 Q	New York, NY Los Angeles, CA	10:30 a.m. (Eastern)	1:30 p.m. (Pacific)	6 hours
b. Select	453 Q	Phoenix, AZ Anchorage, AK	8:00 p.m. (Mountain)	_____ (Alaska)	7 hours
c. Select	34 Q	Chicago, IL Halifax, NS	12:00 p.m. (Central)	_____ (Atlantic)	3 hours 30 minutes
d. Select	733 Q	Detroit, MI Dallas, TX	8:00 a.m. (Eastern)	_____ (Central)	4 hours

5. **Complete the article. Use the words in the box. (You will use two words more than once.) Use your dictionary for help.**

Atlantic   daylight saving   earlier   later   Pacific   ~~standard~~   time zones

It's A Question of Time

In 1884, people in different countries agreed to have ___standard___ time. They divided the
                                                                              a.
world into 24 _____ . Some large countries have more than one. The continental
                      b.
United States, for example, has four. They are Eastern, Central, Mountain, and _____ .
                                                                                        c.
Alaska and Hawaii have their own time zones. Canada has two others. They are Newfoundland and

_____ time. The time difference between one zone and the next is one hour. For
        d.
example, when it's noon Eastern time, it's 1:00 p.m. _____ time. (That's one hour
                                                              e.
_____ .) At the same time, it's 11:00 a.m. Central time. (That's one hour
        f.
_____ .) Many countries change the clock in order to have more hours of light in the
        g.
summer. This is called _____ time. In the United States, it begins the second Sunday
                              h.
in March and ends the first Sunday in November. The country then returns to _____
                                                                                    i.
time.

CHALLENGE   Look at page 261 in this book. Follow the instructions.

The Calendar

1. **Look at page 21 in your dictionary. Which month . . . ?**

   a. begins on a Sunday _____ May _____

   b. begins on a Tuesday and has 30 days _____

   c. begins on a Thursday and has four 7-day weeks _____

   d. begins on a weekday and ends on a weekend _____, _____, and _____

2. **Read Eva's email.** *True* or *False?*

My Mail	
Subject:	your visit
Date:	3-18-17 11:51:11 PM EST
From:	EvaL@uol.us
To:	DaniaX@uol.us

   Hi Dania!

   It's Saturday night. I just returned to Miami yesterday. There were no classes for a week, so I flew to Chicago last Saturday to visit my parents. Classes begin again on Monday. It's a busy semester. I have English three times a week (Mondays, Wednesdays, and Fridays). I usually have language lab every Thursday, too. Next week, however, there's no language lab—I go to computer lab instead. In addition to English, I'm studying science. Science meets twice a week on the days that I don't have English. And there's science lab on Tuesdays.

   Last Sunday, daylight saving time began. Do you have that in Canada? I like it a lot. The days seem much longer.

   I'm glad it's the weekend. Tomorrow I'm seeing Tom. (I told you about him in my last email.) I've got to go now. On Saturdays I go to the gym to work out. We can go together when you come! I'm really looking forward to your visit. Just two weeks from today!

   Oh, and bring your appetite! On Sunday there's a cake sale at the school cafeteria. See you soon.

   Eva

   a. It's March. _____ true _____

   b. It's summer. _____

   c. It's the weekend. _____

   d. Eva is in Chicago. _____

   e. Science meets three days every week. _____

   f. Eva goes to the gym every day. _____

3. Complete Eva's calendar. Use the information in Exercise 2.

March

Sunday	Monday	Tuesday	Wednesday	Thursday	Friday	Saturday
			1	2	3	4
5	6	7	8	9	10	11
12	13	14	15	16	17 *return to Miami*	18
19	20	21	22	23	24	25
26	27	28	29	30	31	

4. What about you? Complete your calendar for this month. Write the month, the year, and the dates. Then write your schedule in the calendar.

_____

Sunday	Monday	Tuesday	Wednesday	Thursday	Friday	Saturday

CHALLENGE Write a letter or an email to a friend. Describe your schedule for this month.

Calendar Events

1. **Look at page 22 in your dictionary. Complete the chart.**

Legal Holidays—U.S. 2017	
a. Christmas	*12/25*
b. *Columbus Day*	10/9 (2nd Mon. of the month)
c. Independence Day	
d.	9/4 (1st Mon. of the month)
e.	1/16 (3rd Mon. of the month)
f.	5/29 (last Mon. of the month)
g. New Year's Day	
h.	2/20 (3rd Mon. of the month)
i.	11/23 (4th Thurs. of the month)

2. **Read the sentences. Write the events. Use the words in the box.**

anniversary	appointment	~~birthday~~	religious holiday
legal holiday	parent-teacher conference	vacation	wedding

a. "I'm twenty-one today!"   *birthday*

b. "Your son is an excellent student, Mrs. Rivera." _____

c. "Let's light candles and celebrate together!" _____

d. "The doctor will see you in a minute, Mr. Chen." _____

e. "The post office is closed today." _____

f. "I really needed this! Two weeks and no work!" _____

g. "We were married ten years ago today!" _____

h. "Jennifer looks beautiful in her white dress." _____

3. **What about you? Check (✓) the events and holidays you celebrate. How do you celebrate?**

☐ birthdays _____

☐ anniversaries _____

☐ New Year's Day _____

☐ Other: _____

CHALLENGE Look online for five holidays from around the world. For each one, write the country, the date, and the name of the holiday.

22

1. **Look in your dictionary. Write all the words that end in -y. Then write their opposites.**

   a. ___empty___ ___full___   d. _____ _____

   b. _____ _____   e. _____ _____

   c. _____ _____   or _____

2. **Look at the classrooms. Find and describe six more differences. Use your own paper.**

   Example: *The June classroom has a little clock, but the clock in the September classroom is big.*

June

September

3. **What about you? How does your classroom compare to the classrooms in Exercise 2? Write about the differences. Use your own paper.**

CHALLENGE Write six sentences that describe this workbook. Use words from page 23 in your dictionary.

Colors

1. Look at <u>page 160</u> in your dictionary. What color is the . . . ?

   a. electric vehicle   <u> silver </u>

   b. SUV   _____

   c. limousine   _____

   d. sports car   _____

   e. hybrid   _____

   f. convertible   _____

   g. hatchback   _____

   h. school bus   _____

2. Complete the article. Use the information in the bar graph.

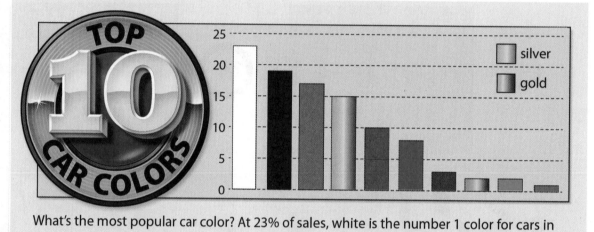

What's the most popular car color? At 23% of sales, white is the number 1 color for cars in

the United States. Why? Some experts say people like light colors because they look clean.

But <u> black </u> (the darkest color of all) is number 2 in popularity. _____ ,
  a.   **b.**

another light color, is number 3 and gets 17% of sales. A similar color, _____ ,
                                                                                      c.

reminds people of technology. _____ is also a light, metallic color, but it only gets
                                        d.

2% of sales. Sports car owners like bright colors such as _____ . At number 5 in sales,
                                                                      e.

this color makes people think of speed. _____ cars also stand out on the road. They
                                                  f.

get 8% of car sales. _____ cars are not as popular. They sell at the same rate as gold
                              g.

cars. Earth colors are becoming more popular. At number 7, _____ cars are more
                                                                        h.

popular than green cars. The last on the list is orange. Now that's a colorful list!

Based on information from: PPG Industries: Automotive Color Trends for 2015.

[CHALLENGE] What are the three favorite car colors of your classmates? Take a survey. Are they the
same as the top three colors in Exercise 2?

1. **Look at __page 24__ in your dictionary. Complete the sentences. Write the locations.**

   a. The white sweaters are ___under___ the black ones, on the ___right___.

   b. The violet sweaters are _____ the turquoise ones, in the _____.

   c. The light blue sweaters are _____ the green and the brown ones.

   d. The green sweaters are _____ the orange ones, on the _____.

2. **Look at the checklist and the picture of the school supply room. Check (✓) the items that are in the correct place.**

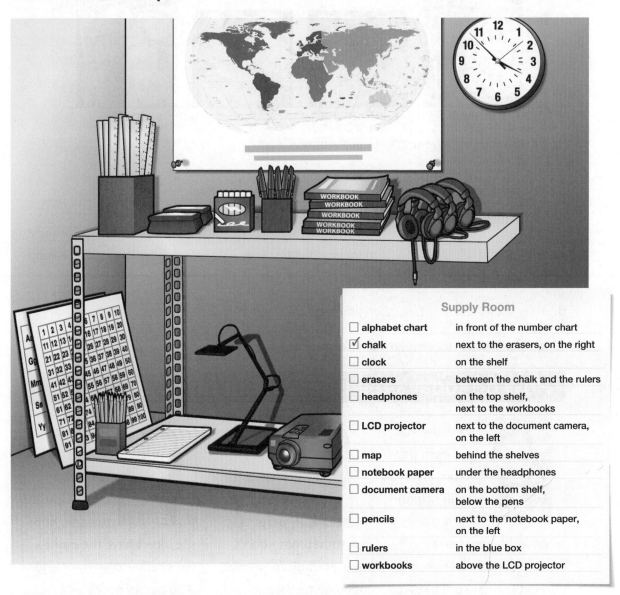

Supply Room	
☐ alphabet chart	in front of the number chart
☑ chalk	next to the erasers, on the right
☐ clock	on the shelf
☐ erasers	between the chalk and the rulers
☐ headphones	on the top shelf, next to the workbooks
☐ LCD projector	next to the document camera, on the left
☐ map	behind the shelves
☐ notebook paper	under the headphones
☐ document camera	on the bottom shelf, below the pens
☐ pencils	next to the notebook paper, on the left
☐ rulers	in the blue box
☐ workbooks	above the LCD projector

3. **Look at Exercise 2. Write about the items that are in the wrong place. Use your own paper.**

   Example: *The alphabet chart is behind the number chart. It isn't in front of it.*

   [CHALLENGE] Write ten sentences about items in your classroom.

Money

1. **Look at page 26 in your dictionary. On your own paper, write the fewest coins and bills you can use to make . . .**

   a. $7.05   **b.** $.64   **c.** $1.37   **d.** $380

   Example: *$7.05: a five-dollar bill, two one-dollar bills or coins, and . . .*

2. **Look at the chart. Complete the sentences.**

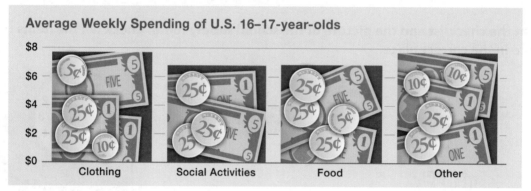

   Average Weekly Spending of U.S. 16–17-year-olds

   Based on information from: Bright Hub Education.
   Bright Hub Education, 2012.

   a. The average 16- to 17-year-old spends _____ $28.90 _____ a week.

   b. These teens spend _____ a week on clothing.

   c. They spend _____ on social activities. They also spend _____ on food outside the home.

   d. They spend _____ on other things, like phone costs and gas.

3. **Circle the words to complete the sentences.**

   ## How do today's teens feel about money?

 At the end of each day, I put all my <u>bills</u> /(coins) in a glass bottle. It's how I save money, and I never need to <u>get change / pay back</u> when I go to the soda machine!

 I get a weekly allowance from my parents, but sometimes I don't have enough for a new video game. I hate to <u>borrow / lend</u> money from my friends, but...

 My best friend wanted to buy a new sweater, but she didn't have the money. I was happy to <u>borrow / lend</u> it to her. I know she'll <u>borrow / pay back</u> the money as soon as she can.

   CHALLENGE   Write at least ten combinations of bills and coins that equal $2.10.

26

1. **Look at page 27 in your dictionary. *True* or *False*? Correct the underlined words in the false sentences.**

   One shopper . . .

   debit card
   a. used a National First Bank ~~credit card~~.   _____false_____

   b. used a $15 gift card.   _____

   c. wrote a traveler's check to pay for a lamp.   _____

   d. paid $27.06 cash.   _____

2. **Circle the words to complete the shopper's advice column.**

   # Ask Sam the Smart Shopper!

   Q: Recently I bought a lamp at the (regular) / sale price. A week later I saw it at the
   a.
   same store for 20% less. Is there anything I can do?

   A: When that happens, some stores will give you the cheaper price if you show your
   sales tax / receipt. That's why you should always keep it.
   b.

   Q: I gave my nephew a sweater for his birthday. He wants to buy / return it and use the
   c.
   money for some video games. When I cashed / bought the sweater, it was $29.99,
   d.
   but now it's on sale for only $19.99. How much will they give him?

   A: Give him the receipt / gift card and SKU number / price tag to bring to the store.
   e.   f.
   He should get $29.99.

   Q: I bought three pairs of jeans. The sales tax / price tag showed $14.99 each, but the
   g.
   cash register showed only $26.97. The clerk said the jeans just went on sale. How
   did the cash register know?

   A: The new price / total was in the store computer. When the computer "read" the
   h.
   receipt / bar code (those black lines), the cash register showed the correct tax / total.
   i.   j.
   What a nice surprise!

CHALLENGE Write a question for the shopper's advice column. Give it to a classmate. Try to answer
your classmate's question.

Same and Different

1. **Look at pages 28–29 in your dictionary. *True* or *False*? Correct the <u>underlined</u> words in the false sentences.**

   sweater
   a. There was a ~~shoe~~ sale at the store.   *false*

   b. Manda and Anya have <u>the same</u> birthday.   _____

   c. Mrs. Kumar bought two matching <u>red</u> sweaters.   _____

   d. She paid <u>$19.99</u> for each sweater before tax.   _____

   e. She bought the sweaters on <u>October 20th</u>.   _____

   f. Manda <u>kept</u> her sweater.   _____

   g. Anya was <u>happy</u> with hers.   _____

   h. She exchanged her green sweater for a <u>white</u> sweater.   _____

2. **Look at the pictures. Complete the email with the words in the box.**

sweaters	twins	~~matching~~	return	disappointed	the same
matching	happy	shop	different	matching	keep

From: TwinsMom

Re: Matching clothes—*Yes* or *No*?

Sometimes *Yes* and sometimes *No*. When my boys were babies,

I always dressed them in ___*matching*___ clothes. They are
    a.

_____, so in those clothes, they looked exactly
  b.

_____. I thought that was really cute, and I loved going to
 c.

the store to _____ for them. They looked adorable in their
      d.

navy blue _____ and red pants. As kids, they were great
    e.

friends and they did everything together, especially baseball, their

favorite sport. Then, in their teens, Mike wanted to play

_____ sports. And he definitely didn't want to wear
 f.

_____ clothes. Leo was really _____ . Now
 g.   **h.**

they're grown up, and they're best friends. This year, I gave both of

them _____ baseball hats, and Mike didn't
   i.

_____ his. He decided to _____ it! I was so
 j.   **k.**

_____ .
 l.

28

3. Look in your dictionary. Match.

_5_ a. Mrs. Kumar went to a store, and   1. she bought sweaters.

____ b. The store had a sale, so   2. she exchanged it for a navy blue one.

____ c. There were many colors, but   3. she didn't want to look the same.

____ d. Anya didn't want a matching sweater because   4. they're warm and happy.

____ e. Manda kept her green sweater, but   5. she shopped for her twins.

____ f. Anya likes navy blue, so   6. Mrs. Kumar chose green.

____ g. Now both twins have sweaters they like, and   7. Anya returned hers.

4. Circle the words to complete the sentences.

My cousins Bena and Myra are twins. They (have) / don't have the same birthday,
                                                  a.

but they don't look or act the same / different. Bena was a noisy / quiet
                                 b.   **c.**

child, and you always knew when she was in the room. She was a good / bad
                                                                    d.

student because she just wasn't happy at school. Today, Bena is a big / small
                                                                        e.

woman, more than six feet tall. She's never in a hurry about anything—

especially shopping. She only buys things on sale, and she doesn't pay the

regular price / sale price for anything. She's never happy / disappointed
                         f.   **g.**

with her purchases. I love to shop with her.

5. Now complete the sentences about Myra. Use words from Exercise 4.

Myra _____was a quiet child_____, and you never knew she was in the room. She
                   a.

_____ because she liked school. Today, Myra _____,
          b.   **c.**

less than five feet tall. She's always in a hurry—especially in stores. She buys the first thing

she sees, and I don't think she _____ for anything. She's often
                                                    d.

_____ her purchases. When Myra says, "Let's go shopping," I usually say,
          e.

"Sorry, I'm busy today."

6. What about you? Should parents dress twins the same? Why or why not? Discuss your answers with a classmate.

CHALLENGE   Write a paragraph. Compare two people you know. Use Exercises 4 and 5 as a model.

Adults and Children

1. **Look at pages 30 and 31 in your dictionary.** *True* or *False*? **Correct the <u>underlined</u> words in the false sentences.**

          seven
   a. There are <u>~~six~~</u> men and women at the round table.   <u> *false* </u>

   b. A <u>man</u> is holding an infant.   <u>   </u>

   c. The <u>toddler</u> wants to sit in a chair.   <u>   </u>

   d. The <u>six-year-old boy</u> is having a bad time.   <u>   </u>

   e. The <u>senior citizen</u> is talking to a man.   <u>   </u>

   f. The <u>baby</u> is sleeping.   <u>   </u>

2. **Put the words in the box in the correct category.**

~~baby~~	boy	girl	infant	man
senior citizen	teen	toddler	woman	

   Males

   <u>   </u>

   <u>   </u>

   Females

   <u>   </u>

   <u>   </u>

   Males or Females

   <u> *baby* </u>

   <u>   </u>

   <u>   </u>

   <u>   </u>

   <u>   </u>

3. **Look at pages 30 and 31 in your dictionary.** *Male* or *Female*? **Check (✓) the answers.**

	Male	Female			Male	Female
a. baby	✓	☐	c. senior citizen		☐	☐
b. teenager	☐	☐	d. toddler		☐	☐

4. **What about you? Look in your dictionary. Imagine you are at the dinner. Who would you like to sit next to? Why?**

   Example: *I'd like to sit next to the baby. I love babies.*

5. **Look at pages 30 and 31 in your dictionary. Guess their ages. Then match.**

_5_ **a.** man   **1.** one year old

___ **b.** senior citizen   **2.** fourteen years old

___ **c.** toddler   **3.** ten years old

___ **d.** teen   **4.** six years old

___ **e.** boy   **5.** forty years old

___ **f.** infant   **6.** sixty-eight years old

___ **g.** baby   **7.** thirty-eight years old

___ **h.** woman   **8.** two months old

___ **i.** girl   **9.** three years old

6. **Look at the pie chart. Circle the words to complete the sentences.**

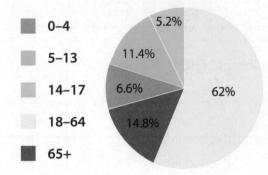

U.S. Population by Age

- 0–4
- 5–13
- 14–17
- 18–64
- 65+

5.2%
11.4%
6.6%
62%
14.8%

Based on information from: The U.S. Census Bureau.

a. Five percent of the U.S. population are senior citizens / (teenagers.)

b. Men and women / Boys and girls are 62% of the population.

c. Babies, infants, and teens / toddlers are in the 6.6% group.

d. A ten-year-old girl / fifty-year-old woman is in the 62% group.

e. There are more children than adults / teens.

f. The biggest percent of the population are babies, infants, and toddlers / men and women.

7. **What about you? Look at the chart in Exercise 6. Which percentage group are you in?**

CHALLENGE   What's a good gift for a baby girl? A baby boy?
A teenage girl? A teenage boy? Discuss your answers with a partner.

Describing People

1. **Look at page 32 in your dictionary. Cross out the word that doesn't belong.**
   Write the category.

   a. ___Weight___   heavy   thin   ~~physically challenged~~   average weight

   b. _____   tattoo   mole   pierced ear   elderly

   c. _____   elderly   pregnant   middle-aged   young

   d. _____   sight impaired   deaf   middle-aged   physically challenged

   e. _____   short   cute   average height   tall

2. **Circle the words to complete the article.**

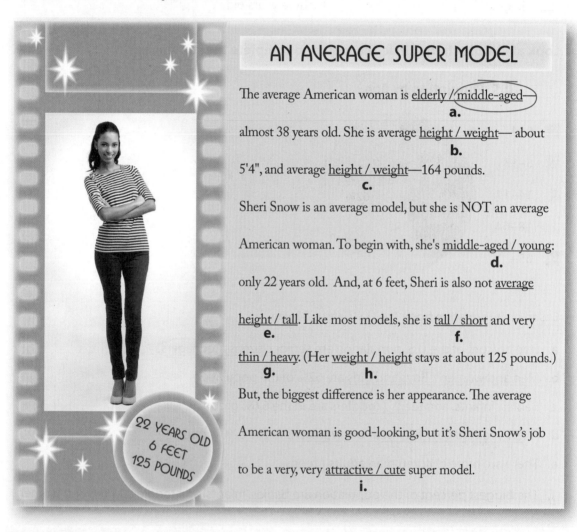

AN AVERAGE SUPER MODEL

The average American woman is elderly / (middle-aged—)
a.

almost 38 years old. She is average height / weight— about
b.

5'4", and average height / weight—164 pounds.
c.

Sheri Snow is an average model, but she is NOT an average

American woman. To begin with, she's middle-aged / young:
d.

only 22 years old. And, at 6 feet, Sheri is also not average

height / tall. Like most models, she is tall / short and very
e.   **f.**

thin / heavy. (Her weight / height stays at about 125 pounds.)
g.   **h.**

But, the biggest difference is her appearance. The average

American woman is good-looking, but it's Sheri Snow's job

to be a very, very attractive / cute super model.
i.

22 YEARS OLD
6 FEET
125 POUNDS

3. **What about you? Write a paragraph about a person you know. Describe the person's**
   age, height, weight, and appearance.

   Example: *My Uncle Tony is middle-aged. He is tall and . . .*

   CHALLENGE Compare yourself or someone you know to the average American man or woman.

32

1. **Look at page 33 in your dictionary. *True* or *False*? Correct the <u>underlined</u> words in the false sentences.**

   a. The bald hairstylist has a ~~sanitizing jar~~ in his hand.   *blow dryer* (above)   _____*false*_____

   b. The woman in his chair has <u>brown</u> hair.   _____

   c. The hairstylist with red hair is using <u>shears</u>.   _____

   d. The hairstylist with blond hair is <u>perming</u> hair.   _____

2. **Complete the advice column with the words in the box.**

beard	blond	blow dryer	color	wavy
dye	~~gray~~	mustache	perm	

   ## Ask Harry

   Q: I'm only twenty, but I've got a lot of

   _____*gray*_____ hair.
   a.

   A: Why not _____ it? You can
   b.

   _____ it black, brown, red, or
   c.

   _____ . Ask your hairdresser
   d.
   about the shade.

   Q: I want _____ hair, but I hate rollers.
   e.

   A: _____ it. You'll have the style
   f.
   you want with no work.

   Q: I always use a _____ after I
   g.
   wash my hair. Is hot air bad for my hair?

   A: Yes. Use a towel some of the time.

   Q: My husband says he spends too much time
   shaving.

   A: Tell him to grow a _____ and a
   h.
   _____ . He'll have to shave
   i.
   less!

3. **Find and correct four more mistakes in this ad.**

   long (above)
   Erica has ~~shoulder-length~~, wavy, brown hair.
   Bob has long, curly, black hair.
   Ann has beautiful shoulder-length, straight, blond hair with bangs.

   They all have great haircuts from Kindest Cut.
   Still only $20.

   KINDEST**CUT**

   Erica   Bob   Ann

   [CHALLENGE] Look in a magazine, a newspaper, or your dictionary. Find a hairstyle you like.
   Describe what a stylist did to create the style.

Families

1. **Look at the children on page 34 in your dictionary. Who said . . . ?**

   a. "I play softball with my two brothers."   <u>   Lily   </u>

   b. "My baby brother just started to walk."   _____

   c. "I don't have any brothers or sisters."   _____

   d. "Aunt Ana made a pretty dress for me."   _____

2. **Complete the family tree. Show the people's relationship to Danica.**

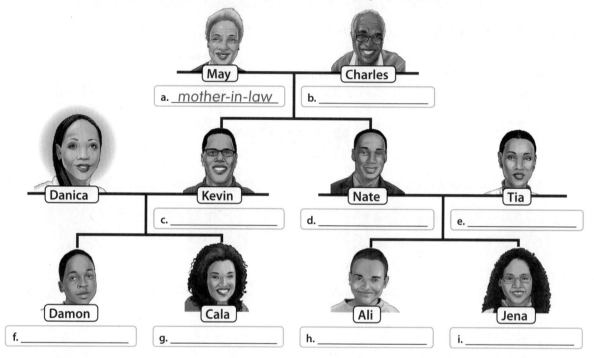

   a. <u> mother-in-law </u>   b. _____

   c. _____   d. _____   e. _____

   f. _____   g. _____   h. _____   i. _____

3. **Look at Danica's niece Jena in Exercise 2. Use information from the family tree to complete Jena's blog post.**

   Jena's Blog: Posted on May 6 at 3:45 PM

   This week my ____cousin____ Cala turned sixteen, so my _____ Kevin and
             a.   **b.**

   my _____ Danica gave her a big party. My _____ Ali and I played with
               c.   **d.**

   the other kids, and my _____ were very busy too—Mom served the
                            e.

   food, and Dad took pictures of Cala, their only _____. Suddenly
                                                   f.

   someone shouted, "May is on the phone." It was our _____
                                                                   g.

   calling from San Francisco!

4. **What about you? Draw your family tree. Use your own paper.**

5. **Look at page 35 in your dictionary.** *True* or *False*?

a. David's father is Lisa's stepfather. _____true_____

b. Kim's mother is married to Lisa's father. _____

c. Mary is Kim's stepsister. _____

d. Carol is divorced from Bill's stepfather. _____

6. **Complete the entries from Lisa's diary. Use the words in the box.**

~~divorced~~	half sister	married	remarried	single father
stepfather	stepsister	stepmother	wife	

3/15/15—Dad moved away this week. He and Mom got ___divorced___. That means
                                                                    a.
they're not _____ anymore. I feel bad, but Mom says I didn't do anything wrong.
                    b.

4/1/15—Dad's new apartment is cool. He says he'll always be my father, but now

he's a _____, not a married one.
            c.

10/4/17—Mom says she wants to get _____ someday. That man Rick
                                                    d.
seems nice. Maybe she'll be his _____ someday.
                                        e.

12/10/17—Mom and Rick got married! Rick's my _____ now.
                                                            f.
I wonder—can I still visit Dad?

12/12/17—I had a great time at Dad's this weekend. Bill and Kim were there. When

Dad and Sue get married, I'll be Bill and Kim's _____. Dad will be their
                                                        g.
stepfather, and Sue will be my _____.
                                    h.

11/14/18—We have a new baby! Her name is Mary. I'm her _____. Mom says I
                                                                i.
can help take care of her.

CHALLENGE Look at page 261 in this book. Follow the instructions.

1. **Look at page 36 in your dictionary. Read the sentences. Write the activities.**

   a. "Mmm. This looks good. Now open your mouth!" _feed the baby_

   b. "You're having a nice bath." _____

   c. "Don't cry, sweetie. You're going to be fine." _____

   d. "Great! That's right. The spoon goes there, next to the plate." _____

   e. "Good. Now we can drive to Grandma's!" _____

   f. "Once upon a time, there was a little boy who had a big dog." _____

   g. "Goodnight, honey. Sleep well and sweet dreams." _____

   h. "Don't touch it! It's hot!" _____

2. **Circle the words to complete the instructions to the babysitter.**

If Tommy cries, try comforting / disciplining him by
a.
dressing / rocking him or give him baby lotion / a pacifier. When
b. c.
you change / bathe his diapers, please use the cloth / disposable
d. e.
ones. You can put the dirty ones in the diaper bag / diaper pail in
f.
his room. We'll wash them tonight. Please don't hold / feed him
g.
or give him a bottle / rattle after 2:30. I'll bathe / nurse him
h. i.
when I get home at 5:00.

If Sara has trouble sleeping, you can read / sing a lullaby
j.
to her from her new book of nursery rhymes.

Thanks. Call me at 555-3234 with any problems!

Monica

3. Cross out the word that doesn't belong. Give a reason.

a. high chair   ~~diaper bag~~   car safety seat

   Babies don't sit in a diaper bag.

b. nipple   training pants   diaper

   _____

c. formula   baby food   teething ring

   _____

d. safety pins   rattle   teddy bear

   _____

e. carriage   stroller   night light

   _____

4. Complete these thank-you notes. Use the words in the box.

| bib   booster car seat   carriage   ~~high chair~~   nursery rhymes   teddy bear |

a.

THANK YOU

Dear Elisa,

   Thanks for the ___high chair___!
Now Johnny can sit and eat with us
at the table. The _____
is great, too. It's pretty.

Melissa

b.

THANK YOU

Dear Aunt Alice,

   Thank you for the
_____ . Now when we
drive to visit Grandma, Julie will be
able to see out the window!

Love, Angela and Scott

c.

THANK YOU

Dear Lili and Quon,
   We all love the _____ !
We read them to Louisa every day. The
_____ is great, too.
Louisa loves playing with him and
can't sleep without him!
Love, Jason

d.

THANK YOU

Dear Bill,
   The _____ is great!
I put Tommy in it yesterday when
I went to the market. He slept
happily and I didn't have to carry
him. Thanks so much!
Love, Amanda

CHALLENGE   Look at page 37 in your dictionary. Imagine someone gave you a baby gift.
Choose an item and write a thank-you note for it.

Daily Routines

1. **Look at pages 38 and 39 in your dictionary. Who does what in the Lim family? Check (✓) the correct box or boxes.**

TO DO

	Mom	Dad	Tess	Marc
a. make lunch	✓	☐	☐	☐
b. take the children to school	☐	☐	☐	☐
c. drive to work	☐	☐	☐	☐
d. go to class	☐	☐	☐	☐
e. go to the grocery store	☐	☐	☐	☐
f. pick up the kids	☐	☐	☐	☐
g. clean the house	☐	☐	☐	☐
h. exercise	☐	☐	☐	☐
i. do homework	☐	☐	☐	☐
j. read the paper	☐	☐	☐	☐
k. check email	☐	☐	☐	☐

2. **Read this article about the family in your dictionary. <u>Underline</u> six more mistakes.**

The Fast Track Family

David and Mai Lim want a lot from life, and their daily routine shows it. They both get up early in the morning. At 6:30 David <u>takes a shower</u>. Then Mai makes breakfast while David eats with the kids. At 7:30 David takes the kids to school. Then David goes to work, and Mai drives to school. At 4:30 Mai picks up the children. Then she cleans the house with the kids and cooks dinner. At 5:00 David leaves work and goes home. The family has dinner together. After dinner the children always do homework. At 8:00 Mai reads the paper and David checks email. Then David watches TV. They go to sleep at 10:30. It's a busy schedule, but the Lims enjoy it.

3. **Correct the mistakes in Exercise 2. Write the correct activity.**

a. _At 6:30 David doesn't take a shower. He gets dressed._

b. _____

c. _____

d. _____

e. _____

f. _____

g. _____

38

4. **Make questions from the scrambled words.**

a. time What you up do get _____What time do you get up?_____

b. eat breakfast When you do _____

c. you leave When the house do _____

d. home come you do time What _____

e. to bed go do When you _____

5. **What about you? Complete the first smartphone with information about your daily routine. Then interview another person. Use questions like the ones in Exercise 4.**

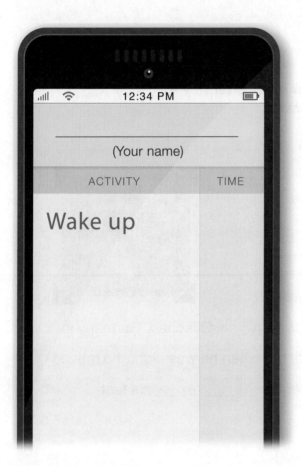

ACTIVITY	TIME
Wake up	

(Your name)

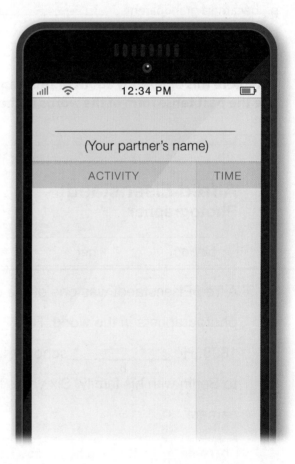

ACTIVITY	TIME

(Your partner's name)

CHALLENGE Compare the routines in Exercise 5. Write six sentences. **Example:** *I get up at 6:00, but Kyung gets up at 7:00. We both leave for class at 8:00.*

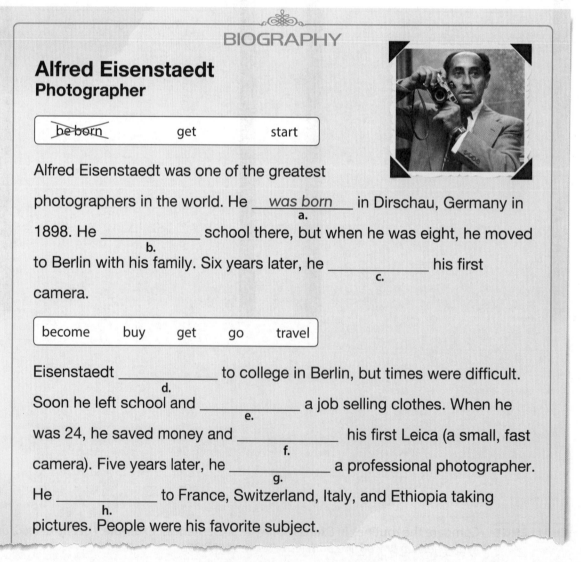

Life Events and Documents

1. **Look at pages 40 and 41 in your dictionary. How old was Martin Perez when he . . . ?**

   a. learned to drive _18 years old_

   b. graduated _____

   c. became a citizen _____

   d. got married _____

   e. had a baby _____

   f. bought his first home _____

   g. became a grandparent _____

   h. died _____

2. **Complete this biography about photographer Alfred Eisenstaedt. Use the past tense form of the words in the boxes.**

BIOGRAPHY

Alfred Eisenstaedt
Photographer

~~be born~~   get   start

Alfred Eisenstaedt was one of the greatest

photographers in the world. He ___was born___ in Dirschau, Germany in
  a.

1898. He _____ school there, but when he was eight, he moved
  b.

to Berlin with his family. Six years later, he _____ his first
  c.

camera.

become   buy   get   go   travel

Eisenstaedt _____ to college in Berlin, but times were difficult.
  d.

Soon he left school and _____ a job selling clothes. When he
  e.

was 24, he saved money and _____ his first Leica (a small, fast
  f.

camera). Five years later, he _____ a professional photographer.
  g.

He _____ to France, Switzerland, Italy, and Ethiopia taking
  h.

pictures. People were his favorite subject.

---

die	get	get married	immigrate	retire

In 1935, Eisenstaedt left Germany and _____ to the United
                                              i.
States. A year later, he _____ a job at *Life* magazine. He worked
                              j.
there for 36 years. After he _____ , he and his wife Alma (the
                                  k.
two _____ in 1949) lived in their house on Martha's Vineyard. He
        l.
_____ there in 1995, at the age of 96.
        m.

3. **Read the sentences about Alfred Eisenstaedt.** *True* **or** *False***? Put a question mark (?)**
   if the information isn't in the reading in Exercise 2.

   a. Alfred Eisenstaedt was born in the United States.   *false*

   b. He went to college in Dirschau.   _____

   c. He became a citizen of the United States.   _____

   d. Eisenstaedt got married before he immigrated to the U.S.   _____

   e. He and his wife had a baby in 1951.   _____

   f. He lived in the United States for 60 years.   _____

4. **Check (✓) the documents Alfred Eisenstaedt probably had. Use the information**
   in Exercise 2.

   [✓] high school diploma   [ ] deed   [ ] college degree

   [ ] marriage license   [ ] passport   [ ] birth certificate

5. **Complete the timeline for Alfred Eisenstaedt. Use the information in Exercise 2.**

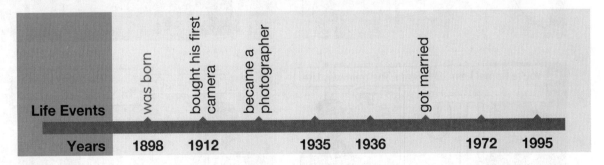

6. **What about you? Draw a timeline with your own information. Then write a short**
   autobiography. Use your own paper.

CHALLENGE Think of a famous person and look up biographical information about him or her in an
           encyclopedia or online. Draw a timeline and write a paragraph about the person's life.

Feelings

1. Look at pages 42 and 43 in your dictionary. Find and write the opposite of these words.

a. worried *relieved*

b. hot _____

c. nervous _____

d. sick _____

e. happy _____

f. full _____

2. Complete the sentences. Use the words in the box.

| disgusted | full | ~~homesick~~ | in pain | relieved |

a. What's wrong?
I'm really *homesick*.

b. Ow!
What's wrong? Are you _____?

c. Yuck! What IS that!?
You look _____!

d. You're home! I am SO _____!
Sorry. The train was late.

e. More turkey?
No, thanks. I'm _____.

3. Circle the words to complete the story.

Minh Ho had so many feelings his first day of school. When he left home, he felt (scared)/ excited.
a.
His mother looked <u>nervous / calm</u>, but his little brother just looked <u>sad / sleepy</u>. When he got to
b. **c.**
school, he walked into the wrong class. The teacher looked <u>bored / surprised</u>, and Minh Ho was
d.
very <u>embarrassed / thirsty</u>. He felt much better in math class. He was <u>proud / frustrated</u> when he
e. **f.**
did a problem correctly. His teacher looked <u>upset / happy</u>. At lunchtime, he looked at his food
g.
and was <u>confused / relieved</u>. "What is this?" He wasn't <u>angry / hungry</u> at all. As he sat in the
h. **i.**
cafeteria, Minh Ho was feeling very <u>full / sad</u> and <u>tired / lonely</u>. Then someone said, "Can I sit here?"
j. **k.**
Suddenly his feelings changed. He felt <u>happy / homesick</u>. Was he <u>in love / in pain</u>?
l. **m.**

4. What about you? How did you feel on your first day of school? Write sentences on your own paper.

CHALLENGE   Look at the picture on page 262. Follow the instructions.

Go to page 249 for Another Look (Unit 2).

A Family Reunion

1. **Look at pages 44 and 45 in your dictionary.** *True* or *False*? **Rewrite the false sentences. Make them true.**

   a. Ben has a <u>small</u> family.   <u>   *false*   </u>

       <u>*Ben has a big family.*   </u>

   b. <u>Every year</u>, his family has a reunion.

   _____   _____

   c. The reunion is at <u>his aunt's</u> house.

   _____   _____

   d. This year, he decorated with <u>balloons and a banner</u>.

   _____   _____

   e. His grandfather and his aunt are talking about <u>the baseball game</u>.   _____

   _____

   f. Some <u>adults</u> are misbehaving.

   _____   _____

   g. Ben's relatives are laughing and Ben is having a <u>good</u> time.   _____

   _____

   h. There are <u>two</u> new babies at the reunion this year.

   _____   _____

   i. Ben's mother-in-law is talking about <u>families</u>.   _____

   _____

   j. Ben is <u>sorry</u> the reunion is only once a year.   _____

   _____

2. **Look at pages 44 and 45 in your dictionary. Who is saying . . . ? Match.**

   <u> 6 </u> **a.** "The Mets are terrible this year!"   **1.** Ben's grandmother

   ____ **b.** "Let's stop talking and watch the game."   **2.** Ben's aunt

   ____ **c.** "In my opinion, you should have two more children."   **3.** Ben's sister

   ____ **d.** "The babies are laughing. I guess they're having a good time!"   **4.** Ben

   ____ **e.** "May, stop misbehaving! Take your hand off the cake."   **5.** Ben's mother-in-law

   ____ **f.** "Aunt Terry! I'm so glad you came."   **6.** Ben's grandfather

44

3. **What about you? Imagine you are at Ben's reunion. What are you doing? Write three sentences.**

   Example: *I'm drinking soda.*

   a. _____

   b. _____

   c. _____

   What aren't you doing? Write three sentences.

   Example: *I'm not eating cake.*

   d. _____

   e. _____

   f. _____

4. **Complete Ben's aunt's email. Use the words in the box.**

baby	baseball game	father	glad	~~nephew~~
good time	big	opinions	relatives	~~reunion~~

   > ### My Mail
   >
   > Every year I go to a family ___*reunion*___ at my _____'s
   >   **a.**   **b.**
   >
   > house. All of my _____ are there. I'm always
   >   **c.**
   >
   > _____ to see them. We have a _____ family,
   >   **d.**   **e.**
   >
   > and next year it will be even larger. Ben and his wife are going to have a new
   >
   > _____ ! This year,
   >   **f.**
   >
   > my _____ and I watched
   >   **g.**
   >
   > a _____ . We had very different
   >   **h.**
   >
   > _____ about it, but we also
   >   **i.**
   >
   > had a _____ !
   >   **j.**

CHALLENGE Imagine you are one of the people at the Lu family reunion. Write about the reunion. Use the email in Exercise 4 as an example.

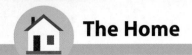

The Home

1. **Look at pages 46 and 47 in your dictionary. *True* or *False*? Correct the <u>underlined</u> words in the false sentences.**

   bedrooms
   a. This home has two <s>bathrooms</s> and a baby's room.   <u>*false*</u>

   b. The <u>bedroom</u> door is open.   _____

   c. The <u>kitchen</u> has three windows.   _____

   d. Mr. Marino is in the <u>attic</u>.   _____

   e. Mrs. Marino and the baby are in the <u>dining area</u>.   _____

   f. One daughter is in the <u>basement</u>.   _____

2. **Look at pages 46 and 47 in your dictionary. Label the floor plans.**

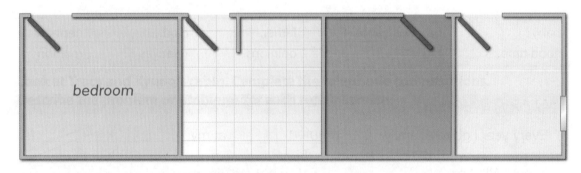

bedroom

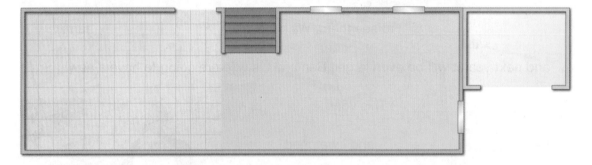

3. **What about you? Draw a floor plan of your home. Label the rooms.**

   My Home

4. **Look in your dictionary. Where are these items?**

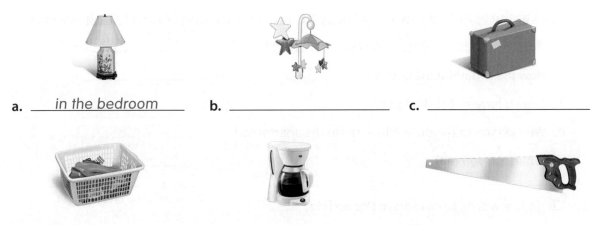

a. ___in the bedroom___   b. _____   c. _____

d. _____   e. _____   f. _____

5. **Look in your dictionary. Circle the words to complete the ad.**

Great for a Family!

Two-bathroom /(bedroom) house with baby's room. One <u>bathroom / bedroom</u>. Large
     a.   **b.**

<u>attic / kitchen</u> with dining <u>area / window</u>. <u>Basement / Living room</u> with a lot of
     c.   **d.**   **e.**

light (three <u>doors / windows</u>). <u>Floor / Basement</u> and attic. One-car <u>attic /garage</u>.
          f.   **g.**   **h.**

Call 555-2468 for more information.

6. **What about you? Describe your "dream" home.**

a. How many bedrooms does it have? _____

b. How many bathrooms? _____

c. Does it have a dining area or a separate
   dining room? _____

d. Does it have a garage? _____
   If *yes*, how many cars can go in the garage? _____

e. Does it have a basement? _____
   If *yes*, what is in the basement? _____

f. How many windows are there? _____
   Which rooms have windows? _____

g. Does it have a large yard? _____

CHALLENGE Write an ad for your "dream" house. Use the ad in Exercise 5 as an example.

1. **Look at the apartment listing on page 48 in your dictionary. Answer the questions.**

   a. How many bedrooms does the apartment have? _____2_____

   b. How many bathrooms does it have? _____

   c. Does it have air conditioning? _____

   d. Who do you call if you're interested in the apartment? _____

   e. When can you call? _____

2. **Circle the words to complete the article.**

← → C ≡

Home Improvement
By James Esposito

It's time to stop using the (apartment search tool) / utilities to look for a bigger apartment. You're
                                         a.
not going to <u>sign a rental agreement / arrange the furniture</u> and pay rent every month anymore.
                  b.
You're going to make the BIG MOVE and <u>rent an apartment / buy a house</u>! You're excited but
                                              c.
nervous. Here are some suggestions that will make things easier. First, make a checklist. What's

important to you? Next, <u>meet with a realtor / call the manager</u>. Explain how much you can pay
                             d.
and go over your checklist. Be patient. Most buyers <u>look at / take ownership</u> of seven to twelve
                                                          e.
houses before they decide. When you find your dream house, <u>make an offer / move in</u> quickly,
                                                                  f.
or you might lose it to another buyer. If you and the sellers agree on the price, it's time to

unpack / <u>get a loan</u>. Finally the happy day comes. The seller hands you
      g.
the keys and you <u>sign a rental agreement / take ownership</u>! Now all you
                      h.
have to do is move in, <u>ask about the features / unpack</u>, and arrange
                            i.
the furniture. Oh, and <u>pay the rent / make the mortgage payments</u>,
                            j.
of course. Welcome to home ownership!

---

3. **Look at page 49 in your dictionary. What are they doing?**

   a. "I think we need some more boxes!" _____ *packing* _____

   b. "How about $125,000?" _____

   c. "Let's put the table there, in front of the love seat." _____

   d. "The keys to our new house! Thank you." _____

   e. "Thank you. Now we have the money for the house!" _____

4. **Look at the classified ads. Answer the questions.**

Smithfield New 2br 2ba house large with AC near schools and shopping $300,000

Greenville 3br 2ba house large sunny kit close to transportation. Move-in condition! $258,000

Lincoln Small 2br, 1ba for sale or rent. Just painted! $185,000

   a. Which house is the biggest? How many bedrooms does it have? _____ *the house in Greenville* _____

   b. What is the price? _____

   c. Which house is the smallest? How many bathrooms does it have? _____

   d. Which house is the least expensive? What is the price? _____

   e. Which house is best for a family with one child? Why? _____

   f. Which house has air conditioning? _____

5. **What about you? Check (✓) all the items that are important to you.**

Type	☐ Apartment	☐ House	☐ Other: _____
Location	☐ City	☐ Suburbs	☐ Country
Near	☐ School	☐ Shopping	☐ Work
Space	☐ Number of rooms	☐ Size of rooms	
Cost	☐ Rent	☐ Mortgage	*CITY* **REALTY**

CHALLENGE Write a paragraph about a time you looked for and found a new home.

Apartments

1. **Look at pages 50 and 51 in your dictionary. Where can you hear . . . ?**

   a. "Bye. I'm going up now." _the elevator_

   b. "The water looks great! I'll go in after this chapter." _____

   c. "All I ever get are bills and ads." _____

   d. "I watch this program every Monday night." _____

   e. "Just sign here, and the apartment is yours!" _____

   f. "Oh, good. My clothes are all dry." _____

2. **Circle the words to complete the ad.**

NewWAVE

THE GLENWOOD MANOR

Enjoy Suburban Living In The Middle Of The City! The Glenwood Has It All ...

We just put up a fire escape / (vacancy sign!) 1- and 2- bedroom apartments now available!
   a.

SAFETY

♦ Full-time manager / prospective tenant lives in the apartment complex
         b.
♦ Intercom / Trash chute in every apartment
      c.
♦ Security camera / Buzzer in all public areas
            d.

COMFORT

♦ Beautiful roof garden / peephole
            e.
♦ Some apartments available with balconies / vacancy signs
                     f.

CONVENIENCE

♦ 60-car courtyard / garage with one free emergency exit / parking space per apartment
        g.   **h.**
♦ Laundry room / Swimming pool on every floor (all new washers and dryers)
      i.
♦ Elevator / Playground for children
      j.
♦ Alley / Recreation room with big-screen TV and pool table
      k.

For more information, contact our building manager / tenant: John Miller 555-4334
                l.

3. **Complete the safety pamphlet. Use the words in the box.**

buzzer	deadbolt lock	door chain	elevator	fire escape
~~intercom~~	smoke detector	peephole	key	stairs

Better Safe Than Sorry

▶ Don't allow strangers into the building. Always use your _____intercom_____ to ask
a.
"Who's there?" <u>before</u> you use your
_____.
b.

▶ Look out your _____ before
c.
you open your apartment door. When you're
at home, keep your _____ on.
d.

▶ Install a _____. It's the
e.
strongest lock.

▶ Give a copy of your _____
f.
to the building manager. In case of an
emergency, it will be easier to enter your
apartment.

▶ Keep a _____on the wall or
g.
ceiling between your bedroom and your
apartment door. Check it every month!

▶ In case of fire, do not use the
_____. (The heat can cause it
h.
to stop between floors.) Use the
_____instead.
i.

▶ Feel the door of your apartment. If it's hot,
the fire may be out in the hall. Use the
_____ to leave your apartment.
j.

*For serious emergencies, dial 911. All
other times, call your local police or fire
department.*

4. **What about you? How safe is your home? Check (✓) the things your home has.**

☐ deadbolt lock ☐ door chain ☐ emergency exit ☐ fire escape

☐ intercom ☐ peephole ☐ security camera ☐ security gate

☐ smoke detector ☐ Other: _____

CHALLENGE Describe your ideal apartment building.

Different Places to Live

1. **Look at page 52 in your dictionary. Where can you hear . . . ?**

   a. "My roommate is studying chemistry." <u>a college dormitory</u>

   b. "I became homeless after I lost my job." _____

   c. "We raise horses." _____

   d. "All four houses look the same." _____

2. **Complete the letter. Use the words in the box.**

city	condo	country	~~farm~~	mobile home
nursing home	senior housing	suburbs	townhouse	

   Dear Fran,

       You asked me to tell you about the places I've lived. I grew up on a potato

   _____<u>farm</u>_____ . After your grandfather and I got married, we bought a small
       a.

   _____ in a very large building. I didn't like living in a big
       b.

   _____ like Boston. I really prefer living in the _____ , where
       c.   **d.**

   I grew up. I was happy when we bought a _____ in the
                                               e.

   _____ , only fifteen miles from the city. When your grandfather retired,
       f.

   we wanted to travel. We bought a _____ and for a while, we moved our
                                                g.

   little home every few years! After your grandfather died, I wanted to be around more

   people my age, so I moved to _____ . Then I got sick and needed more
                                              h.

   help, so I moved here to this _____ . When you were younger, you used
                                           i.

   to think all the elderly people here were your grandparents, too! We're all looking

   forward to your next visit.

   Love,
   Grandma

3. **What about you? Where have you lived? Make a chart like the one below.**

Name of Place	City, Suburbs, or Country	Type of Home	Year You Moved There	How Long You Lived There
New York	city	apartment	2010	6 years

   CHALLENGE   Write a paragraph about the places you've lived. Use information from Exercise 3.

52

1. **Look at page 53 in your dictionary. What can you use to . . . ?**

   a. eat outside   _patio furniture_

   b. cook outside   _____

   c. take a nap   _____

   d. water the lawn   _____ and _____

   e. grow your own tomatoes   _____

2. **Look at the houses. Find and describe 8 more differences. Use your own paper.**

   Example: _House A's mailbox is red, but House B's is blue._

3. **What about you? Plan your ideal yard. Check (✓) the items you would like.**

   ☐ a patio   ☐ flower beds   ☐ a hammock   ☐ Other: _____

   CHALLENGE   Draw your ideal yard and write a paragraph describing it.

A Kitchen

1. **Look at page 54 in your dictionary. Complete the sentences.**

   a. The _____teakettle_____ is on the right back burner of the stove next to the pot.

   b. The _____ is on the counter, to the right of the sink.

   c. The _____ are on the wall, under the cabinet and above the dish rack.

   d. The _____ is below the oven.

   e. The boy is holding a _____.

   f. The _____ is on the table next to the electric mixer.

2. **Look at the chart.** *True* or *False*? **Correct the** <u>underlined</u> **words in the false sentences.**

   ## Average Number of Years That Appliances Last

   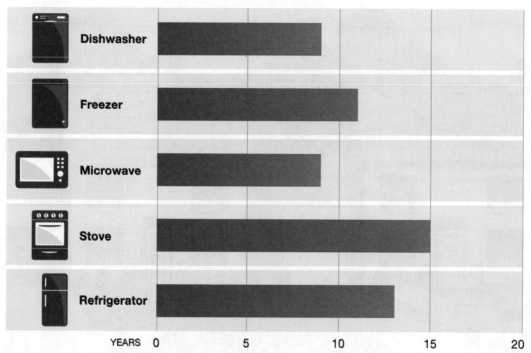

   Based on information from: *Consumer Reports 2009.*

   thirteen
   a. A refrigerator lasts an average of about ~~ten~~ years.   _____false_____

   b. A dishwasher lasts an average of about <u>nine</u> years.   _____

   c. A microwave lasts about as long as a <u>refrigerator</u>.   _____

   d. The average life of a dishwasher is <u>longer</u> than the life of a freezer.   _____

   e. A <u>refrigerator</u> lasts longer than the other appliances.   _____

   CHALLENGE Which five kitchen appliances do you think are the most important? Why?

1. **Look at page 55 in your dictionary. List the items on the dining room table and on the tray. Use your own paper.**

   Example: *4 placemats*

2. **Complete the conversations. Use the words in the box.**

| fan | hutch | platter | serving bowl | ~~tablecloth~~ | tray | vase |

   a. **Alek:** I'm setting the table. Are we going to use placemats?

      Ella: No. Put on the white _____*tablecloth*_____ instead.

   b. **Alek:** Are we going to serve each guest a piece of fish?

      Ella: No. I'll put the fish on a big _____ in the middle of the table.

   c. **Alek:** Where are the good plates?

      Ella: They're in the _____. The _____ for the vegetables is there, too.

   d. **Alek:** Where should I put the coffee mugs?

      Ella: I'll carry them out on a _____ after we finish eating.

   e. **Alek:** Is it hot in here?

      Ella: Yes. Why don't you turn on the _____?

   f. **Alek:** The flowers are beautiful!

      Ella: I'll get a _____ for them.

3. **What about you? Draw a picture of the table at a dinner you had. Label the items.**

   CHALLENGE   Find a picture of a dining area in a newspaper or magazine. Describe it to a classmate. Your classmate will draw a picture of it.

1. **Look at page 56 in your dictionary.** *True* or *False*? **Correct the <u>underlined</u> words in the false sentences.**

   entertainment center

   a. There's a painting on the wall over the ~~mantle~~.   *false*

   b. The DVR is to the left of the <u>stereo system</u>.   _____

   c. The <u>houseplant</u> is next to the sofa.   _____

   d. There are throw pillows on the <u>armchair</u>.   _____

   e. There's a candle holder and candle on the <u>coffee table</u>.   _____

2. **Look at the pictures. Circle the words to complete the sentences.**

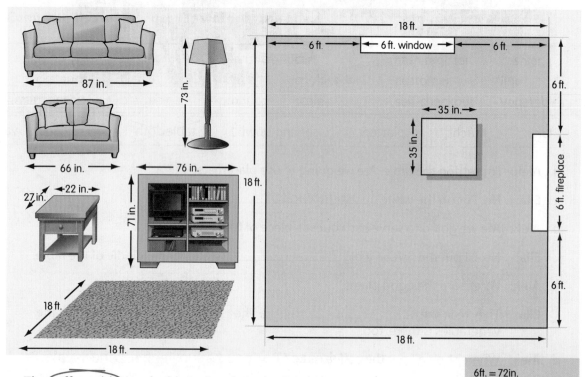

   a. The (coffee table) / end table is already in the living room.

   b. The <u>entertainment center / love seat</u> can go to the left of the window.

   c. The <u>love seat / sofa</u> won't fit to the right of the fireplace.

   d. The carpet is <u>bigger than / the same size as</u> the living room.

   e. The floor lamp is <u>shorter / taller</u> than the entertainment center.

3. **What about you? Draw a floor plan of your living room. Label the items.**

   CHALLENGE   How would you decorate the living room in Exercise 2? Write sentences. **Example:**
   I'd put the sofa in the middle of the living room, across from the window.

1. **Look at page 57 in your dictionary. Which item is each person talking about?**

   a. "It's in the toothbrush holder."   <u>toothbrush</u>

   b. "Can I put my dirty jeans in <u>here</u>?"   _____

   c. "I'm going to hang your bath towel and washcloth <u>here</u>."   _____

   d. "There's hair in <u>it</u>. The water isn't going down."   _____

2. **Complete the article. Use the words in the box.**

medicine cabinet	hot water	grab bar	soap dish	sink	showerhead
shower curtain	wastebasket	faucets	bath mat	~~bathtub~~	rubber mat	toilet

   # Keep bath time safe and happy by following these safety rules:

   1. Never leave a young child alone in the _____<u>bathtub</u>_____.
      a.
      Even small amounts of water can be dangerous.

   2. Avoid burns from _____. Turn the temperature on your water heater down to
      b.
      100°F. Fix all dripping _____ and don't forget the _____
      c.   **d.**
      —hot drops from above can hurt, too.

   3. Prevent falls. Keep a _____ in the bathtub and a nonslip _____
      e.   **f.**
      on the floor. And don't forget to put that slippery soap back in the _____ after
      g.
      you wash. Never hold onto the _____ when you get out of the bathtub. Install a
      h.
      _____ on the bathtub wall. Provide a stool so that children can reach the
      i.
      _____ safely to wash their hands and brush their teeth.
      j.

   4. Keep medicines locked in the _____. Never throw old medicines away in a
      k.
      _____ where children can get them. Flush them down the _____.
      l.   **m.**

3. **What about you? What do you do to prevent injuries and accidents in the bathroom? Write sentences on your own paper.**

   Example: *We put a rubber mat in the bathtub.*

   CHALLENGE   Draw a picture of your bathroom. Label the items.

A Bedroom

1. **Look at page 58 in your dictionary.** *True* or *False*? **Correct the <u>underlined</u> words in the false sentences.**

   on the wood floor
   a. The cat is <s>under the bed.</s>   _____false_____

   b. There is a <u>full-length mirror</u> in the closet.   _____

   c. The alarm clock is on the <u>dresser</u>.   _____

   d. The <u>light switch</u> and the outlet are on the same wall.   _____

   e. The woman is lifting the <u>mattress</u> and the dust ruffle.   _____

2. **Read the letter and look at the picture. Complete Tran's list. Use your own paper.**

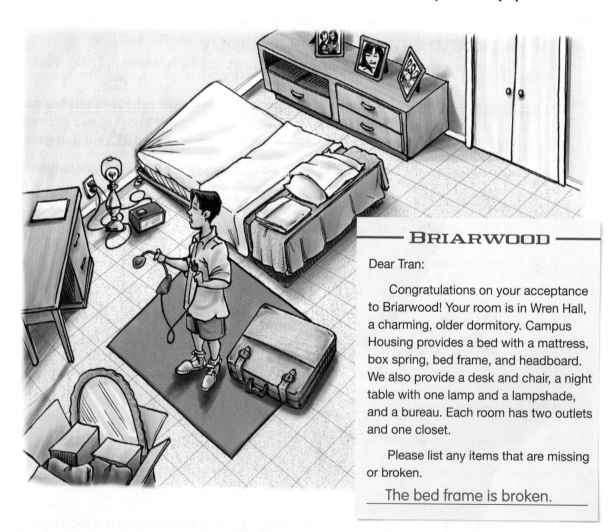

BRIARWOOD

Dear Tran:

Congratulations on your acceptance to Briarwood! Your room is in Wren Hall, a charming, older dormitory. Campus Housing provides a bed with a mattress, box spring, bed frame, and headboard. We also provide a desk and chair, a night table with one lamp and a lampshade, and a bureau. Each room has two outlets and one closet.

Please list any items that are missing or broken.

The bed frame is broken.

3. **Look at Exercise 2. What did Tran bring? Make a list.**

   Example: *sheets*

   [CHALLENGE] Write a paragraph about your ideal bedroom.

58

1. **Look at page 59 in your dictionary. Cross out the word that doesn't belong.**

   a. **For sleeping** crib ~~puzzle~~ bunk bed cradle

   b. **For safety** baby monitor safety rail bumper pad blocks

   c. **For playing** ball changing pad doll crayons

   d. **Furniture** changing table chest of drawers toy chest coloring book

2. **Complete the article. Use the words in the box.**

mobile	changing table	wallpaper	stuffed animals
~~crib~~	bedspread	chest of drawers	

Expecting a new family member?

HERE'S WHAT YOU'LL NEED TO MAKE YOUR BABY'S ROOM A SAFE AND HAPPY PLACE.

The biggest item is the ____crib____. The mattress
                              a.
must fit tightly, with no spaces that a baby's head can fit

through. A pretty _____ will help keep baby
                        b.
warm, but it should fit loosely on top of the mattress. You can change your

baby on a bed, but a _____ is better for your back. Finally,
                            c.
you will need a _____ for baby's clothing.
                      d.
For decoration, hang a _____ where baby can watch it (some
                              e.
of them play music, too). Paint the room or put up colorful

_____. And don't forget some soft, cuddly _____
      f.   **g.**
for baby to play with.

3. **What about you? Describe your favorite toy or game as a child.**

   Example: *I loved my teddy bear. It was...*

[CHALLENGE] Look at page 262 in this book. Follow the instructions.

Housework

1. **Look at page 60 in your dictionary. Correct the <u>underlined</u> words.**

   a. The man in B is ~~putting away~~ *recycling* newspapers.

   b. The man in D is <u>sweeping</u> the floor.

   c. The girl in N is <u>washing</u> the dishes.

   d. The woman in O is <u>dusting</u> the counter.

2. **Look at the room. Circle the words to complete the note.**

Hi! I wasn't quite able to do everything.

I polished the (desk) / dresser, but I didn't
                a.
dust the <u>desk / dresser</u>. I <u>swept /</u>
      b.   **c.**
<u>vacuumed</u> the floor, and I washed the

<u>dishes / windows</u>. I also washed the
      d.
<u>sheets / glasses</u>, but didn't make
      e.
<u>lunch / the bed</u>. Sorry! Could you
      f.
<u>take out / empty</u> the garbage and
      g.
put away the <u>dishes / books</u>? *Viktor*
             h.

3. **What about you? Which would you prefer to do? Tell a classmate. Do you agree?**

   Example: *I'd prefer to dry the dishes.*

   a. wash the dishes / dry the dishes

   b. dust the furniture / polish the furniture

   c. sweep the floor / vacuum the carpet

   d. make the bed / change the sheets

   CHALLENGE Take a survey. Ask five people about their favorite and least favorite kinds of housework. Write their answers.

1. **Look at page 61 in your dictionary. Add a word to complete the list of cleaning supplies.**

    a. glass _cleaner_   d. dish _____   g. trash _____

    b. oven _____   e. recycling _____   h. scrub _____

    c. rubber _____   f. furniture _____   i. sponge _____

2. **Complete the conversations. Use the words in Exercise 1.**

    a. **Paulo:** Do you have any _____ trash bags _____?
    I want to empty the wastebasket.

    Sara: Sorry. I used the last one.

    b. **Ben:** The mirror has a lot of fingerprints on it.

    Ann: Use some _____.

    c. **Ada:** Can you help me with these? If you wash, I'll dry.

    Mario: Sure. Here's a _____.

    d. **Taro:** What should we do with the empty bottles?

    Rika: Don't throw them away. Put them in the _____ in the alley.

    e. **Amber:** I dusted the desk, but it still doesn't look clean.

    Chet: Try some _____ on it.

    f. **Luis:** You're doing a great job on that stove, but that _____ isn't good for your hands.

    Vera: You're right. Do we have any _____?

    g. **Layla:** The kitchen floor is really dirty. The _____ isn't getting it clean.

    Zaki: I know. You have to get down and use the _____ on it.

3. **Cross out the word that doesn't belong. Give a reason.**

    a. dustpan   broom   ~~disinfectant wipes~~   sponge mop

    You don't use them to clean the floor. _____

    b. steel-wool soap pads   dishwashing liquid   dish towel   bucket

    _____

    c. scrub brush   sponge   feather duster   sponge mop

    _____

CHALLENGE Imagine you have just moved into a new home. You need to dust the furniture, clean the oven, wash the windows, and mop the kitchen floor. Make a shopping list.

Household Problems and Repairs

1. **Look at pages 62 and 63 in your dictionary. Who should they call?**

    a.
    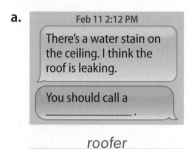

    Feb 11 2:12 PM

    There's a water stain on the ceiling. I think the roof is leaking.

    You should call a _____ .

    _____ *roofer* _____

    b.

    May 20 11:25 AM

    Mike's toy is stuck in the toilet!

    Call a _____ .

    _____

    c.
    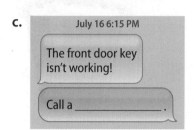

    July 16 6:15 PM

    The front door key isn't working!

    Call a _____ .

    _____

    d.

    Oct 24 4:47 PM

    Sorry, Mom. I kicked my soccer ball through the front window.

    OK. I'll call a _____ .

    _____

2. **Look at Tracy and Kyung's cabin. Complete the telephone conversations. Describe the problem or problems for each repair service.**

    a. Repairperson: Bob Derby Carpentry. Can I help you?

    Tracy: _The door on our kitchen cabinet is broken._ _____

    b. Repairperson: Plumbing Specialists, Ron here.

    Kyung: _____ ,

    _____ , and _____

    c. Repairperson: Chestertown Electricians. This is Pat.

    Kyung: _____

    d. Repairperson: Nature's Way Exterminators. What's the problem?

    Tracy: _____

3. **Look at the chart.** *True* or *False*? **Write a question mark (?) if the information isn't in the chart.**

Pests	Where They Live	How to Prevent Them	How to Get Rid of Them
	on pets, carpets, and furniture	Keep pets either inside or outside all the time.	Vacuum often. Comb pets daily. Wash them with water and lemon juice.
	behind walls, under roofs and floors	Repair cracks and holes in roofs and walls. Keep garbage in tightly closed garbage cans.	Poison is dangerous to humans. Put traps along walls. Put a piece of cheese in the trap.
	in wood, especially wet or damaged places	Repair cracks and holes. Repair leaks in pipes. Check every 1–2 years.	Call the exterminator. You need a professional to get rid of these pests, which destroy your house by eating the wood.
	gardens and lawns	Repair wall cracks. Clean floors and shelves often. Wipe spilled honey or jam immediately.	Find where they enter the house and repair that hole. Put mint leaves in food cupboards.
	behind walls, in electric appliances	Clean carefully. Keep food in closed containers. Repair all cracks and holes.	Make a trap by putting a piece of banana in a wide-mouthed jar. Put petroleum jelly around the inside of the jar to keep trapped bugs inside. Place in corners or under sinks. Call an exterminator.
	in sheets, blankets, mattresses, and cracks in the bed; in cracks on the wall	Don't buy used sheets, blankets, or mattresses. Clean up around the outside of the house. Don't allow birds or squirrels to build nests on or in the house.	Wash sheets and blankets in hot water; vacuum the bed and mattress. A professional exterminator is often necessary.

a. To prevent most pests, you must repair household problems. _____*true*_____

b. You have to use poison to get rid of mice. _____

c. Sometimes cockroaches get into the toaster oven. _____

d. Fleas like sweet food. _____

e. You have to buy cockroach traps. _____

f. Ants carry diseases. _____

g. Mint leaves help get rid of ants. _____

h. Mice eat people's food. _____

i. You should put a piece of fruit in a mouse trap. _____

j. Bedbugs live only in beds. _____

CHALLENGE   Write some other ways of dealing with household pests.

Go to page 250 for Another Look (Unit 3).

1. **Look at pages 64 and 65 in your dictionary.** *True* or *False*? **Rewrite the false sentences. Make them true.**

   a. Tina and Sally are <u>sisters</u>.   <u>*false*</u>

            <u>*Tina and Sally are roommates.*</u>

   b. They had a <u>DJ</u> for their party.   _____

   _____

   c. The neighbors were <u>irritated</u> about the music at the first party.   _____

   _____

   d. There was a big mess in the <u>rec room</u> after the first party.   _____

   _____

   e. The tenants made two <u>rules</u> at the tenant meeting.   _____

   _____

   f. Sally and Tina were <u>happy</u> at the tenant meeting.   _____

   _____

   g. Now it's against the rules to have loud music on <u>weekends</u>.   _____

   _____

   h. Their neighbors got invitations to the <u>second</u> party.   _____

   _____

2. **Circle the words to complete the conversations.**

   Ms. Sanders: Look at this (mess)/ noise! What happened?
                                    a.

   Mr. Clark: There was a big <u>meeting / party</u> in 2B last night. All the <u>tenants / roommates</u> are
                                          b.   **c.**

                 <u>irritated / happy</u>.
                    d.

   Mr. Dean: We need to make some <u>rules / invitations</u> about parties. Any suggestions?
                                             e.

   Mr. Clark: No loud <u>mess / music</u>!
                       f.

   Tina: Ms. Sanders, we're very <u>sorry / irritated</u> about our party.
                                  g.

   Ms. Sanders: Thanks, girls. I know it won't happen again.

   Sally: Did you get our invitation to the <u>rec room / hallway</u> party?
                                        h.

   Mr. Clark: Yes, I did! Thanks. I'll be there.

3. **What about you? Do you have some rules where you are living now? Are they good rules? Why or why not? What are some good rules for people in an apartment or a dormitory room?**

4. **Look at pages 64 and 65 in your dictionary. When did Tina and Sally . . . ?**
   Put the sentences in order (1–8).

   ____ **a.** clean the mess in the hallway

   ____ **b.** dance with their neighbors in the rec room

   __1__ **c.** clean the apartment for the first party

   ____ **d.** make Mr. Clark in 2A very irritated

   ____ **e.** make some rules at the tenant meeting

   ____ **f.** give out the invitations to the neighbors

   ____ **g.** have a party in 2B

   ____ **h.** get an invitation to the tenant meeting

5. **Complete Sally and Tina's sign with the words in the box.**

mess	noise	dance	rec room	rules
sorry	~~neighbors~~	irritated	apartment	tenants

   # To Our ___Neighbors___
   a.

   We made a lot of _____ at our party last night, and we
   b.

   _____ our neighbors. We're very _____ about the
   c. **d.**

   loud music and the _____ in the hallway. We agree with the
   e.

   new _____ , and it won't happen again. We've given all the
   f.

   _____ in the building invitations to our party on
   g.

   Saturday, December 13th. We'll have great food and music, so please

   come and _____ with your neighbors in the _____.
   h. **i.**

   Tina and Sally, _____ 2B
   j.

Plan a party. Work with a group. When is your party? What do you have to do and
   when? Use the ideas in the word box or your own.

choose the place	choose the music	send out invitations
plan the food	clean up after the party	

Back from the Market

1. Look at pages 66 and 67 in your dictionary. Which food comes from a . . . ?

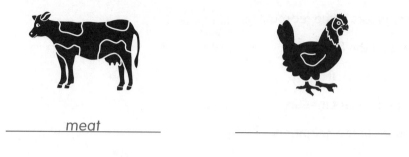

_____ *meat* _____   _____

_____   _____

2. Marisol is going to make these meals. Write the foods she needs.

eggs
_____
_____
_____
_____
_____
_____
_____

3. Look at Marisol's shopping list in Exercise 2. Check (✓) the coupons she can use.

☐ **Save $1.00** on every package of Paulo's

☐ **SAVE 50¢** on all brands!

☐ **Freshly Baked** Buy 12, get the 13th one FREE!

☐ **Farm Fresh!** SAVE $1.00 on 12

4. **Complete the conversations. Use the words in the box.**

coupons	fruit	grocery bag	meat	~~milk~~	shopping list	vegetables

Ana: What would you like to drink?

Luis: _____*Milk*_____, please.
   a.

Liza: Would you like a hamburger?

Elek: No, thanks. I don't eat _____.
   b.

Hoa: Do you like bananas?

Lan: I love bananas. They're my favorite _____.
   c.

Dan: I'm going to the market. Do we need more milk?

Eva: Yes, I wrote it on the _____.
   d.

Dan: What about carrots or peas?

Eva: No. We have enough _____.
   e.

Eva: Oh. Don't forget to take these _____.
   f.

Dan: Great. We'll save a lot of money with them!

Mike: Can I have another _____?
   g.

Cashier: Sure. Paper or plastic?

5. **What about you? Do you eat . . . ? If *yes*, what types? Use pages 68–71 and page 76 in your dictionary for help.**

	Yes	No	Examples
vegetables	☐	☐	_____
fruit	☐	☐	_____
cheese	☐	☐	_____
meat	☐	☐	_____
fish	☐	☐	_____
eggs	☐	☐	_____
bread	☐	☐	_____

CHALLENGE Work with a classmate. Plan a meal together. Use the food on pages 66 and 67 in your dictionary.

Fruit

1. **Look at page 68 in your dictionary. Complete the sentences.**

   a. A ___bunch of bananas___ costs 50¢.

   b. The _____ are between the prunes and dates.

   c. The _____ are tall and have green leaves on top.

   d. The _____ are above the blueberries.

2. **Look at the pictures. Complete the chart.**

Fruit	Best during	Buy ones that are
a. ___watermelons___	June, July, August	cut open, dark red inside
b. _____	June and July	dark red and big
c. _____	July and August	bright orange, with soft skins
d. _____	December to June	heavy
e. _____	April to July	dry and dark red, size not important
f. _____	July and August	dark green

3. **Look at Exercise 2. Circle the words to complete the sentences.**

   a. The best (grapefruits)/ mangoes are heavy.

   b. Don't buy a watermelon / kiwi unless it is cut open.

   c. Plums / Strawberries are good in April.

   d. Grapefruits / Peaches are good in the winter.

   e. When you buy cherries / strawberries, size is important.

   f. Summer is a good time to buy lemons / limes.

   g. Apples / Peaches should have soft skins.

4. **What about you? List your favorite types of fruit. When do you buy them?**

   CHALLENGE   Make a chart like the one in Exercise 2 for your favorite fruit.

1. **Look at page 69 in your dictionary. Put these vegetables in the correct category.**

~~artichokes~~	~~beets~~	~~bell peppers~~	bok choy	cabbage
chili peppers	corn	cucumbers	eggplants	carrots
peas	radishes	spinach	string beans	lettuce
sweet potatoes	tomatoes	turnips	zucchini	squash

Root Vegetables

beets

Leaf Vegetables

artichokes

Vegetables with Seeds

bell peppers

2. **Complete the recipe with the amounts and names of the vegetables in the picture.**

Healthy Vegetable Stew

Put three cups of water on the stove to boil. While it is heating, use a sharp knife to slice

_____ _four_ _____ _potatoes_____ , _____ _____ ,
a.   b.   c.   d.

_____ _____ , and _____ _____ .
e.   f.   g.   h.

Cut _____ _____ into quarters and crush four cloves of _____
i.   j.   k.

with the back of a spoon. Add these ingredients to the boiling water and cook over low for

20 minutes. Add _____ cups of _____ and cook for three more minutes.
l.   m.

3. **What about you? Which vegetables do you like in a stew? Make a list.**

CHALLENGE Write the recipe for a vegetable dish. Look online, in a recipe book, or ask a friend.

Meat and Poultry

1. **Look at page 70 in your dictionary. Cross out the word that doesn't belong. Write the category.**

   a. _____Poultry_____   chicken   duck   ~~lamb~~   turkey

   b. _____   bacon   ham   sausage   tripe

   c. _____   chops   leg   shanks   wings

   d. _____   drumsticks   ribs   steak   veal cutlets

2. **Complete the article with information from the charts.**

FAT FACTS

A 3 1/2 ounce serving of _____*sausage*_____ has 31 grams of fat.
a.

A serving of _____ and a serving of _____ have the same
            b.   **c.**
amount of fat.

_____ has the highest amount of fat.
     d.

_____ has the lowest amount of fat.
     e.

A chicken _____ with skin on it has two times as much fat as a skinless one.
            f.

With 18 grams of fat, _____ has 13 more grams than _____
               g.   **h.**
from the same animal.

Fat Grams per 3 1/2 Ounce Serving of Cooked Meat

10 grams
5 grams
2 grams
18 grams
8 grams
4 grams
20 grams
13 grams
49 grams
31 grams
10 grams
8 grams

CHALLENGE   Keep a record of the meat you (or another person) ate last week. Figure out the fat content. Use the information in Exercise 2.

1. **Look at page 71 in your dictionary. *True* or *False*? Correct the underlined words in the false sentences.**

   a. The swordfish is ~~frozen~~. *fresh*   *false*

   b. The cod is next to the <u>tuna</u>.   _____

   c. The <u>scallops</u> are to the right of the mussels.   _____

   d. Salami and pastrami are in the <u>deli</u> section.   _____

   e. The <u>wheat bread</u> is between the white bread and the rye bread.   _____

   f. The woman is reaching for the <u>mozzarella</u> cheese.   _____

   g. The Swiss cheese is between the cheddar and the <u>American</u> cheese.   _____

   h. There's a special price for the <u>whole salmon</u>.   _____

2. **Look at the seafood prices and the recipe cards. How much will the seafood for each recipe cost? (You can use page 75 in your dictionary for information about weights and measures.)**

   Note: doz. = dozen = 12 pieces   1 lb. = 1 pound, 2 lbs. = 2 pounds

a. **Linguine with clams**	b. **New Orleans shrimp**	c. **Steamed mussels with orange**
36 fresh raw clams	1 1/2 lbs. of medium shrimp	6 lbs. of mussels
<u>$23.97</u>	_____	_____

d. **Southern style crab cakes**	e. **Trout with mushrooms**	f. **Grilled salmon with corn**
1 lb. fresh or frozen crab meat	2 lbs. whole trout	4 salmon steaks 8 oz. each
_____	_____	_____

3. **What about you? Work with a classmate. Order lunch from the deli.**

   Example: *I'll have a smoked turkey sandwich on wheat bread with mozzarella cheese. What about you?*

   CHALLENGE   What other seafood and deli foods do you know? Make a list.

A Grocery Store

1. **Look at pages 72 and 73 in your dictionary. Cross out the item that doesn't belong. Write the section of the store.**

   a. _Canned Foods_ beans ~~frozen dinner~~ soup tuna

   b. _____ bagels bananas oranges tomatoes

   c. _____ ice cream margarine sour cream yogurt

   d. _____ apple juice coffee oil soda

   e. _____ bagels cake cookies nuts

   f. _____ candy bars nuts pop potato chips

   g. _____ flour oil pet food sugar

2. **Complete this article. Use the words in the box.**

aisles	basket	beans	cart	cash register	cashier
checkstands	clerk	coffee	~~cookies~~	customer	line
manager	margarine	produce	scale	self-checkout	vegetables

SAVE TIME and MONEY
at the supermarket

■ Never shop when you're hungry. Those chocolate ____cookies____ will
   _{a.}
be hard to resist on an empty stomach. You should also stay away

from _____ with snack foods!
     b.

■ Do you really need a large shopping _____ or is a smaller
                                          c.

shopping _____ enough? Having too much room may
          d.

encourage you to buy more than you need.

■ Be a smart _____. Shop with a list. That makes it easier to
              e.

buy only what you need.

72

- Keep a price book of items that you buy frequently. *Example*: If you drink a lot of _____, compare prices at different stores.
  f.

- Always check the unit price. *Example*: It may be cheaper to buy a large can of black _____ than a small can. Check: How much does it cost per pound?
  g.

- Do you need a pound of potatoes? Don't guess. Use the _____ and buy the exact amount.
  h.

- Watch for sales. Buy a lot of the items you need.

- Buy the store brand. *Example*: The supermarket brand of butter or _____ will probably cost less than the famous brands.
  i.

- If the _____ doesn't look fresh, buy frozen _____. They'll look and taste better.
  j. k.

- Avoid standing in _____. Try to shop when the store is less crowded. If all of the _____ aren't open, speak to the store _____. Remember: Sometimes the _____ is faster.
  l. m. n. o.

- Always watch the _____ when the _____ is ringing up your order. Is the price right? Mistakes can happen!
  p. q.

- If you can't find an item, don't waste your time looking for it. Ask a grocery_____ for help.
  r.

3. **What about you? Which of the shopping tips in Exercise 2 do you use? What other ways do you save time and money when you go food shopping? Write about them.**

CHALLENGE   Look at page 263 in this book. Follow the instructions.

Containers and Packaging

1. Look at page 74 in your dictionary. Complete the flyer.

♺ **RECYCLE—It's the Law!**

The packaging for many items on your grocery list belongs in your recycling bin, not your garbage can.
Follow the recycling guidelines as you use these items.

YES

a. ✔ plastic or glass _____bottles_____ (water)

b. ✔ plastic or glass _____ (jam)

c. ✔ metal _____ (soup)

d. ✔ cardboard _____ (cereal)

e. ✔ cardboard _____ (paper towels)

NO

f. ✖ plastic _____ (bread)

g. ✖ plastic _____ (yogurt)

h. ✖ cardboard _____ (milk)

i. ✖ plastic _____ (cookies)

j. ✖ plastic _____ (toothpaste)

Note: Recycling guidelines are different in different places.

2. Look at the groceries that Mee-Yon bought this week. Which items have packaging
that she can recycle? Which items don't? Use information from Exercise 1.
Make two lists. Use your own paper.

Example: *She can recycle the packaging for the bottle of oil. She can't recycle the two bags of bread.*

3. What about you? What can and can't you recycle in your community? Make two lists.

CHALLENGE Look in your dictionary. Write six sentences about other items that come in the same
containers and packaging. **Example:** *Beans and vegetables also come in cans.*

1. **Look at the charts on page 75 in your dictionary. Circle the larger amount.**

    a. 3 teaspoons / (3 tablespoons)   d. 2 pints / 1 liter

    b. 100 ml / 2 fluid ounces   e. 2 pounds / 36 ounces

    c. 8 pints / 6 quarts   f. 5 quarts / 2 gallons

2. **Look at the nutrition facts. Answer the questions. Use your dictionary for help.**

Nutrition Facts
Kidney Beans – Serving Size 1/2 cup

Amount Per Serving	
Calories 110	Calories from Fat 0
Protein	8g
Carbohydrate	22g
	% Daily Value
Calcium	6%
Iron	10%

Nutrition Facts
Skim Milk – Serving Size 1 cup

Amount Per Serving	
Calories 90	Calories from Fat 0
Protein	8g
	% Daily Value
Calcium	30%
Vitamin D	25%

Nutrition Facts
Rice – Serving Size 1/4 cup raw (about 1 cup cooked)

Amount Per Serving	
Calories 170	Calories from Fat 0
Protein	4g
Carbohydrate	38g
	% Daily Value
Calcium	2%
Iron	8%

Nutrition Facts
Chocolate Candy – Serving Size 1 piece (1/2 oz.)

Amount Per Serving	
Calories 90	Calories from Fat 30
Total Fat	4g
Protein	1g

Note: % Daily Value = % of the total amount you should have in one day

a. Which has more protein, a cup of beans or a cup of milk? _____ *a cup of beans* _____

b. How many pieces of chocolate candy are there in one pound? _____

c. How many pints of milk give 100% of the daily value of vitamin D? _____

d. How much fat is there in three ounces of chocolate candy? _____

e. How many cups of milk do you need for 90% of the daily value of calcium? _____

f. What percent of the daily value of calcium do you get from a pint of milk and two

    servings of rice? _____

g. A serving of rice and beans contains a quarter cup of beans and a half cup of cooked rice.

    How much carbohydrate is there in a serving? _____

h. What percent of the daily value of iron is there in a serving of rice and beans? _____

[CHALLENGE] Look at page 263 in this book. Follow the instructions.

Food Preparation and Safety

1. **Look at page 76 in your dictionary. Then look at the pictures here. What does Laura do right? What does she do wrong? Check (✓) the correct box. Write sentences.**

	Right	Wrong	
a.	✓		*She cleans the counters.*
b.		✓	*She doesn't*
c.			
d.			
e.			

2. **Look at the chart. Complete the sentences.**

Calories in 3 oz. Chicken Breast

150   161   222

172   168   175

a. ___Roasted___ chicken has 172 calories.

b. _____ chicken has 11 more calories than boiled chicken.

c. _____ chicken has the most calories.

d. _____ chicken has the lowest number of calories.

e. With 168 calories, _____ chicken has 7 more calories than grilled chicken.

f. _____ chicken has 175 calories, but fewer calories than fried chicken.

3. Look at page 77 in your dictionary. Circle the words to complete the cookbook definitions.

a. (beat)/ stir: Make mixture smooth by quick motion with a spoon, fork, whisk, or mixer.

b. boil / sauté: Cook in very hot liquid (212°F for water).

c. peel / chop: Cut into pieces with a knife.

d. slice / dice: Cut into very small pieces with a knife (smaller than chopping).

e. grate / grease: Cut into small pieces using small holes of a grater.

f. mix / spoon: Combine ingredients, usually with a spoon.

g. grate / peel: Take off the outer skin.

h. boil / simmer: Cook slowly in liquid just below the boiling point.

i. preheat / steam: Cook over boiling water, not in it.

4. Look at Paulo's recipe. It got wet, and now he can't read parts of it. Complete the recipe. Use the words in the box.

| add | bake | grease | microwave | mix | ~~preheat~~ | slice | spoon |

FISH

Baked cod in sour cream

1/2 pound cod   1/4 c. mayonnaise

1 TBS. butter   1 c. sour cream

salt and pepper   10 oz. mushrooms

Preheat   the oven to 350°F.   a baking dish with a
     a.   b.

little butter. Place the fish in the dish, top with the rest of the butter.

           salt and pepper.   the mayonnaise and
        c.   d.

sour cream together and   it over the fish.
                      e.   f.

the mushrooms, and add them to the dish.   in the oven for
                                   g.

45 minutes or   on high for about 7 minutes.
                 h.

Servings: 2

CHALLENGE   Write one of your favorite recipes.

1. **Look at page 78 in your dictionary.** *True* or *False*? **Correct the <u>underlined</u> words in the false sentences.**

   a. There are two *cake* ~~pie~~ pans above the cookie sheets.   _____*false*_____

   b. There's a lid on the <u>casserole dish</u>.   _____

   c. There's a roasting rack in the <u>mixing bowl</u>.   _____

   d. There's butter in the <u>saucepan</u>.   _____

   e. There's a <u>garlic press</u> between the wooden spoon and the casserole dish.   _____

   f. One of the cooks is using the <u>can opener</u>.   _____

   g. One of the cooks is using the <u>vegetable peeler</u>.   _____

2. **Circle the words to complete the cookbook information.**

Some utensils you need in your kitchen

Grater / **Whisk**: to beat eggs, cream, etc.

Steamer / Colander: to remove water from cooked pasta, vegetables, etc.

Ladle / Spatula: to spoon soup, sauces, etc. out of a pot

Paring / Carving knife: to cut up small fruits and vegetables

Lid / Tongs: to cover pots and pans

Storage container / Strainer: to keep food fresh

Pot / Potholders: to handle hot utensils

Eggbeater / Wooden spoon: to stir soups, sauces, etc.

Double boiler / Roasting rack: to cook food slowly on top of the stove

Cake and pie pans / pots: to bake desserts

> **CHALLENGE**   Think of a recipe. Make a list of all the utensils you need for the recipe. What do you need each one for? **Example:** *I need a whisk to beat the eggs.*

1. **Look at page 79 in your dictionary. Cross out the word that doesn't belong.**

   a. cheeseburger   ~~chicken sandwich~~   hamburger   hot dog

   b. burrito   ice-cream cone   nachos   taco

   c. ketchup   straw   mustard   mayonnaise

   d. muffin   onion rings   ice-cream cone   donut

2. **Look at the menu. _True_ or _False_?**

Typical Nutritional Values for Fast Food

calories: 540 fat: 28g sugar: 10g	calories: 300 fat: 16g sugar: 1g	calories: 170 fat: 10g sugar: 1g	calories: 360 fat: 6g sugar: 10g	calories: 151 fat: 13g sugar: 3g
calories: 365 fat: 17g sugar: 4g	calories: 480 fat: 30g sugar: 6g	calories: 195 fat: 11g sugar: 11g	calories: 356 fat: 8g sugar: 63g	calories: 182 fat: 0g sugar: 44g

a. A soda doesn't have any fat, but it has a lot of sugar.   _true_

b. The cheeseburger has more calories than anything else on this menu.   _____

c. The French fries have more calories than the onion rings.   _____

d. The chicken sandwich has more sugar than the pizza.   _____

e. The cheeseburger has more fat than anything else on this menu.   _____

f. The hot dog has fewer calories than the taco.   _____

g. The milkshake has more calories than the donut.   _____

h. The onion rings have 30 grams of sugar.   _____

CHALLENGE   Take a survey of your classmates' top five fast foods.

A Coffee Shop Menu

1. **Look at pages 80 and 81 in your dictionary. What comes with . . . ?**

   a. steak and _____*baked potato*_____

   b. roast chicken and _____

   c. _____, rice, and lemon

   d. grilled cheese sandwich and a _____

   e. _____ and honey

   f. _____ and jelly

   g. a chef's salad with _____, eggs, and _____

   h. _____ and/or _____ with butter and syrup

   i. spaghetti with _____ and _____

   j. meatloaf and _____

2. **Complete the conversation. Use the words in the box.**

cake	coffee	pie	~~potatoes~~
salad	soup	vegetables	

   Hyun: I'll have the steak and _____*potatoes*_____.

a.

   Server: Baked or mashed? Or maybe potato salad?

   Hyun: Baked potato, please. And the steamed
   _____.

b.

   Server: OK. Anything to start?

   Hyun: I think I'd like a cup of _____ to begin with.

c.

   Server: We only have chicken noodle today. OK?

   Hyun: Er, no. I'll have a small house _____ instead.

d.

   Oh, and bring me some garlic bread, please.

   Server: Very good. Would you like something for dessert?

   Hyun: Do you have apple _____?

e.

   Server: Sorry, we don't.

   Hyun: Well, then, I'll have the layer _____ and a cup of decaf

f.

   _____. Thank you.

g.

3. **Look at Exercise 2. Write the order.**

```
                    CARL'S Coffee Shop
  ──────────────────────── ORDER FORM ────────────────────────
  _____   steak     _____
  _____      _____
  _____      _____
  _____
```

4. **Read the order in Exercise 3. Look at the food the server brought Hyun. The server made six mistakes. Describe the mistakes.**

a. _The server gave him rolls, but he asked for garlic bread._

b. _____

c. _____

d. _____

e. _____

f. _____

5. **What about you? Look at the menu in your dictionary.**
   What would you like? Write your order.

```
                    CARL'S Coffee Shop
  ──────────────────────── ORDER FORM ────────────────────────
  _____      _____
  _____      _____
  _____      _____
```

CHALLENGE Imagine you own a coffee shop. Write your own dinner menu.

A Restaurant

1. **Look at the top picture on pages 82 and 83 in your dictionary. Who says . . . ?**

   a. "Your table is ready, Mr. and Mrs. Smith."   _____hostess_____

   b. "Would you like asparagus or zucchini with that?"   _____

   c. "Here. Have some bread."   _____

   d. "We also have chocolate, coconut, and mango ice cream."   _____

   e. "The dishes are clean now."   _____

   f. "I'm coming through with some more dirty dishes!"   _____

   g. "I need to beat this a little more."   _____

2. **Circle the words to complete this restaurant review.**

A. J. Clarke's 290 Park Place 555-3454

At Clarke's, you'll relax in the comfortable, green (dining room) / kitchen that can serve about
a.

50 chefs / diners. The hostess seated / served my guest and me in a quiet booth / high chair, and we got a
b.   **c.**   **d.**

breadbasket / soup bowl filled with fresh rolls. The service was great. The patron / server continued to
e.   **f.**

pour / clear water throughout the meal.
g.

And what a meal it was! The check / menu had something for everyone. Our busser / server, Todd,
h.   **i.**

recommended the fish of the day, tuna. My friend ordered / served the chicken l'orange. After Todd
j.

carried / took our orders, he brought us two salad plates / saucers with the freshest lettuce I've ever eaten. This was
k.   **l.**

followed by two large bowls / plates of onion soup. Our main dishes did not disappoint us. The tuna was so tender
m.

that you could cut it without a steak knife / teaspoon. The chicken, too, was wonderful.
n.

When we were finished, the busser cleared the dishes / set the table. Time for dessert! Todd
o.

carried / left out the dessert fork / tray filled with cakes and pies—all baked in the restaurant's
p.   **q.**

kitchen / dish room. Raspberry pie and a cup / saucer of delicious hot coffee ended our perfect meal. We
r.   **s.**

happily paid / poured the check and left / took Todd a nice tip. My tip to you: Eat at A. J. Clarke's.
t.   **u.**

And don't forget to ask for a napkin / to-go box to take home the food you can't finish!
v.

Reservations recommended.

3. **Look at the picture. Complete the article.**

A Formal __Place Setting__
a.

A _____ is in the center, usually with
b.

the _____ on top of it. The utensils
c.

are on both sides. To the left of the plate are

(from closest to farthest) a _____ and a _____.
d.   e.

To the right of the plate are a _____, a _____, and a
f.   g.

_____. Above the plate is a water _____ and to the
h.   i.

right are two _____. There is also a small _____
j.   k.

above and to the left of the dinner plate. The butter _____ is on
l.

top of it.

4. **What about you? Most people's table settings do not look like the formal one in Exercise 3. Draw your table setting. How is it the same as the table setting in Exercise 3? How is it different? Write sentences.**

Example: *We put the napkin under the fork.*

_____

_____

_____

_____

_____

_____

_____

CHALLENGE Write a description of a meal you had at a restaurant or at someone's home.

Go to page 251 for Another Look (Unit 4).

1. **Look at pages 84 and 85 in your dictionary. *True* or *False*?**

   a. Two men are playing <u>football</u>.   <u>   false   </u>

   b. Cara's sells <u>organic vegetables</u>.   _____

   c. The <u>watermelons</u> are three for $3.00.   _____

   d. The herb vendor sells <u>flowers</u>, too.   _____

   e. A market worker is <u>weighing</u> avocados.   _____

   f. The children are tasting the <u>samples</u>.   _____

   g. Mr. Novak's father is drinking some <u>tea</u>.   _____

   h. The lemonade stand is across from the <u>hot food vendor</u>.   _____

2. **Write the letter of the false sentences in Exercise 1. Make them true.**

   a.   *Two men are playing live music.* _____

   ___   _____

   ___   _____

   ___   _____

   ___   _____

3. **Circle the words to complete the blog post.**

   ← → C   🔍 www.farmersmarket.us   ≡

   Saturday, August 2

   Today I went to the Tenth Street (Farmers' Market) / Grocery Store.
                                                  a.

   I saw the free <u>avocados / samples</u> first, so I tried some
                      b.

   <u>lemonade / fruit</u>—peaches and strawberries. Then I bought some
      c.

   cookies from the <u>bakery / herb vendor</u>. I drank some lemonade
                    d.

   next—it was really <u>hot / sour</u> after those <u>sweets / herbs</u>. I wasn't
                  e.   f.

   planning to buy groceries, but the <u>organic / canned</u> vegetables were beautiful so I got
                                            g.

   some corn and some <u>peaches / avocados</u>. Before I left, I stopped at the <u>hot food / flower</u>
                       h.   i.

   vendor for a taco, and I ate it while I listened to a local band called Sounds of Mexico.

   You can't hear <u>live / radio</u> music at the grocery store!
         j.

4. **Look in your dictionary. What's at the farmers' market? Check (✓) the items.**

- [✓] live music
- [ ] frozen foods
- [ ] baked goods
- [ ] flowers
- [ ] vendors

- [ ] fruit
- [ ] pet food
- [ ] herbs
- [ ] menus
- [ ] samples

- [ ] organic vegetables
- [ ] soup
- [ ] beverages
- [ ] canned foods
- [ ] hot food

5. **Complete the flyer. Use the words in the box.**

dill	samples	cucumbers	hot food	~~farmers' market~~	fruit
basil	lemonade	organic	live music	vegetables	sweets

Tenth Street ____Farmers' Market____
a.

➤ _____—Sounds of Mexico and Fruity Tunes will play this week.
  b.

➤ Free _____—taste before you buy
  c.

➤ _____ food—chemical-free, grown nature's way
  d.

➤ _____—peaches and watermelons are here!
  e.

➤ _____—local corn and _____ , much fresher than the supermarket
  f.   **g.**

➤ Herbs—parsley, _____ , and_____
                    h.   **i.**

➤ _____—tacos, falafel, burgers, and barbecue
  j.

➤ _____—fresh-baked cookies and cakes
  k.

➤ Beverages—herbal teas, _____, and vegetable juices
                          l.

JOIN US THIS WEEKEND

6. **What about you? Look in your dictionary. What do you like about the farmers' market? What do you like about a grocery store? Make a list for each.**

Farmers' market

_____fresh vegetables_____

_____

_____

_____

Grocery store

_____open all week and all year_____

_____

_____

_____

CHALLENGE Work with a classmate. Make a flyer for a farmers' market. Use Exercise 5 as a model.

Everyday Clothes

1. **Look at pages 86 and 87 in your dictionary. Complete the diagram.**

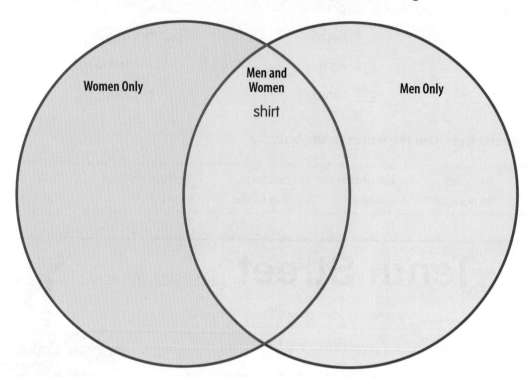

Women Only

Men and Women

shirt

Men Only

2. **Look in your dictionary. What can people wear . . . ?**

   a. under a sweater _____*shirt*_____ _____ _____ _____

   b. with a skirt _____ _____ _____ _____

   c. on their feet _____ _____ _____

   d. on their heads _____

3. **What about you? Check (✓) the clothes you have. Where do you wear them?**

   Where?

   ☐ jeans _____*at home,*_____

   ☐ sneakers _____

   ☐ T-shirt _____

   ☐ suit _____

   ☐ sweater _____

   ☐ baseball cap _____

   ☐ socks _____

   ☐ slacks _____

4. Look at pages 86 and 87 in your dictionary. Circle the words to complete the sentences.

a. The man in the blue shirt is wearing (jeans) / slacks.

b. The woman in the blue blouse has a handbag / sweater.

c. The man at the ticket window is wearing a blue shirt / T-shirt.

d. The woman in the yellow dress / white skirt is putting on a sweater.

e. The girl with the handbag / baseball cap is tying her shoe.

f. The girl in the sneakers / shoes is wearing socks.

g. The man in jeans / the suit is looking at his watch.

5. *A pair* means "two." Look at pages 86 and 87. What items come in two pieces or have two legs? Complete the phrase *a pair of...*

a. _____ jeans _____

b. _____

c. _____

d. _____

e. _____

6. What about you? What will you wear? Imagine you are going to .... You can use your dictionary for help.

a. a jazz concert _____

b. a job interview _____

c. the park _____

d. school _____

e. a Friday night party with your classmates _____

f. a family reunion _____

g. the grocery store _____

CHALLENGE Look at Exercise 1. Name two more pieces of clothes for . . .
You can use pages 86–91 in your dictionary for help.

Women Only _____ _____

Men and Women _____ _____

Men Only _____ _____

Casual, Work, and Formal Clothes

1. **Look at pages 88 and 89 in your dictionary. Who is . . . ?**

    a. wearing sandals   *the woman in capris*

    b. carrying a briefcase   _____

    c. wearing a bow tie   _____

    d. talking to the man in the tank top   _____

    e. wearing a pullover sweater   _____

    f. wearing high heels   _____

    g. talking on the phone   _____

    h. helping a woman with her luggage   _____

    i. sitting on the couch   _____

    j. sitting on the floor   _____

2. **Circle the words to complete the advice column.**

Clothes Encounters

Q I'm looking for a job as an office manager.

   What should I wear on interviews?

A You can't go wrong with a dark blue
   (business suit) / tuxedo. Wear it with
                  a.
   a white shirt and <u>bow tie / tie</u>. Then
                          b.
   just grab your <u>briefcase / clutch bag</u>
                       c.
   and you're good to go! After you get

   the job, you can change to a

   <u>sport jacket / vest</u>. Wear it with
           d.
   <u>shorts / a sport shirt</u> or a
             e.
   <u>cardigan / pullover</u> sweater for a neat look.
            f.

Q I'm going on a business trip to Florida. Can you suggest something casual to wear between meetings? I don't want to wear jeans, but I want to feel comfortable.

A After work, relax in a pair of <u>capris /sweatpants</u>, a T-shirt, and
g.
<u>high heels / sandals</u>. You'll feel very
h.
comfortable and look great. If it gets

cool, put on a <u>knit top / tank top</u>.
i.

Q My husband and I got invited to a wedding. The invitation says "Black tie."
What does that mean?

A For men, "black tie" means a <u>tuxedo / uniform</u>, and usually a <u>bow tie / tank top</u>.
j.   k.
Many men don't own these items, but they can rent them! For women, black tie

can mean either a <u>cocktail dress / sweatpants</u> or <u>an evening gown / overalls</u>.
l.   m.
Complete the outfit with <u>high heels / sandals</u> and have fun!
n.

3. **What about you? What do you think are the most important items of clothing to have? Where do you wear these clothes?**

Example: *a sport shirt—I wear it at work, at school, and at home.*

[CHALLENGE] Choose five people from your dictionary. Describe their clothes.

Example: *On page 73, the woman near the snacks is wearing a black skirt, a purple pullover sweater, and black high heels.*

Seasonal Clothing

1. **Look at page 90 in your dictionary. Cross out the word that doesn't belong. Write the weather condition.**

   a. ___Windy___   overcoat   ~~cover-up~~   winter scarf   jacket

   b. _____   poncho   rain boots   umbrella   ski hat

   c. _____   straw hat   swimsuit   parka   sunglasses

   d. _____   down jacket   leggings   ski mask   windbreaker

2. **Correct the ad.**

   > It's windy out there, but Jillian is dressed for the weather in a warm, brown
   > *jacket*
   > leather ~~parka~~, bright red earmuffs, and a red and yellow headband.
   >
   > That straw hat protects her from the autumn wind.
   >
   > **Jillian**

3. **Write ads for Abdulla, Polly, and Julio's clothing. Use Exercise 2 as an example.**

   Abdulla   **Polly**   **Julio**

   a. ___It's sunny out there, but Abdulla_____

   _____

   _____

   b. _____

   _____

   _____

   c. _____

   _____

   _____

CHALLENGE   What do you like to wear in different weather conditions? Write short paragraphs like the ones in Exercise 3.

Underwear and Sleepwear

1. **Look at page 91 in your dictionary. Find the words that complete *a pair of* . . .**

    long underwear _____ _____ _____

    _____ _____ _____ _____

    _____ _____ _____ _____

    _____ _____ _____ _____

2. **Put the items in the correct list.**

Mom	Dad	Amy	Brian
bikini panties	_____	_____	_____
_____	_____	_____	
_____	_____	_____	
_____	_____	_____	
_____	_____		
_____	_____		
_____			

CHALLENGE You're going on a trip next weekend. List the underwear and sleepwear you'll take.

91

Workplace Clothing

1. **Look at pages 92 and 93 in your dictionary. What is it?**

   a. It protects his clothes when he cooks.　　　　*chef's jacket*

   b. It has her name on it.　　　　_____

   c. He keeps his hammer in it.　　　　_____

   d. He wears it with his blazer.　　　　_____

   e. It's blue and he wears his badge on it.　　　　_____

   f. It helps him breathe.　　　　_____

2. **Circle the words to complete the article.**

Dressing for Safety

Part of a job is wearing the right clothes. A manager wants to look good in

a (blazer) / work shirt and smock / tie. But many workers need to dress for safety, too.
　　　　a.　　　　　　　　　b.
Here are some examples—from head to toe.

★ **Protect your head.** Construction workers need hairnets / hard hats to protect
　　　　　　　　　　　　　　　　　　　　　　　　　c.
themselves from falling objects.

★ **Protect your face.** A medical technician needs a surgical gown / face mask to
　　　　　　　　　　　　　　　　　　　　　　　　　　　d.
avoid breathing in dangerous substances.

★ **Protect your eyes.** You only have two. That's the reason why many jobs

require special safety glasses / ventilation masks.
　　　　　　　　　　　　e.

★ **Protect your body.** Working on the road? Cars need to see you. That's why

road workers need to wear high visibility waist aprons / safety vests.
　　　　　　　　　　　　　　　　　　　　　　f.

★ **Protect your feet.** Things can fall on your feet, too. That's why road workers,

construction workers, and other workers wear coveralls / steel toe boots.
　　　　　　　　　　　　　　　　　　　　　　　　g.

Many workers need to protect *other* people, too. A surgeon, for example, needs a

helmet / scrub cap and a surgical mask / smock to protect patients from germs.
　　h.　　　　　　　　　　　i.

*Wearing the right clothes at the right time can help make the workplace a
safe place.*

3. **Look in your dictionary. Cross out the word that doesn't belong. Give a reason.**

a. cowboy hat   bump cap   bandana   ~~badge~~

     You don't wear a badge on your head.

b. safety glasses   ventilation mask   blazer   surgical mask

c. work pants   jeans   lab coat   security pants

d. polo shirt   smock   apron   waist apron

4. **Look at the pictures. What are the problems? Write sentences.**

a.

     He isn't wearing a hard hat.

     He isn't wearing steel toe boots.

b.

c.

d.

5. **What about you? Look in your dictionary. What workplace clothing do you have? When do you wear this clothing?**

Example: *I wear an apron when I cook.*

CHALLENGE Look at pages 170–173 in your dictionary. Find three jobs. What work clothing do people wear? **Example:** *A dental assistant wears a surgical mask and medical gloves.*

Shoes and Accessories

1. **Look at pages 94 and 95 in your dictionary. Read the sentences. What are the people talking about?**

   a. "I always keep my coins in <u>one</u>—separate from my bills." _____change purse_____

   b. "According to this <u>one</u>, it's 10:08." _____

   c. "Wow! <u>This</u> has even more room than the backpack!" _____

   d. "Ow, my finger! <u>This</u> is pretty, but it's sharp!" _____

   e. "John gave <u>one</u> to me. I put his photo in it." _____

   f. "Oh, no. I forgot to put my credit card back in <u>it</u>." _____

   g. "<u>It</u>'s a little too big for my finger." _____

2. **Look at the ad. Complete the sentences.**

Accessories East

Black leather ____belt____ ,
            a.
silver _____ , and
        b.
black _____
       c.

Foot Smart

White _____
       d.

ER JEWELERS

Gold _____ ,
       e.
pierced _____ ,
          f.
and _____ for her hand
      g.

The Bag House

Red _____
      h.

NEWPORT MALL

YOUR ONE STOP FOR
FALL FASHIONS

94

3. **Look at the shopping list. Where can you buy these items?**
   Use the stores from Exercise 2.

NEWPORT MALL

YOUR ONE STOP FOR
FALL FASHIONS

brown purse	The Bag House
gold bracelet	_____
backpack	_____
string of pearls	_____
black flats	_____

4. **Circle the words to complete the information from a shoe store.**

Foot Smart
at the
NEWPORT MALL

YOUR ONE STOP FOR
FALL FASHIONS

If the Shoe Fits

Be a smart (customer) / salesclerk. When you purchase / wait in
   a.   b.

line for shoes, always try them on / assist a customer at the
                            c.

end of the day—your feet are bigger then! Ask yourself:

Is there enough room at the sole / toe? There should be at least
                                  d.

1/2 inch between the end of your foot and the beginning

of the shoe. And remember: you need different kinds

of shoes for different kinds of activities. Women may want

to wear high heels / oxfords to an evening party, but
         e.

tennis shoes / pumps are a better choice for the office.
         f.

The lower the heel / pin, the more comfortable the shoe.
              g.

Both women and men can relax at home in a pair of

hiking boots / loafers, but you'll want shoes with
         h.

scarves / shoelaces for walking.
   i.

CHALLENGE Which accessories make good gifts? Explain who you would buy them for and why.
Example: *I'd buy a backpack for my girlfriend because she loves to hike.*

Describing Clothes

1. **Look in your dictionary. Cross out the word that doesn't belong. Write the category.**

   a. ___*Sweater styles*___   V-neck   crewneck   ~~wide~~   turtleneck

   b. _____   light   print   paisley   floral

   c. _____   large   medium   small   too small

   d. _____   ripped   sleeveless   unraveling   too big

2. **Look at the pictures. Complete the sentences.**

Lisa   Ana

   a. Lisa's skirt is a ___*miniskirt*___ .

   b. Ana's skirt is _____-length.

   c. The zipper on Ana's skirt is _____ .

   d. Ana's belt is _____ . Lisa's belt is _____ .

   e. Ana's blouse is _____-sleeved, but the sleeves are too _____ .

   f. Lisa's blouse is _____-sleeved too, but the sleeves are too _____ .

   g. Lisa's blouse is _____ .

   h. Both women are unhappy with the clothes. And at $500, they are much too _____ !

3. Look at the pictures. Circle the words to complete the article.

Suitable Dressing

1500s
1700s
after 1789
end of 1800s

Men's formal business suits never seem to change very much these days. However, it took a long time for men to get to this basic piece of clothing.

During the 1500s in Europe, fashionable men wanted to look fat. Their pants were (short) / long and baggy / tight. They wore short / long, light / heavy jackets that were
a.   b.   c.   d.
sleeveless / long-sleeved, and they even stuffed their clothes to look bigger!
e.

In the 1700s, men preferred to look thinner and taller. The rich and stylish wore their

pants shorter / longer and very tight / baggy, and they wore shoes with low / high heels.
       f.   g.   h.
Jackets became longer / shorter and looser / tighter, and men wore fancy / plain shirts
             i.   j.   k.
under them. After the French Revolution in 1789, it became dangerous to dress like the

rich. Instead, many men dressed like workers in long / short pants and loose jackets.
                                     l.
This outfit was a lot like the modern suit, but the parts did not match. The man in the

picture, for example, is wearing striped / checked brown pants with a fancy
                              m.
polka-dotted / paisley vest and a solid / plaid green jacket.
        n.   o.

Finally, at the end of the 1800s, it became stylish to match the pants, jacket, and vest.

As you can see, today's business suit has not changed much since then.

CHALLENGE Describe traditional clothing for men or women from a culture you know well.
Example: *In Oman, women wear long, baggy pants. The weather is very hot, so clothing is usually light.*

Making Clothes

1. **Look at pages 98 and 99 in your dictionary. Cross out the word that doesn't belong. Write the category.**

   a. _Parts of a Sewing Machine_   needle   bobbin   ~~velvet~~   feed dog

   b. _____   wool   pattern   leather   linen

   c. _____   fringe   zipper   snap   hook and eye

   d. _____   beads   sequins   appliqué   buckle

2. **Write the name of the material.**

   a. 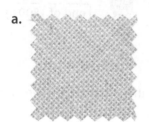   b.    c.    d.

   a. ___linen___ This was the first woven material. Ancient people learned how to make thread from the blue-flowered flax plant and weave it into cloth. Today it is often used to make light jackets and suits.

   c. _____ This material is made from the hair of sheep and some other animals. It is soft, warm, and even waterproof! It is often used to make coats, sweaters, mittens, and scarves.

   b. _____ Very early, people learned how to make animal skins into this strong material. They rubbed the skins with fat to make them soft. Today it is often used to make shoes, boots, jackets, and purses.

   d. _____ For thousands of years, only the Chinese knew how to make clothing from this beautiful material. The fabric is often used to make underwear, blouses, and ties.

3. **Circle the words to complete the conversation in a fabric store.**

   Isabel: I'm making a blouse for my daughter.

   Kim: What type of material are you thinking of?

   Isabel: (Lace)/ Thread or maybe cotton / ribbon. I'm not sure yet.
             a.   **b.**

   Kim: OK. What kind of fabric / closure are you going to use?
                                    c.

   Isabel: Buttons / Beads.
             d.

   Kim: Do you need a rack / pattern?
                       e.

   Isabel: No. I always like to design clothes myself.

   Kim: Really? That's great. Do you use a sewing machine / bobbin?
                                                        f.

   Isabel: No. I don't have one. I sew by hand / machine. All I need is a needle and thread / feed dog!
                                             g.   **h.**

4. **Look at pages 98 and 99 in your dictionary.** *True* or *False*? **Correct the <u>underlined</u> words in the false sentences.**

   a. The sewing machine operators are sewing by ~~hand~~. *machine*   _____false_____

   b. There are seven <u>bolts of fabric</u> in the garment factory.   _____

   c. The shirts on the <u>rack</u> in the garment factory are purple, green, and blue.   _____

   d. The <u>bobbin</u> is above the presser foot.   _____

   e. The women in the fabric store are looking at <u>hook and loop fasteners</u>.   _____

5. **Write the name of the material.**

   a.   b.   c.   d.

   a. ___corduroy___ This material is made from cotton. It can have a wide or narrow pattern of raised ridges (vertical lines). It is often used to make jackets and pants.

   c. _____ This strong material is usually made from cotton. In the 1800s, clothing maker Levi Strauss used it to make the first pair of jeans. Today this very popular material is worn all over the world, especially by young people.

   b. _____ This material is usually made from linen thread. It has a beautiful open design, often of flowers or leaves. It is often sewn by hand, but it can also be made by machine. It is used for blouses, dresses, curtains, and tablecloths.

   d. _____ This material comes from the chemistry laboratory, not from a plant or animal. It is very strong, and it is used to make stockings, pantyhose, windbreakers, and many other items of clothing.

6. **What about you? What are you wearing today? Complete the chart.**

Clothing Item	Material	Type of Closure	Type of Trim

CHALLENGE   Design a piece of clothing. Draw it and write a description.

Making Alterations

1. **Look at page 100 in your dictionary. What can you use to . . . ?**

   a. repair a rip when you don't have needle and thread   *safety pin*

   b. cut material   _____

   c. hold pins and needles   _____

   d. remove threads from a hem   _____

   e. measure a sleeve or waistband   _____

   f. protect your finger when you sew   _____

   g. put clothes on while you make alterations   _____

2. **Circle the words to complete the instructions to the tailor.**

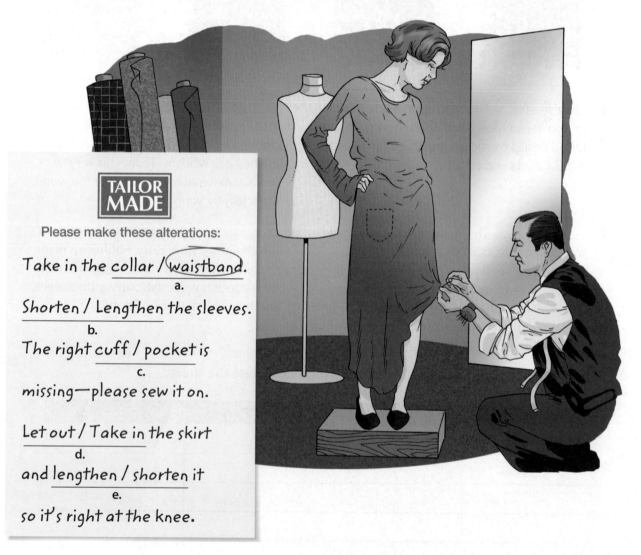

TAILOR MADE

Please make these alterations:

Take in the collar / (waistband).
                          a.

Shorten / Lengthen the sleeves.
              b.

The right cuff / pocket is
                   c.

missing—please sew it on.

Let out / Take in the skirt
            d.

and lengthen / shorten it
             e.

so it's right at the knee.

CHALLENGE   Look at the sewing supplies in your dictionary. Choose five and write their functions.
           Example: *A thimble protects your finger.*

100

1. **Look at page 101 in your dictionary. What do you need to . . . ?**

   a. make clothes softer _____*fabric softener*_____

   b. iron the clothes _____ and _____

   c. sort the laundry _____

   d. make clothes whiter _____

   e. dry wet clothes without a dryer _____ and _____

   f. dry wet clothes quickly _____

   g. hang up clean clothes in your closet _____

2. **Circle the words to complete the laundry room instructions.**

▌▌CLEANMACH   QUICK WASH

WASHING INSTRUCTIONS

1. Pour (laundry detergent)/ spray starch [a.] into the washer / dryer. [b.]

2. Load / Sort [c.] the machine. DO NOT OVERLOAD.

3. Choose the correct temperature.

4. Close door. Hanger / Washer [d.] will not operate with door open.

5. Insert coins or payment card into slot.

6. To add bleach / dryer sheets [e.]: wait until laundry basket / washer [f.] has filled.

7. When the rinse light goes on, add fabric softener / laundry detergent [g.] if you want.

DRYING INSTRUCTIONS

1. Clean the iron / lint trap [h.] before using the dryer.

2. Load / Unload [i.] the machine. DO NOT OVERLOAD. Overloading causes dirty / wrinkled [j.] clothes.

3. Add dryer sheets / clothespins [k.] if you want.

4. Close door. Dryer / Washer [l.] will not operate with door open.

5. Choose the correct temperature.

6. Insert coins or payment card into slot. Push *start* button.

For service, call (800) 000-WASH

CHALLENGE Look at some of your clothing labels. Write the laundry instructions.

Go to page 252 for Another Look (Unit 5).

A Garage Sale

1. **Look at pages 102 and 103 in your dictionary. *True* or *False*? Correct the underlined words in the false sentences.**

   tree
   a. There's a flyer on the ~~folding card table~~.   _____false_____

   b. A woman is <u>browsing</u> near the garage.   _____

   c. A <u>blue</u> sticker means the price is $2.00.   _____

   d. They have <u>new</u> clothing for sale.   _____

   e. A woman is bargaining for a <u>VCR</u>.   _____

2. **Complete the chart of items for sale at a garage sale.** ▮ = $10.00, ▮ = $5.00, ▮ = $2.00

Type of Item	Item	Price
Electronics	VCR	$10.00
Furniture		$5.00
	jacket	
Accessories	hat	
		$2.00

3. **Circle the words to complete the conversations. Use information from Exercise 2.**

   Donna: Hi. How much is this blue <u>jacket</u> / (sweatshirt)?
   a.

   Eddy: It's <u>$2.00 / $5.00</u>.
   b.

   Donna: But look, it's <u>stained / torn</u>.
   c.

   Alya: Do you need a folding <u>chair / card table</u>? This one's only $5.00.
   d.

   Chen: Why don't you <u>bargain / browse</u> a little? They might take $2.00 for it.
   e.

   Paz: What does the green <u>sticker / flyer</u> mean?
   f.

   Lia: It means the price is <u>$10.00 / $5.00</u>.
   g.

   Paz: That seems expensive for a <u>CD/cassette player / VCR</u>. Most people use DVRs now.
   h.

4. **What about you? Work with a partner. Imagine you are at a garage sale.
   Bargain for some of the items. Talk about the items in Exercise 2 or in your dictionary.**

5. **Look at pages 102 and 103 in your dictionary. Write the total for each group.**

They bought . . .	They paid . . .
a. an ironing board and a pair of cowboy boots	$10.00
b. a pair of black shoes, two purses, and a pair of jeans	_____
c. an iron, a gray coat, and a sport jacket	_____
d. a pair of sneakers, a pink robe, and a purse	_____
e. a hard hat, a pair of brown shoes, a blue T-shirt, and a CD / cassette player	_____

6. **Complete the article. Use the words in the box.**

browse	clock radio	folding chair	used clothing	~~garage sale~~
bargain	stickers	flyers	folding card table	VCR

TIPS FOR A SUCCESSFUL ___Garage Sale___
                                              a.

1 Find things to sell. You have a new alarm clock, so you don't need that old

_____ anymore. You watch DVDs, so why keep that old
         b.

_____?
         c.

2 Show the date, time, and address on your _____ .
                                                        d.

3 Give information about sizes of _____ —for example, size
                                              e.

10 women's dresses.

4 Set up your _____ and _____ early. People will arrive
                         f.   g.

before the sale starts.

5 Use colored _____ for prices. It's easier than price tags.
                         h.

6 Let people just look around and _____ , but also ask them what they
                                              i.

are looking for.

7 People love to _____ , so don't insist on the full price. You want the
                            j.

money more than that old pair of shoes—that's why you're having the garage

sale, right?

CHALLENGE Work with a group. Plan a garage sale for your class. Look at pages 53–56 and 86–87 in your dictionary. Choose items to sell and decide on the prices. How will you use the money?

1. **Look at pages 104 and 105 in your dictionary. Complete the definitions.**

   a. We use them to touch, to pick things up, and to type.   *fingers*

   b. We use them to hear.   _____

   c. We use them to see.   _____

   d. We use it to breathe and to smell.   _____

   e. It connects our head to our shoulders.   _____

   f. They are at the end of our feet. They help us walk.   _____

   g. It's the front part of our body, below the neck.   _____

   h. We use it to eat and to speak.   _____

   i. We have more than 100,000 of them on our head! They help keep our bodies warm.   _____

2. **Complete. Read these as: "Hand is to finger as foot is to toe."**

   a. hand : finger = foot : _____*toe*_____

   b. leg : foot = arm : _____

   c. hear : ears = see : _____

   d. touch : finger = smell : _____

   e. pants : legs = shoes : _____

3. **What about you? What clothes or accessories do you use for these parts of your body?**
   Example: *scarf, . . .*

   a. neck   _____

   b. head   _____

   c. eyes   _____

   d. ears   _____

   e. hands   _____

   f. legs   _____

   g. back   _____

   h. feet   _____

4. **Look at pages 104 and 105 in your dictionary. *True* or *False*?**

a. The man sitting on the park bench has his left leg crossed over his right leg. _____*true*_____

b. The man with the book is holding binoculars in his right hand. _____

c. The woman running has red hair. _____

d. The little boy's arms are in front of him. _____

e. The little boy isn't wearing anything on his feet. _____

5. **Circle the words to complete the article.**

← → C   🔍 www.aboutcomputers/default.us   ☰

COMPUTER HEALTH 101

Computers. They're great. We can't live without them. But sitting at one for
hours every day can cause problems for your body. Here are some tips to help
you work, play, and feel better at the computer.

Keep your (head) / hand up. Don't bend it down or back. Your feet / eyes should
        a.   b.
be at about the same height as the top of your computer screen.

Your arms / toes should be at your sides, close to your body. The bottom part of
        c.

your arms should be parallel to the floor. Relax your

feet / shoulders. Don't raise them. Your hands / feet
        d.   e.

should be relaxed and straight. Don't bend them up

or down. Your back / hair should be straight.
        f.

Sit up "tall." Your feet / ears should be on the floor.
        g.

Don't cross your eyes / legs! And remember: Stop
        h.

and take frequent breaks to rest your body!

CHALLENGE Which type of doctor should you see for problems with your . . . ? Match.

_____ **a.** feet   **1.** optometrist

_____ **b.** eyes   **2.** podiatrist

_____ **c.** ears   **3.** audiologist

Look online or ask someone you know.

Inside and Outside the Body

1. **Look at page 106 in your dictionary. Cross out the word that doesn't belong. Write the category.**

   a. <u>The Arm, Hand, and Fingers</u>   elbow   ~~shin~~   wrist

   b. _____   ankle   heel   knuckle

   c. _____   finger   see   hear

   d. _____   gums   teeth   forehead

2. **Circle the words to complete the instructions.**

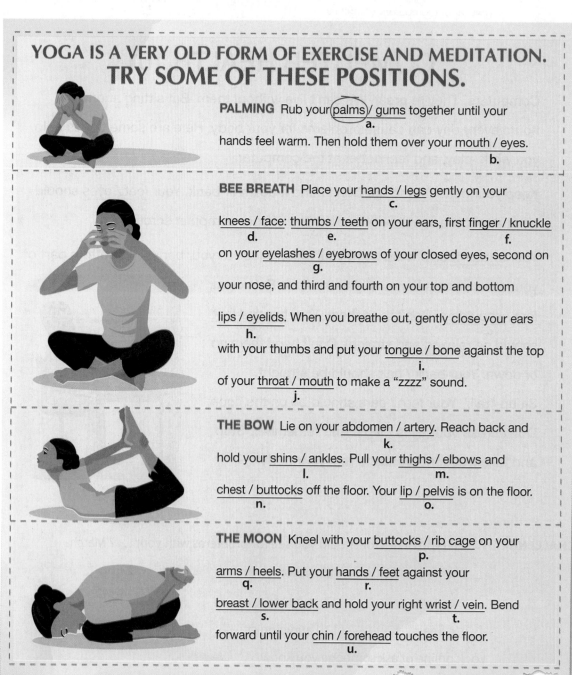

YOGA IS A VERY OLD FORM OF EXERCISE AND MEDITATION. TRY SOME OF THESE POSITIONS.

PALMING Rub your (palms) / gums together until your
                      a.
hands feel warm. Then hold them over your mouth / eyes.
                                                b.

BEE BREATH Place your hands / legs gently on your
                                    c.
knees / face: thumbs / teeth on your ears, first finger / knuckle
d.   **e.**   **f.**
on your eyelashes / eyebrows of your closed eyes, second on
                    g.
your nose, and third and fourth on your top and bottom

lips / eyelids. When you breathe out, gently close your ears
    h.
with your thumbs and put your tongue / bone against the top
                                    i.
of your throat / mouth to make a "zzzz" sound.
        j.

THE BOW Lie on your abdomen / artery. Reach back and
                           k.
hold your shins / ankles. Pull your thighs / elbows and
        l.   **m.**
chest / buttocks off the floor. Your lip / pelvis is on the floor.
n.   **o.**

THE MOON Kneel with your buttocks / rib cage on your
                              p.
arms / heels. Put your hands / feet against your
q.   **r.**
breast / lower back and hold your right wrist / vein. Bend
  s.   **t.**
forward until your chin / forehead touches the floor.
          u.

106

3. Read the article. Label the foot with the matching parts of the body.

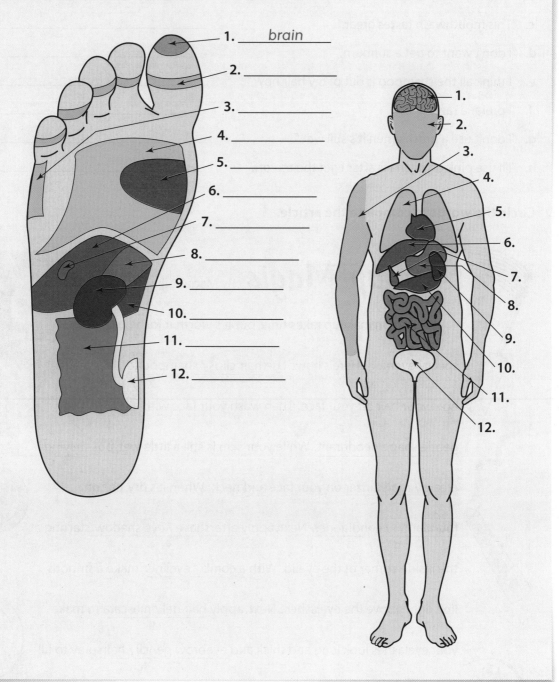

Some people use reflexology to stay healthy. They believe that by pressing certain parts of the foot, you can help certain parts of the body. For example, if you have a headache, you should press the top of your big toe.

1. _____brain_____
2. _____
3. _____
4. _____
5. _____
6. _____
7. _____
8. _____
9. _____
10. _____
11. _____
12. _____

4. What about you? What do you do to relax and stay healthy? What parts of the body are these activities good for? Write at least five sentences.

CHALLENGE   Write instructions for your favorite exercise.

Personal Hygiene

1. **Look at pages 108 and 109 in your dictionary. What is each person doing?**

   a. "This air is really hot."   _drying her hair_

   b. "This cap really keeps my hair dry!"   _____

   c. "This mouthwash tastes great."   _____

   d. "I don't want to get a sunburn."   _____

   e. "I think all the shampoo is out of my hair now." _____

   f. "I prefer a razor."   _____

   g. "I don't use a brush when it's still wet." _____

   h. "I'll use pink on my nails after I get the red off." _____

2. **Circle the words to complete the article.**

Makeup Magic By Magali Silveira

Putting on makeup takes time, but it's worth it for a

special evening. Here's how: Use (hair clips) / shampoo to
a.

hold your hair off your face. Then wash your face with a

gentle soap / deodorant. While your skin is still a little wet, put shaving
b.   **c.**

cream / moisturizer on your face and neck. When it's dry, put on

foundation / conditioner. Next, apply aftershave / eye shadow, starting at
d.   **e.**

the inside corner of the eyelid. With a comb / eyeliner, make a smooth
f.

line right above the eyelashes. Next, apply hair gel / mascara to make
g.

your eyelashes look long and thick and eyebrow pencil / hairspray to fill
h.

in the line of your eyebrows. Outline your lips and then fill in the lines

with lipstick / toothpaste. Finish off with a dusting of bath / face powder,
i.   **j.**

and you're ready to face the world!

108

3. Complete the crossword puzzle. Each clue is two words.

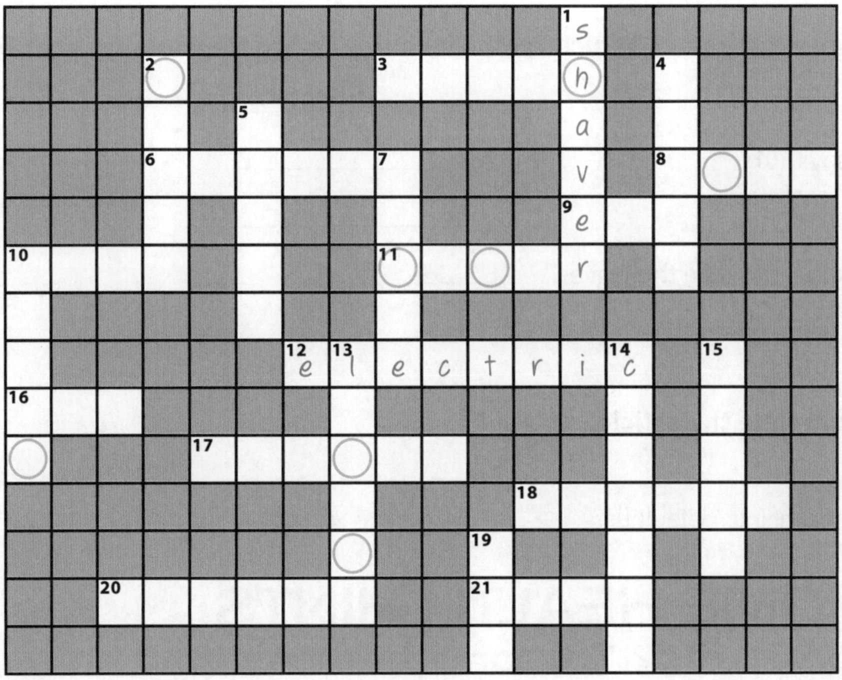

Clues

12 Across + 1 Down	You don't need water when you shave with it.
2 Down + 19 Down	It holds your hair in place.
3 Across + 10 Down	Use it after every meal.
5 Down + 6 Across	Be careful when you shave with them—they're sharp.
8 Across + 18 Across	Color your fingernails and toenails with it.
9 Across + 4 Down	It will make your eyes look bigger.
11 Across + 7 Down	Put it on your skin when you're finished shaving.
10 Across + 13 Down	It makes your skin feel smooth and soft.
14 Down + 21 Across	Style your hair with it.
16 Across and 20 Across	Use it outside to protect your skin from a burn.
17 Across + 15 Down	Remove food from between your teeth with it.

Now use the circled letters to answer this question:

What can you take to relax? _____ _____ _____ _____ _____ _____ _____ _____

4. What about you? What is your personal hygiene routine in the morning? List the steps.

Example: *First, I...*

CHALLENGE Write detailed instructions for one of the following tasks:
Washing and styling your hair   Flossing and brushing your teeth
Shaving   Doing your nails

1. **Look at page 110 in your dictionary. Which symptom or injury are they talking about?**

    a. "This one in the back hurts."   _toothache_

    b. "The thermometer says 101."   _____

    c. "I ate too much ice cream."   _____

    d. "Next time I'll wear gloves to rake the leaves." _____

    e. "Press on it to stop the bleeding."   _____

2. **Circle the words to complete the article.**

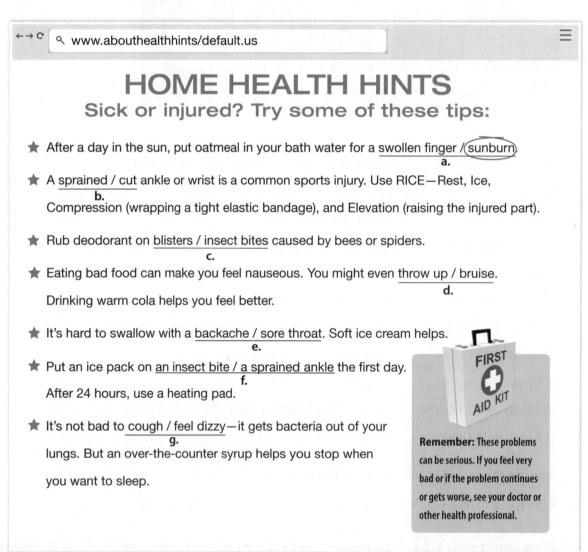

← → C   🔍 www.abouthealthhints/default.us   ☰

HOME HEALTH HINTS
Sick or injured? Try some of these tips:

★ After a day in the sun, put oatmeal in your bath water for a swollen finger / (sunburn).
   a.

★ A sprained / cut ankle or wrist is a common sports injury. Use RICE—Rest, Ice,
   b.
   Compression (wrapping a tight elastic bandage), and Elevation (raising the injured part).

★ Rub deodorant on blisters / insect bites caused by bees or spiders.
   c.

★ Eating bad food can make you feel nauseous. You might even throw up / bruise.
   d.
   Drinking warm cola helps you feel better.

★ It's hard to swallow with a backache / sore throat. Soft ice cream helps.
   e.

★ Put an ice pack on an insect bite / a sprained ankle the first day.
   f.
   After 24 hours, use a heating pad.

★ It's not bad to cough / feel dizzy—it gets bacteria out of your
   g.
   lungs. But an over-the-counter syrup helps you stop when
   you want to sleep.

FIRST AID KIT

Remember: These problems can be serious. If you feel very bad or if the problem continues or gets worse, see your doctor or other health professional.

3. **What about you? What do you do when you have a stomachache? an earache? a rash?**

    Example: *When I have a stomachache, I drink tea.*

CHALLENGE Find out about blisters. What are they? Write about how to prevent and treat them.

1. **Look at page 111 in your dictionary. What are the people talking about?**

   a. "Can you please fill <u>this</u> out for me?" <u>health history form</u>

   b. "According to <u>this</u>, your pressure is fine." _____

   c. "Relax. <u>This</u> will only hurt for a second." _____

   d. "According to <u>this</u>, you have a low fever." _____

   e. "When I listen through <u>this</u>, your lungs sound clear." _____

2. **Complete the pamphlet. Use the words in the box.**

~~appointment~~	check your blood pressure	draw blood
examination table	examine your eyes	examine your throat
health history form	health insurance card	listen to your heart
patient	nurse	receptionist

   # Dr. Gregory Sarett

   ## What to Expect During Your _Appointment_
   a.

   Before you see the doctor, the _____ will ask to see your
   b.

   _____ . If you are a new _____, she will also ask you to
   c.   d.

   complete a _____ . Then a _____ will check your
   e.   f.

   height and weight. She will also _____ to see if it is too high or too low.
   g.

   Then, Dr. Sarett, using a stethoscope, will _____ while you are on the
   h.

   _____ . He will use the stethoscope to listen to your lungs and abdomen,
   i.

   too. Next comes the vision exam. Using an ophthalmoscope (an instrument with a light), the

   doctor will _____ . He will also _____ , nose, and ears.
   j.   k.

   He may do other tests, too. He may, for example, _____ and send it to a lab
   l.

   for testing. At the end of the exam, he will discuss the results and make recommendations.

   CHALLENGE Look in your dictionary. Write about Mr. Zolmar's doctor's appointment.
   Begin: *Andre had a doctor's appointment. First, the receptionist . . .*

Illnesses and Medical Conditions

1. **Look at pages 112 and 113 in your dictionary. Complete the chart.**

Illness or Condition	What is it?	Contagious?	What are some symptoms?
a. *arthritis*	a disease of the joints	no	painful, swollen, stiff joints, often in hands, feet, shoulders, and hips
b.	a medical condition	no	tight feeling or pain in chest, difficulty breathing, wheezing, coughing
c.	a common childhood disease	yes	red, itchy rash on face, on body, and inside throat that turns into blisters; fever
d.	a very common infection of the nose, throat, etc.	yes	runny or stuffy nose, itchy or sore throat, cough, sneezing, low fever, tiredness, watery eyes
e.	a disease of the brain, more common in older people	no	confusion; problems with memory, language, and thinking; personality changes
f.	a condition caused by the pancreas not making enough insulin	no	tiredness, thirst, increased hunger, weight loss, blurred vision
g.	an infection most common in infants and children	no	nervousness, earache, "full" feeling in the ear, fever, difficulty hearing
h.	a condition often caused by hard and narrow arteries	no	(Often no symptoms in beginning) Later: chest pains, heart attack
i.	the virus that causes AIDS	yes	(In the beginning) swollen glands, sore throat, fever, rash
j.	a common childhood disease	yes	fever, dry cough, runny nose, red eyes, tiny spots inside mouth, red rash on forehead and around ears, and, later, whole body
k.	a childhood disease	yes	painful, swollen glands (between ear and jaw) on one or both sides of face, fever, tiredness
l.	a disease in which the cells divide uncontrollably	no	depend on what area of the body is affected; can include tiredness, skin changes, lumps under the skin, pain, and breathing problems

Based on information from: Mayoclinic.org.

2. **Complete the posts. Use the words in the box.**

allergic	allergies	anaphylaxis	breathing	hives	~~rash~~	sneezing	swelling

← → C   Sign In | Register ≡

Allergy Community Message Board   🔍 _____

Home
Discussions
Topics
Tips
Resources

I don't eat shrimp because I develop a very itchy
_____rash_____ on my neck. It's not a strong reaction, but
    a.
I'm afraid to try any other shellfish. What do you think?

130 Replies

I've had a cat for three years, but I think I'm getting
_____ to her. Whenever she's in the house, I
    b.
start _____ and blowing my nose. What should
        c.
I do?

98 Replies

I didn't know I had any _____ until I was a
                            d.
teenager. I was on a class picnic and I got stung by a
bee. Almost immediately, my face started _____
                                              e.
and turning red, and _____ broke out all over my
                          f.
skin. Within a couple of minutes, I was having trouble
_____. It was very scary. An ambulance came
    g.
and the EMTs told me that this kind of reaction is called
_____. Now I carry special medicine with me
    h.
wherever I go in case it happens again.

211 Replies

3. **What about you? Check (✓) the illnesses or medical conditions you had as a child.**

☐ measles   ☐ mumps   ☐ chicken pox
☐ asthma   ☐ flu   ☐ pneumonia

[CHALLENGE] Find out about high blood pressure. What is it? Is it contagious? What are some
             symptoms?

A Pharmacy

1. **Look at page 115 in your dictionary. What should the people buy at the pharmacy? Circle the answers.**

   a. "I need to keep my arm still."   Buy a cast / (a sling.)

   b. "I have a backache."   Try a heating pad / a humidifier.

   c. "I have a sore throat."   Get an antacid / throat lozenges.

   d. "My nose is stuffed."   Try an inhaler / nasal spray.

   e. "I'm coughing and sneezing a lot."   Buy cold tablets / eye drops.

   f. "I have a bad headache."   Get an air purifier / a pain reliever.

2. **Read the prescription labels. Write the type of medicine after each sentence. Use the words in the box.**

capsules	cough syrup	ointment

   Indications:
   Use on insect bites and rashes caused by poison ivy or poison oak.
   Directions:
   Apply a small amount of Corticurall 1 to 3 times a day.
   WARNING:
   FOR EXTERNAL USE ONLY
   CORTICURALL

   ABC/Pharmacy
   RX: 2596
   DATE FILLED: 6/9/18
   BLACK, Ronald
   Take 1 three times a day
   Temox 250 mg.
   Finish all medication.
   Dr. Susan Brown
   Qty: 30

   BCD Pharmacy
   RX: 789
   Date filled: 1/2/16
   Charnov, Rudy
   Take 2 tsp. by mouth
   Polyriscine CS
   every 4 hours
   Dr. Paul Rime
   Exp. 12/31/17
   Amount: 120 ml.

   a. You can use this three times a day. ___ointment___

   b. It's a liquid. _____

   c. The dosage is one, three times a day. _____

   d. This is an over-the-counter medication. _____

   e. Take this for ten days. _____

   f. The expiration date is in 2017. _____

   g. Don't take this by mouth. _____

   h. Don't take this on an empty stomach. _____

   i. Don't drive or operate heavy machinery when taking this medicine. _____

3. **Circle the words to complete the diary entries.**

Feb 11—Woke up in the hospital with crutches / (casts) on both my
                                                        a.
legs! I can't remember anything about the accident. Jim's OK,
thank goodness. He has a sling / walker on his arm, but that's all.
                                 b.
Here comes the nurse . . .

Feb 14—Jim visited me today and pushed me around the hospital in
a wheelchair / humidifier.
        c.

March 24—They took off the casts / canes. Now I can hold my
                                    d.
air purifier / walker in front of me and move around on my own.
        e.
After a couple of weeks, I'll be ready for a pair of crutches / capsules.
                                                          f.

April 8—I can stand, but I have to learn to use my legs again. The
exercises hurt a lot. I put an antacid / a heating pad on my painful
                                       g.
muscles after therapy. At first I used pain relievers / throat lozenges,
                                                      h.
but I don't like to take medicine.

April 28—Tomorrow I go home! It's been more than two months!
I still need to use a cane / an inhaler to get around, but it won't be
                          i.
long now until I can walk without any help.

4. **What about you? What over-the-counter medicine do you have at home?**
   Look at the labels and make a chart like the one below.

Type	Dosage	Indications	Warnings
tablets	1–2 tablets every 4–6 hours	to prevent nausea	Do not take if you have a breathing problem.

CHALLENGE Write about an accident or illness that you or someone you know has recovered from.
What were the treatments and medications? What were the steps to recovery?

1. Look at page 116 in your dictionary. What are the people doing?

a. "I think I'll watch some TV while I'm in bed."   *getting bed rest*

b. "I have to take one capsule two times a day."   _____

c. "This is hard exercise!"   _____

d. "I need to see a doctor. My back really hurts."   _____

e. "I'd like some more salad."   _____

f. "That's OK, Doctor. It only hurt for a second!"   _____

2. Read the doctor's notes and look at the picture. Is the patient following medical advice? What is he doing? What is he NOT doing?

From the Desk of Dr. Wise

a. Get bed rest.

b. Drink fluids.

c. Take medicine.

d. Eat a healthy diet.

e. Don't smoke!!!

a. *He isn't getting bed rest.* _____

b. _____

c. _____

d. _____

e. _____

3. **Look at page 117 in your dictionary. What's the problem?**

   a. "I can't read this. Why are the words so small?"   _vision problems_

   b. "Ow! My leg really hurts!"   _____

   c. "I feel sad all the time."   _____

   d. "What? Could you repeat that again, please?"   _____

   e. "Help! I have too much to do, and no time to do it!" _____

4. **Circle the words to complete the pamphlets.**

Do you have

(Vision Problems)/ Hearing Loss?
            a.
_____

Are you having trouble reading this?

It may be time for new

glasses / hearing aids.
       b.
Or maybe you like contact lenses / fluids.
                            c.
Visit an audiologist / optometrist and have
             d.
your eyes checked.

Are you feeling

tired and sad most of the time?
_____

Maybe you are one of the more than

20 million people suffering from

depression / stress. Don't despair!
       e.
See a physical therapist / therapist for
                  f.
physical / talk therapy. You can also
         g.
get immunized / join a support group.
                    h.

5. **What about you? What do you do when you feel stress?**

   Example: *When I feel stress, I exercise.*

CHALLENGE How do you take care of your health? What do you do? What don't you do?
            Write two paragraphs.

Medical Emergencies

1. **Look at page 118 in your dictionary. What happened? Complete the sentences.**

   a. The little girl in the laundry room _____ *swallowed poison* _____.

   b. The woman in the snow _____.

   c. The man with the toaster _____.

   d. The boy in the doctor's office _____.

   e. The man boiling water in the kitchen _____.

   f. After her car hit a tree, the woman on the ground _____.

   g. The woman near the ambulance _____ when the paramedics arrived.

2. **Circle the words to complete the article.**

How Safe Are You at Home?

Not very. As you probably know, most accidents occur at home. Millions of

people are injured at home every year using everyday products. Over a million

(fall)/ are in shock while using stairs, steps, or bicycles. Falls also cause thousands
   a.

of injuries in tubs and showers. But falling is not the only way that people get hurt

in the bathroom. Some people drown / choke or burn themselves / get frostbite
                                 b.   **c.**

while bathing. Many people also cut themselves and bleed / can't breathe while
                                                        d.

using razors. In the kitchen, people start fires or burn themselves / are unconscious
                                                   e.

while they are cooking. Sometimes children get an electric shock / swallow poison
                                              f.

because household cleaners are not safely stored. Many people are injured / have a
                                                                  g.

heart attack because something large, like a TV or a bookcase, falls on them. And,

of course, people sometimes bleed / get an electric shock because they don't take
                                  h.

care of appliance cords or allow the cords to get wet. Medication can also be

a danger in the home. People sometimes burn themselves / overdose
                                              i.

or have a heart attack / an allergic reaction
         j.

(such as a skin rash) while taking medications.

1. **Look at page 119 in your dictionary. Complete the information from a first aid manual.**

Always keep your medicine chest or first aid kit well supplied. Include:

a. _____gauze_____ for holding sterile pads in place, or (if sterile) for covering cuts

b. _____ for removing pieces of glass or wood from the skin

c. _____ for preventing movement of a broken or sprained arm, finger, etc.

d. _____ for covering large cuts and burns

e. _____ for holding pads and gauze in place

f. _____ for preventing infection of small cuts

g. _____ for covering small cuts

h. _____ for pouring on a new cut to help prevent infection

i. _____ for putting around a sprained ankle

j. _____ for treating rashes and allergic skin reactions

k. _____ for reducing pain and swelling

l. _____ for finding medical information

Note: A deep cut that continues to bleed may need _____ . Contact your doctor or go
m.
to a clinic or hospital emergency room. People with special medical conditions such as diabetes,

heart disease, or serious allergies, should wear a _____ to identify the problem.
n.

2. **Write the name of the life-saving technique. Use the words in the box.**

| CPR | Heimlich maneuver | rescue breathing |

a. _Heimlich maneuver_ Named after the doctor who invented it, this technique is used on people who are choking on food or another object.

b. _____ Performed mouth to mouth, this technique is used on people who have stopped breathing.

c. _____ This technique involves mouth-to-mouth breathing and heart compression on people who have stopped breathing. Special training is needed.

CHALLENGE Are there first aid items that you use that are not in your dictionary? Write about them.
Example: *I use vitamin E for small kitchen burns.*

Dental Care

1. **Look at page 120 in your dictionary. What is the dentist or dental hygienist doing?**

   a. "I'm getting all the plaque off."   _cleaning teeth_

   b. "I'm almost finished. Then I'll fill it."   _____

   c. "This will give us a good picture of that tooth."   _____

   d. "You won't feel any pain after this."   _____

   e. "It's almost out now."   _____

2. **Complete the pamphlet. Use the words in the box.**

cavities	crown	dental instruments	dentist	dentures
fillings	gum disease	hygienist	~~plaque~~	

   ## COMMON DENTAL QUESTIONS

   Q: What is _____plaque_____ ?
   a.

   A: A substance that forms on your teeth.

   After it gets hard, only a

   _____ or dental
   b.

   _____ using special
   c.

   _____ can remove it.
   d.

   Q: I never get _____.
   e.

   Do I still need to make appointments

   every year?

   A: Yes. Dentists also check for other

   problems, including cancer and

   _____, the main
   f.

   reason for tooth loss. The goal is to keep

   your own teeth and avoid needing

   _____.
   g.

   Q: I have a lot of old silver and gold

   _____. Is there
   h.

   anything I can do about their

   appearance?

   A: Yes. Dentists can place a

   _____ over a tooth
   i.

   with old fillings.

CHALLENGE   Write two questions for orthodontists. Try to find the answers.

120

1. **Look at page 121 in your dictionary. Complete the sentences.**

   a. The document that explains your insurance coverage is called an _insurance policy_ .

   b. The person who has the insurance is called a _____.

   c. An insurance company is called a _____.

   d. Most companies offer different _____. They are often called the Bronze, Silver, and Gold levels.

   e. If you pay more, you get more _____.

   f. It's important to _____ to find the one that is right for you.

   g. The law requires insurance companies to _____ soon after they receive it.

2. **Look at the insurance plans. Circle the words to complete the sentences.**

Alpha Company			
	Bronze	Silver	Gold
Monthly Premium*	$289	$345	$428
Deductible	$4,500	$3,000	$1,000
Co-pay	$25	$15	none
Out-of-pocket Maximum**	$10,000	$8,000	$3,000

*Average rate with two dependents
**All rates apply to in-network doctors.

BeWell Health Insurance			
	Bronze	Silver	Gold
Monthly Premium*	$239	$315	$405
Deductible	$6,000	$4,000	$2,000
Co-pay	$35	$20	none
Out-of-pocket Maximum**	$11,000	$9,000	$4,000

*Average rate with two dependents
**All rates apply to in-network doctors.

   a. BeWell's plans have lower (premiums) / deductibles than Alpha Company's plans.

   b. Alpha Company's deductibles / out-of-pocket maximums are $1,000 lower than BeWell's.

   c. If you buy a Gold plan from these companies, you don't have to pay a deductible / co-pay.

   d. These premiums are averages for a person with two dependents / deductibles.

   e. These plans reflect the prices you pay for in-network / out-of-network doctors.

   f. If you see an in-network / out-of-network doctor, you will pay more.

A Hospital

1. **Look at pages 122 and 123 in your dictionary. *True* or *False*? Correct the underlined words in the false sentences.**

   a. The ~~CNA~~ is checking the patient's IV drip.   _____false_____
      RN

   b. The <u>administrator</u> is putting an ID bracelet on a new patient.   _____

   c. The pediatrician's patient isn't wearing a <u>hospital gown</u>.   _____

   d. The <u>surgical nurse</u> is discussing a patient's food.   _____

   e. There's a medical waste disposal container inside the <u>lab</u>.   _____

   f. There's medication on the patient's <u>bed table</u>.   _____

   g. The <u>bedpan</u> is next to the hospital bed.   _____

   h. The <u>volunteer</u> is drawing blood for a blood test.   _____

2. **Circle the words to complete the information from a hospital pamphlet.**

The Operation—What to Expect
Surgery is stressful, but it can help to know what to expect.

In most cases, orderlies will take you to the hospital's emergency /(operating) room on a
                                                           a.

bed table / gurney. They will then carefully move you to the ambulance / operating table,
         b.   c.
where the surgery will take place. Your surgical team (the anesthesiologist, surgical

nurses, and, of course, the dietician / surgeon) will be there. In order to avoid infection,
                                                d.
they will wear surgical caps / gowns on their heads and sterile surgical gloves / stretchers
                    e.   f.
on their hands. All the instruments will be sterilized, too. During

the operation, the administrator / anesthesiologist will monitor
                               g.
all your medical charts / vital signs (blood pressure, breathing,
                   h.
and heart rate). A call button / An IV, attached to a vein in
                    i.
your arm, will provide you with fluids, and, if necessary,

medication. Ask your doctor how long it will take to recover

from your operation. Remember: Knowing what to expect

will help you feel better!

3. **Look at the chart. Write the numbers to complete the sentences.**

Doctors by Specialty and Gender in the United States		
Specialty	Male	Female
anesthesiology	33,917	12,226
cardiology	19,435	2,365
internal medicine	153,236	69,479
obstetrics / gynecology	21,833	23,189
ophthalmology	15,902	4,597
pediatrics	33,357	45,976
psychiatry	41,311	24,968
radiology	33,240	9,613

Based on information from: USA Doctors Data (2014) and Association of American Medical Colleges AAMC (2012).

a. There are _____4,597_____ female eye doctors in the United States.

b. The number of male eye doctors is _____.

c. There are _____ female doctors who are X-ray specialists.

d. _____ male doctors are heart specialists.

e. _____ male doctors specialize in mental illness (for example, depression).

f. _____ female doctors specialize in women's healthcare.

g. _____ male doctors specialize in children's medicine.

4. **What about you? Who would you prefer? Check (✓) the columns.**

	Male	Female	No Preference
a. internist			
b. cardiologist			
c. psychiatrist			
d. ophthalmologist			
e. orderly			
f. obstetrician			
g. pediatrician			
h. nurse			

CHALLENGE   Find out the name of other kinds of medical specialists. What do they do?
Example: *An orthopedist is a bone doctor.*

Go to page 253 for Another Look (Unit 6).

A Health Fair

1. **Look at pages 124 and 125 in your dictionary. *True* or *False*?**

   a. The <u>aerobics</u> class starts at 10:00.   _____true_____

   b. There's a <u>fat-free</u> cooking demonstration.   _____

   c. The health fair opened at <u>9:00</u>.   _____

   d. An acupuncture treatment is <u>free</u>.   _____

   e. You can buy <u>vitamins</u> at the Good Foods booth.   _____

   f. The medical screening is <u>free</u>.   _____

   g. A nurse is <u>taking</u> a woman's <u>temperature</u>.   _____

   h. The eye exam is <u>$2.00</u>.   _____

   i. There's a nutrition label <u>lecture</u>.   _____

2. **Write the letter of the false sentences in Exercise 1. Make them true.**

   _b._   _There's a sugar-free cooking demonstration._ _____

   ____   _____

   ____   _____

   ____   _____

   ____   _____

3. **Circle the words to complete the journal entry.**

   Today, I went to a <u>booth</u> / (health fair) at a local <u>clinic</u> / <u>demonstration</u>. I am so glad I went!
   a. b.
   At the <u>hatha yoga</u> / <u>medical screening</u> booth, I found out that my <u>blood pressure</u> / <u>pulse</u> is a little
   c. d.
   high—135 over 80. The nurse told me that exercise helps, so I watched a very interesting

   <u>acupuncture</u> / <u>aerobic exercise</u> class. It looked easy and fun, and I'll ask my doctor if it's OK for me.
   e.
   Next, I had an <u>ear</u> / <u>eye</u> exam and found out I can see perfectly—no problems there! I wanted to
   f.
   try an acupuncture <u>exam</u> / <u>treatment</u>, but the needles scared me a little. Maybe next time. The last
   g.
   booth had a lecture about <u>nutrition labels</u> / <u>vitamins</u>—very interesting! I'm going to start reading
   h.
   them when I shop for food.

4. **What about you? Do you exercise? Is exercise important to you? Why or why not? Tell a classmate.**

5. Look in your dictionary. Complete the flyer.

Come to the ___Health Fair___ !
a.

Where: Fadool _____ **When:** _____ , 9–4
b.   c.

Learn and have fun at these booths:

1 _____ We'll check your blood pressure and
d.
_____ your _____ for only $2.00.
e.   f.

2 _____ Can you see the big *E*? How about
g.
the little *c*? Find out here—it's _____ !
h.

3 _____ Are you getting enough protein?
i.
Listen and learn about _____ .
j.

4 _____ Exercise and
k.
relax the gentle way. 2–3 p.m.

5 _____ Chef Bill will
l.
show you how to cook sugar-free desserts.

6 _____ Headaches?
m.
Sore feet? Feeling blah? Try a treatment
for only $5.00.

See you there!

---

6. Where can you hear . . . ? Match.

_2_ **a.** "Bend your left leg. Raise your right arm."   **1.** nutrition lecture

___ **b.** "Now cover your left eye, and read the first row."   **2.** aerobic exercise or yoga class

___ **c.** "Seventy-two beats a minute. Excellent."   **3.** acupuncture treatment

___ **d.** "You can make this delicious dessert with no sugar!" **4.** medical screening

___ **e.** "Notice the serving size. It's only a half cup."   **5.** cooking demonstration

___ **f.** "Just relax. The needle won't hurt."   **6.** eye exam

---

CHALLENGE Work with a classmate. Imagine you are planning a health fair. Look at the activities in the word box below and the ones in your dictionary. What are some activities that you will include? Why?

| bicycle safety | talking to your doctor | quitting smoking |
| having a healthy back | making a first aid kit | having healthy teeth |

1. Look at pages 126 and 127 in your dictionary. *True* or *False*? Correct the <u>underlined</u> words in the false sentences.

a. The post office is across from the ~~bank~~.   *courthouse*   _____*false*_____

b. The bank is on Main Street next to the <u>police station</u>.   _____

c. The Chinese restaurant is between the courthouse and the <u>fire station</u>.   _____

d. The gas station is on 6th Street, across from the <u>office building</u>.   _____

e. The parking garage is next to the <u>hotel</u>.   _____

f. The <u>city hall</u> is on the corner of Grand Avenue and Main Street.   _____

g. The <u>bus station</u> is on the corner of Elm Street and Grand Avenue.   _____

2. Complete the ads.

a.

INTOWN _____ *Parking Garage*
Your car is safe with us.
Park long- or short-term.
Low rates.
130 Washington Place

b.

Down City _____
201 Elm Street
International Cooking
Open for dinner
Tues–Sun 6:00–9:00
Reservations suggested
Tel 555-2634   Fax 555-2635

c.

Miram _____
Medicine with a Heart
Patient information 555-4313
Emergency service 555-4310
Visit our website at www.mh.us.

d.

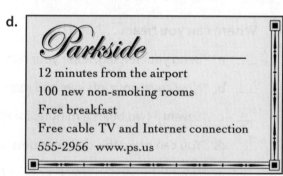

Parkside _____
12 minutes from the airport
100 new non-smoking rooms
Free breakfast
Free cable TV and Internet connection
555-2956   www.ps.us

e.

Rick's _____
Open every day from 6 a.m. to midnight.
Best car wash in town!
Just 2 minutes from the highway

f.

The People's Savings _____
"Where your money is our business!"
Downtown Branch:
210 Main Street
24-hour ATM
555-6666

3. **Look at pages 126 and 127 in your dictionary. Where can you go to . . . ?**

a. have lunch _____the restaurant_____

b. borrow a book or DVD _____

c. visit a sick friend _____

d. spend the night _____

e. get a bus to Boston _____

f. apply for a driver's license _____

g. report a crime _____

h. get married _____

4. **Circle the words to complete the notes.**

a.
> I went to the (bank) / city hall
> to get some money.
> I'll be home around 4:00.
>
> Dan

b.
> I'm driving Suzie to the
> bus station / hospital.
> She's taking the 8:40 to
> Greenville. See you soon.
>
> Alicia

c.
> It's now 3:00. I'm going to the
> gas station / parking garage.
> The tires need air.
> I'll be back soon.
>
> M

d.
> I needed to go to the
> office building / post office
> to buy some stamps.
> Also, your Mom called.
>
> R

5. **What about you? Work with a partner. Complete the chart with information about your community.**

Place	Street Location
library	
courthouse	
bus station	
city hall	
fire station	
police station	
post office	

CHALLENGE Look in a phone book or at an online phone directory.
Find the names of a hotel, a bank, a library, and a hospital in your community.

1. **Look at pages 128 and 129 in your dictionary. Where can you find . . . ?**
   (Do not use *supermarket* or *shopping mall*.)

   a. a sandwich _____coffee shop_____

   b. a cake _____

   c. paper and pens _____

   d. the best view of the city _____

   e. tickets for a football game _____

   f. English classes _____ or _____

   g. a new couch _____

   h. a used car _____

   i. paint for your living room _____

   j. a room for the night _____

   k. a place to exercise _____

2. **Complete the tourist information. Use the words in the box.**

cemetery	church	convention center	school
shopping mall	~~skyscraper~~	stadium	theater

   # PLACES OF INTEREST IN
   # NEW YORK CITY

   Empire State Building Over 1,250 feet tall, this building is the most famous _skyscraper_ in
   a.
   New York City. Go to the top for a wonderful view.

   Yankee _____ Located in the Bronx, this is home to one of the best teams in baseball
   b.
   history—the New York Yankees.

   Trump Tower Inside this modern building at Fifth Avenue and 56th Street, you will find five floors of

   excellent (and very expensive) stores from around the world in a large _____.
   c.

Jacob K. Javits Center Thousands of businesspeople and tourists go to this _____ called "The Marketplace for the World," to see exhibits such as the New York International Auto Show and Book Expo America.
d.

Trinity _____ This is one of the oldest and most beautiful houses of worship in the city. Many historically important people, such as Alexander Hamilton and Robert Fulton, are buried in its _____.
e.

f.

Cooper Union Completed in 1859, this _____ is one of the oldest in the United States. Free classes were given day and night to fit working people's schedules. Students of all ages still study there today.
g.

Broadway and 42nd Street This is a great location if you want to go to the _____. On every night (except Monday), you can choose between more than 30 shows around this famous intersection.
h.

3. **What about you? Would you want to live near a . . . ? Check (✓) the boxes.**

	Yes	No	Why?
construction site	☐	☐	_____
school	☐	☐	_____
supermarket	☐	☐	_____
factory	☐	☐	_____
Other: _____	☐	☐	_____

CHALLENGE Make a list of places for tourists to visit in your city or town. Include information about each of the places.

1. **Look at pages 130 and 131 in your dictionary. Where can a shopper use these coupons?**

a. _fast food restaurant_

b. _____

c. _____

d. _____

e. _____

f. _____

2. **Where can you hear . . . ? Use your dictionary if you need help.**

Dad: I can't read the menu.

Tim: Drive forward a little.

a. _drive-thru window_

Bob: Where's the bleach?

Kim: On top of the dryer.

c. _____

Anne: How much change do I need?

Clerk: Two quarters for ten pages.

b. _____

Pete: Do you get Spanish papers?

Owner: _El Diario_ comes on Tuesdays.

d. _____

3. Look at the picture. <u>Underline</u> six more mistakes in the newspaper article.

LOCAL NEWS

Last week, Fran Bates rode her bike into Mel Smith's <u>car</u>. There were no injuries. A pedestrian entered the book store with a dog and was asked to leave. Two children opened the mailbox on Elm Street. Fire Chief Dane closed it and called their parents. A shopper parked a car at the crosswalk on Main Street and received a parking ticket.

The town council met yesterday and voted to fix the parking space at Main and Elm. Pedestrians say they cannot cross the street safely. Officer Dobbs reported that the parking meter on that corner should also be fixed. Finally, the council voted for another street vendor. Shoppers complained about long lines for the only one in service in front of the photo shop.

4. Look at the picture in Exercise 3. Rewrite the article correctly.

Example: *Last week, Fran Bates rode her bike into Mel Smith's cart.*

CHALLENGE   Look at the picture in Exercise 3. Write about other problems.

1. **Look at pages 132 and 133 in your dictionary. Check (✓) the activities you can do at this mall. Write the kind of store you can do them in. (Do not use *department store*.)**

   ☐ buy cough syrup _____

   ✓ buy a birthday card _____card store_____

   ☐ look at digital video recorders _____

   ☐ get clothes dry-cleaned _____

   ☐ plan a vacation _____

   ☐ get new eyeglasses _____

   ☐ get a hamburger _____

   ☐ buy flowers _____

   ☐ buy a dictionary _____

   ☐ buy a dog _____

   ☐ mail letters _____

   ☐ buy chocolates _____

2. **Two teenagers are shopping at a mall. Look at the mall directory on page 133 of this book. Read the conversations and write the kind of place for each one.**

   a. **Server:** What flavor?
      Emma: Strawberry, please. _____ice cream shop_____

   b. **Amy:** What do you think? Too curly?
      Emma: No. It's a terrific perm. _____

   c. **Amy:** I love that new song by King.
      Emma: Let's go buy the CD. _____

   d. **Emma:** Hey! Do you want to take the elevator?
      Amy: No. Let's take this instead. It'll be faster. _____

   e. **Emma:** Let's go here for your high heels.
      Amy: Good idea. I usually don't like shopping at Crane's. _____

   f. **Amy:** Do you like these earrings?
      Emma: Yeah. You look good in gold. _____

   g. **Emma:** I need to get a new cell phone.
      Amy: Well, there's Cell Town right over there. _____

   h. **Amy:** Excuse me. Where's the main entrance?
      Clerk: Right over there. Next to the restrooms. _____

3. Look at Exercise 2. Circle the numbers and symbols on the map and draw Amy and Emma's route.

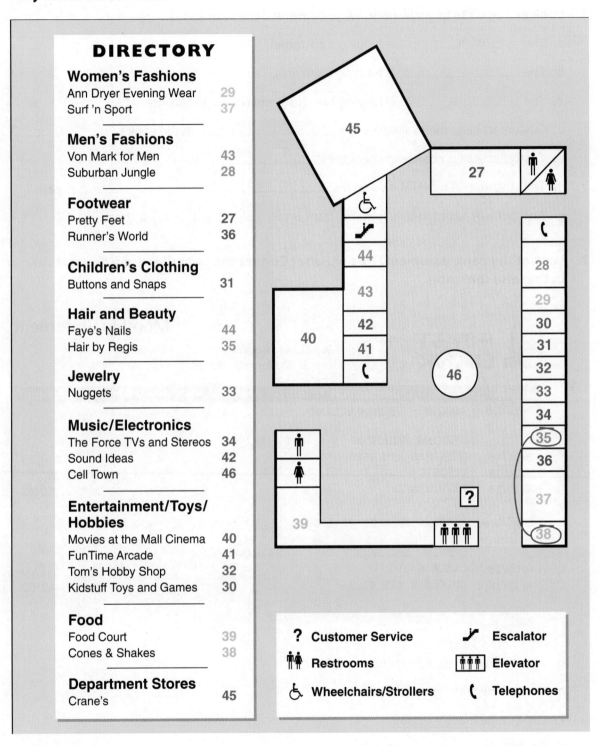

DIRECTORY

Women's Fashions
| Ann Dryer Evening Wear | 29 |
| Surf 'n Sport | 37 |

Men's Fashions
| Von Mark for Men | 43 |
| Suburban Jungle | 28 |

Footwear
| Pretty Feet | 27 |
| Runner's World | 36 |

Children's Clothing
| Buttons and Snaps | 31 |

Hair and Beauty
| Faye's Nails | 44 |
| Hair by Regis | 35 |

Jewelry
| Nuggets | 33 |

Music/Electronics
The Force TVs and Stereos	34
Sound Ideas	42
Cell Town	46

Entertainment/Toys/Hobbies
Movies at the Mall Cinema	40
FunTime Arcade	41
Tom's Hobby Shop	32
Kidstuff Toys and Games	30

Food
| Food Court | 39 |
| Cones & Shakes | 38 |

Department Stores
| Crane's | 45 |

? Customer Service
Restrooms
Wheelchairs/Strollers
Escalator
Elevator
Telephones

4. What about you? Look at the mall in Exercise 3. Where would you like to go? Why?

CHALLENGE Where do you prefer to shop—downtown (the business center of a town or city) or a shopping mall? Think about weather conditions, the transportation you can use to get there, the kinds of stores, prices, and entertainment. Write at least five sentences.

1. Look at page 134 in your dictionary. Complete the sentences.

a. The _____teller_____ is helping a customer.

b. The _____ is wearing a uniform.

c. The _____ is helping two customers open an account.

d. Customers keep their valuables in a _____ in the bank's _____.

e. Customers can go online to check their _____.

f. The customer at the ATM is using his _____ to _____ cash.

g. Another way to get money from the bank is to _____ a check.

2. Look at the bank statement. *True* or *False*? Correct the underlined words in the false sentences.

FIRST BANK

Monthly Statement

Jamal Al-Marafi
March 31–April 30, 2018

DATE	TRANSACTION		AMOUNT	BALANCE
SAVINGS	ACCOUNT NUMBER: 0125-00			
	OPENING BALANCE: $1,117.20			
3/31/18	QUIKCASH ATM #123	W	50.00	1,067.20
4/01/18	DEPOSIT	D	1,283.47	2,350.67
4/20/18	WITHDRAWAL	W	100.00	2,250.67
CHECKING	ACCOUNT NUMBER: 0135-08			
	OPENING BALANCE: $849.00			
4/05/18	CHECK #431	W	732.00	117.00
4/11/18	QUIKCASH ATM #123	W	75.00	42.00

      checking

a. Jamal's ~~savings~~ account number is 0135-08. _____*false*_____

b. On 3/31, he <u>withdrew cash</u>. _____

c. On 4/01, he <u>made a deposit</u>. _____

d. On 4/05, he used his <u>checkbook</u>. _____

e. On 4/11, the balance in his checking account was <u>$849.00</u>. _____

f. On 4/11, he used <u>a deposit slip</u>. _____

CHALLENGE Compare the balances and transactions in Jamal's savings and checking accounts.
      Example: *Jamal made one deposit in his … .*

1. **Look at page 135 in your dictionary. Complete the sentences.**

   a. You can look up the Nile River in an _____ atlas _____.

   b. The little girl and her mother are looking at a _____.

   c. You'll need a _____ to check out library books.

   d. The library clerk is at the _____.

   e. If you keep a book too long, you have to _____.

2. **Complete the librarian's answers. Use the words in the box.**

author	biography	~~e-book~~	magazines	newspaper
online catalog	periodicals	reference librarian	title	

   Patron: Do you have the novel *Tom Sawyer*?

   Librarian: No, it's checked out, but we have it

   as an _____ e-book _____.
   a.

   Patron: I'm looking for a job. Do you have this weekend's

   job ads?

   Librarian: The Sunday _____ is over there
   b.

   along with the other _____.
   c.

   Patron: Where can I find information about fashion and makeup?

   Librarian: We get several fashion _____ every month. Try those.
   d.

   Patron: I'm looking for a novel by Jane Austen, but I can't remember what it's called.

   Librarian: You don't need the _____. Just type the name of the
   e.
   _____ into the _____ and press *Enter*.
   f. **g.**

   Patron: Can you recommend a good _____ about John F. Kennedy?
   h.

   I have to write a report about his life.

   Librarian: Sorry. I'm the library clerk. Ask the _____. She's over there.
   i.

   CHALLENGE   Look at the library in your dictionary. What is each person doing?
   Example: *The reference librarian is showing a man an atlas.*

1. **Look at pages 136 and 137 in your dictionary. Answer the questions.**

   a. What comes in books of 20?   _____stamps_____

   b. What says *Newton, New York*?   _____

   c. What has a Los Angeles postmark?   _____

   d. What tells you the weight of a package?   _____

   e. Where can you buy stamps?   _____ or

                                                    _____

   f. Who delivers the mail?   _____

2. **Circle the words to complete the information about the U.S. postal services.**

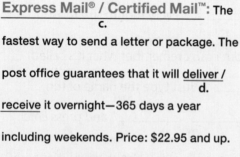

HOW TO SEND YOUR MAIL   *U.S. MAIL*

First-Class Letter / Package: For
a.
envelopes weighing 13 oz. or less. Price: First

oz. $0.47, each additional oz. $0.21.

Postcard / Postmark: Price: $0.34.
b.

Priority Mail®: Mail weighing more than 13

oz. Price: $6.45 and up.

Express Mail® / Certified Mail™: The
c.
fastest way to send a letter or package. The

post office guarantees that it will deliver /
d.
receive it overnight—365 days a year

including weekends. Price: $22.95 and up.

Ground post: For scales / packages weighing
e.
from 1–70 lbs. Price: $6.75 and up.

Certified Mail™ / Priority Mail®: The safest
f.
way to address / mail important, valuable letters
g.
and packages. You get a mailing receipt, and the

receiver's post office also keeps a record.

You can find postal forms / return addresses for
h.
this service at your post office. Price: $3.30 plus

postage.

Airmail / Media Mail® (Book Rate): For
i.
small and large packages containing books, CDs,

DVDs, and other media. Price: $2.61 and up.

Note: Rates change. Check your local post office or go to www.usps.com.

3. **What about you? What kinds of mail service do you use? How much do they cost?**

4. Look at the information in Exercise 2. Answer the questions.

a. You are mailing a very important document to a school. What's the safest way to mail it?
   __Certified Mail™__

b. Your letter must arrive tomorrow. What's the fastest way to send it? _____

c. You are mailing DVDs to your nephew. How should you send them? _____

d. You are mailing gifts to your family. They live in the same state as you. You need the package to arrive in 10 days. What's the cheapest way to send them? _____

e. You are mailing a 14-oz. envelope to a friend. It's OK if it doesn't arrive tomorrow.
   What's the cheapest way to send it? _____

5. Complete this email. Use the words in the box.

addressed	delivered	envelope	~~greeting card~~	letter carrier	mailbox
mailed	put on	received	return address	stamp	wrote

My Mail

To: LibraGuy@iol.us
Subject: Sorry!

Hi Enrique!

I really didn't forget your birthday on October 4! Two weeks ago, I went to the store and got you

a beautiful _____*greeting card*_____. I _____ a note in the card, put the card in
                        a.   **b.**

the green _____, _____ the envelope, walked to the nearest
              c.   **d.**

_____, and _____ the card. Yesterday I was very surprised when the
     e.   **f.**

_____ _____ the card—to ME!!! Guess what! I forgot to _____
     g.   **h.**   **i.**

a stamp! (Luckily, I didn't forget to write my _____ on the envelope!) So, long story
                                                      j.

short, that's the reason you never _____ a card from me this year.
                                          k.

Next year I'll send you an e-card, so I won't need a _____!
                                                            l.

CHALLENGE   Use the information in Exercise 2 to calculate the postage within the United States for . . . .

   a. a 3-oz. letter   _____   c. a 3-oz. certified letter   _____

   b. a small postcard   _____   d. a 1-oz. letter for next-day delivery   _____

137

Department of Motor Vehicles (DMV)

1. **Look at the DMV office on page 138 in your dictionary.** *True* or *False*? **Correct the <u>underlined</u> words in the false sentences.**

    DMV handbook
    a. You can get a form or a <u>p̶h̶o̶t̶o̶</u> at the information stand.   *false*

    b. Three people are taking a test in the <u>testing area</u>.   _____

    c. A DMV clerk is taking a man's <u>fingerprint</u>.   _____

    d. Another clerk is giving a man a <u>vision exam</u>.   _____

    e. One <u>window</u> is closed.   _____

2. **Look at the pictures. Answer the questions.**

PROOF OF INSURANCE	KEEP IN VEHICLE AS EVIDENCE OF INSURANCE	
POLICYHOLDER: ROSA RODRIGUEZ	**POLICY NUMBER:** 54323-45HG	**ABC** **AUTO INSURANCE** 14601 Young Street Houston, TX 77034
ADDRESS: 79 MAIN ST HOUSTON, TX 77002	**EXPIRATION DATE:** 12/01/2018	
MAKE: HONDA CIVIC	**YEAR:** 2013	

   a. What is Rosa's license plate number?   *LVD 123*

   b. What is her driver's license number?   _____

   c. When is the expiration date for her license?   _____

   d. Is there a registration sticker on her license plate?   _____

   e. When is the expiration date for her proof of insurance?   _____

3. Circle the words to complete the information from the website.

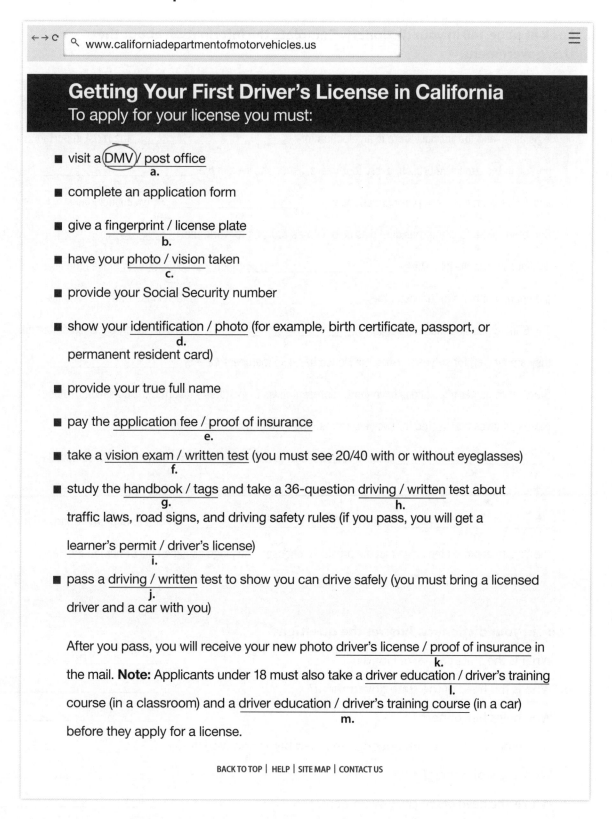

www.californiadepartmentofmotorvehicles.us

Getting Your First Driver's License in California
To apply for your license you must:

- visit a (DMV) / post office
  a.

- complete an application form

- give a <u>fingerprint / license plate</u>
  b.

- have your <u>photo / vision</u> taken
  c.

- provide your Social Security number

- show your <u>identification / photo</u> (for example, birth certificate, passport, or
  d.
  permanent resident card)

- provide your true full name

- pay the <u>application fee / proof of insurance</u>
  e.

- take a <u>vision exam / written test</u> (you must see 20/40 with or without eyeglasses)
  f.

- study the <u>handbook / tags</u> and take a 36-question <u>driving / written</u> test about
  g.   **h.**
  traffic laws, road signs, and driving safety rules (if you pass, you will get a

  <u>learner's permit / driver's license</u>)
  i.

- pass a <u>driving / written</u> test to show you can drive safely (you must bring a licensed
  j.
  driver and a car with you)

  After you pass, you will receive your new photo <u>driver's license / proof of insurance</u> in
  k.
  the mail. **Note:** Applicants under 18 must also take a <u>driver education / driver's training</u>
  l.
  course (in a classroom) and a <u>driver education / driver's training course</u> (in a car)
  m.
  before they apply for a license.

BACK TO TOP | HELP | SITE MAP | CONTACT US

CHALLENGE Compare getting a license in California to getting a license in your native country or
another state in the United States. **Example:** *In Germany, you can sometimes get your
driver's license when you are 17...*

Government and Military Service

1. **Look at page 140 in your dictionary. Complete the information about the U.S. government.**

There are three _____branches_____ of government: the _____ , the
          a.   **b.**

legislative, and the judicial. There is an election for _____ , the most important
                                                    c.

person in the executive branch, every four years. He or she lives in the _____
                                                         d.

and runs the country. The president chooses a _____ , which includes a
                                               e.

Secretary of State. If the president dies or becomes too sick to work, the _____
                                                         f.

continues to do the job. The _____ branch, called Congress, makes the laws of
                                  g.

the country. It has two "houses": the _____ and the House of Representatives.
                                            h.

The Senate has 100 members called _____ . There are two from each state and
                                            i.

they are elected for six-year terms. The House has 435 members called _____ .
                                                          j.

States with bigger populations have more representatives than states with smaller populations. These

representatives are elected for two-year terms. The third branch of government, the

_____ branch, reviews laws to make sure they follow the U.S. Constitution. The
                    k.

highest court is called the _____ . Its decisions are final. Eight
                                       l.

_____ and one _____ "sit" on the Supreme Court. After
          m.   **n.**

the Senate approves the judge that the president chooses, the judge can keep his or her job for life.

2. **Look in your dictionary. Answer the questions.**

   a. What is the state capital of Florida?   _____*Tallahassee*_____

   b. Who is the head of the state government?   _____

   c. Who helps him or her?   _____

   d. Which branch of government does an assemblyperson work for?   _____

   e. Who else works there?   _____

   f. Who is the head of the city government?   _____

   g. Which branch of government does a councilperson work for?   _____

CHALLENGE   Compare a branch of the U.S. government with another country's government that you know. **Example:** *In the U.S., a president runs the country. In Jordan, a king runs the country.*

3. Look at the pie chart. Circle the words to complete the sentences.

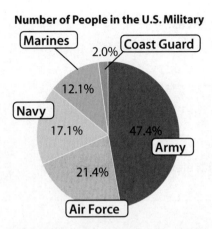

Number of People in the U.S. Military

Marines
2.0% Coast Guard
12.1%
Navy
17.1%
47.4%
Army
21.4%
Air Force

Based on information from: 2013 Demographics Report: Profile of the Military Community.

a. The (Army) / Navy is the biggest branch of the military.

b. The Air Force / Marines is bigger than the Navy / Army.

c. The Marines / Coast Guard is the smallest branch.

d. The chart does not include the National Guard / Navy.

4. Complete the article. Use the words in the box.

active duty	admiral	airman	general	officer	on reserve
Pentagon	recruit	~~Secretary of Defense~~	soldier	veterans	

Quick Facts about the U.S. Military

○ The ___Secretary of Defense___ is the main advisor to the president on military matters. Only the
       a.
president has more power over the military.

○ The headquarters of the Department of Defense is the _____, an enormous
                                    b.
office building in Arlington, Virginia, named for its unusual shape.

○ Normally, to become an _____ in the military, you must have a four-year
                     c.
college degree and receive special training. The highest officer in the Army is called a

_____. In the Navy, the highest officer is an _____ .
       d.   **e.**

○ The U.S. military has over 1,300,000 members who are on _____ around the
                                      f.
world. In addition, there are 811,000 people _____. These people can be
                              g.
called if they are needed.

○ There are thousands of recruiting stations across the country. If you want to be a

_____ , you can go to an Army recruiting station, if you want to be an
       h.
_____, you can go to an Air Force recruiting station, and so on. Every
       i.
_____ needs to pass a physical exam, an academic test, and a background check.
       j.

○ There are many benefits for _____ of the Armed Forces, including
                         k.
healthcare, education, and access to housing loans.

Civic Engagement

1. **Look at page 142 in your dictionary. Complete the sentences.**

   a. To avoid a $500 fine, you must ___*obey the law*___.

   b. Anne Johnson reads the newspaper in order to _____.

   c. Alena Smolka decided to _____ *yes* in the election.

   d. Charles Li uses a check to _____.

   e. This year, Ana Guzman must _____ with eleven other citizens.

   f. As an eighteen-year-old male, Todd McBain must _____.

2. **Read the sentences. Which right is each person thinking about? Use the words in the box.**

   | ~~fair trial~~ free speech freedom of the press freedom of religion peaceful assembly |

   I know they will find me Not Guilty!

   We can march in the park.

   We can say what we want.

   a. ___*fair trial*___   b. _____   c. _____

   I can go to a church, synagogue, or mosque. It's *my* choice.

   The newspaper can print what it wants.

   d. _____   e. _____

3. **Read the information. Who can take a citizenship test? Check (✓) the correct box.**

   a. ☐ Luisa is 17 years old. She has lived in the U.S. for 10 years.

   b. ☐ Mehmet is 50 years old. He has lived in the U.S. for 4 years.

   c. ☐ Mei-ling is 20 years old. She has lived in the U.S. for 6 years.

   CHALLENGE Which right of citizens is the most important to you? Why?

4. **Complete the newspaper article. Use the words in the box.**

City Council	councilperson	ran for office	debated	elected officials
got elected	opponent	campaigned	serve	~~election results~~

Dan Chen Wins!

By Roland Cormier
Smithfield, Wednesday, Nov 7

The ___election results___ are in. The city of Smithfield has a new _____,
   a.   **b.**
forty-five year old Dan Chen. Mr. Chen, a Smithfield resident, _____ in
                                                                      c.
yesterday's election. He beat his _____, Liz Larson, by 35,000 votes. This
                                        d.
was the first time Chen _____. The candidates _____ for two
                              e.   **f.**
months. Hundreds of people watched as he and Larson _____ the issues
                                                              g.
last month at the Smithfield City College Auditorium. Mr. Chen will _____
                                                                          h.
on the Smithfield _____ for a term of four years. There are four other
                        i.
_____ on the council.
      j.

5. **What about you? Look at page 143 in your dictionary. Answer the questions. Discuss your answers with a partner.**

   a. When was the most recent election in your area? _____

   _____

   b. Who or what was on the ballot? _____

   _____

   c. Have you ever been in a polling booth? _____

   _____

   d. Are you interested in political debates? Why or why not? _____

   _____

   e. Would you attend a political rally? Why or why not? _____

   _____

The Legal System

1. **Look at page 144 in your dictionary. Who is . . . ?**

    a. wearing handcuffs _____ *the suspect* _____

    b. talking to the witness _____

    c. typing _____

    d. shaking hands with the defendant _____

    e. sitting in jail _____

    f. standing in a corner in the courtroom _____

2. **Circle the words to complete the interview with a former convict.**

A HARD LESSON

PS MAGAZINE: Tell us about your experience with the legal system.

You (went to prison) / stood trial for several years, didn't you?
   a.

DAN LEE: Yes—for burglary. I was released / arrested three
                              b.
years ago. It was the happiest day of my life.

PS MAGAZINE: You didn't have a job when you were arrested.

How did you hire a lawyer / stand trial?
                c.

DAN LEE: I didn't. The court gave me one. And she was good. In fact, when we appeared in

court / jail, she got the guard / judge to lower the bail to $1,000.
   d.   e.

PS MAGAZINE: So what happened when you sentenced the defendant / stood trial?
                                                              f.

DAN LEE: She did her best, but the prosecuting / defense attorney had a lot of
                                              g.
evidence / handcuffs against me.
   h.

PS MAGAZINE: Were you surprised when the police officer / jury gave a verdict / witness
                                                    i.   j.
of "guilty"?

DAN LEE: No, but I *was* surprised when the judge sentenced / released me. Seven years!
                                                  k.
Now I tell young people what it's like to spend years in jail / court.
                                                            l.

CHALLENGE Write the story of the man in the dictionary who was arrested.

1. Look at page 145 in your dictionary. Put each crime in the correct category.

Crimes Against People	Crimes Against Property (buildings, cars, etc.)	Substance Abuse Crimes (drugs and alcohol)
_____	*vandalism*	_____
_____	_____	_____
_____	_____	
_____	_____	
_____		

2. Look at the chart. Complete the sentences. Use the words in the box. (You will use one word twice.)

assaults	burglaries	murders	victim

Number of Crimes in the U.S. per 100,000 People

Year	Assault	Burglary	Murder
2000	324.0	728.8	5.5
2005	290.8	726.9	5.6
2010	252.8	701.0	4.8
2014	232.5	542.5	4.5

Based on information from: The Federal Bureau of Investigation (FBI). Crime in the United States (2014).

a. In 2000, there were 324 _____*assaults*_____ per 100,000 people in the U.S.

b. In 2000, there were about 729 _____ per 100,000 people in the U.S.

c. Between 2000 and 2005, the number of _____ went up.

d. You were less likely to be a _____ of a crime in 2014 than you were in the early 2000s.

e. The number of _____ has dropped the most since 2000.

CHALLENGE Look at page 263 in this book. Follow the instructions.

Public Safety

1. **Look at page 146 in your dictionary. Complete the poster with the correct advice.**

Neighborhood Lookout   *Safety Tips*

a. _____*Lock your doors.*_____ A deadbolt is your best protection. Door chains are also good.

b. _____ Always ask, "Who's there?" If you don't know them, don't let them in!

c. _____ Who else is on the street? Notice other people.

d. _____ For men, the best place is an *inside* jacket pocket. For women, keep it *closed* and *close* to your body at all times.

e. ATMs are great, but be careful using one. _____

f. _____ There's safety in numbers. Remember: muggers usually look for *easy* victims.

g. _____ Remember: Criminals don't want witnesses, so lights are your friends.

h. _____ Whose suitcase is that? If its owner isn't there, contact the police.

i. Be careful on the Internet, too. Only _____ where you see the 🔒 symbol.

j. _____ If you witness a crime or become a crime victim, dial 911 immediately!

The East Village Neighborhood Lookout — Looking Out for You!

2. **Look at the picture. What safety mistakes is the man making? Use the information in Exercise 1.**

a. ___*He isn't staying on well-lit streets.*___

b. _____

c. _____

d. _____

e. _____

3. **What about you? Which of the safety tips in Exercise 1 do you follow? Make a list.**

CHALLENGE Interview five people. Find out about the safety tips they follow.

1. **Look at page 147 in your dictionary. Write a different way to say each item.**

   a. pictures and other things that children shouldn't see ___*inappropriate material*___

   b. adults who want to hurt children _____

   c. watch what your children do online _____

   d. when children are mean to other children online _____

   e. a way to control your children's Internet browser _____

2. **Complete the Internet safety rules. Use the words in the box.**

secure sites	phishing	block	hacking	~~delete~~	secure	update

   To: All Employees
   Re: INTERNET SAFETY

   The security of our computer system is important to all of us. Please observe the following rules to keep our data safe and our network free from viruses:

   - Do not open attachments from unknown sources. ___*Delete*___ all suspicious emails immediately.
     a.

   - Be aware of _____ scams. Remember that banks and other institutions
     b.
     will never ask you for personal information in an email. Only use _____
     c.
     when you are providing account numbers, Social Security numbers, and other sensitive information.

   - Keep your eyes open for suspicious activity on our sites.
     If you suspect _____ , contact the IT Department immediately.
     d.

   - Be sure to create _____ passwords. Do not use your birthday, easy
     e.
     number sequences, or the word "password."

   The IT Department is doing its best to protect your information and keep the work environment professional. We _____ the security system regularly.
   f.
   In addition, we _____ inappropriate sites. Please contact us if you have
   g.
   any questions or need further assistance.

1. **Look at pages 148 and 149 in your dictionary. Which disaster is the news reporter talking about?**

   a. "The same one erupted five years ago."   _volcanic eruption_

   b. "All homes near the beach were destroyed by the ocean water."   _____

   c. "The two vehicles were badly damaged, but the drivers were not hurt in the crash."   _____

   d. "Store detectives found the little girl sitting on the floor."   _____

   e. "The twister destroyed several farms in its path."   _____

   f. "The search and rescue team arrived at the house quickly."   _____

2. **Complete the news articles. Use the words in the box.**

airplane crash	avalanche	blizzard	drought
~~earthquake~~	explosion	fire	firefighters
hurricane	search and rescue team		

   a.
   # DISASTER STRIKES KOBE, JAPAN

   TOKYO, JAN 17 —An ____earthquake____ measuring 7.1 on the Richter scale hit the city of Kobe, Japan killing more than 5,000 people and injuring 26,500 others. More than 100,000 buildings were destroyed.

   b.
   _____ # KILLS 109

   Miami, May 11—A DC-9 jet en route to Atlanta went down in the Florida Everglades just a few minutes after takeoff from Miami. All 109 passengers were killed. The cause of the disaster is not yet known.

   c.
   # INFERNO IN LONDON UNDERGROUND

   London, November 18—Thirty died and thirty-one were seriously injured in a _____ in one of the busiest subway stations in the world. "As soon as I got on the escalator, I could smell burning," said one witness. Seconds later she saw the red flames and dark smoke. _____ rushed to the scene.

d.

BOMB _____ in Oklahoma City Kills 169

Oklahoma City, April 19—A car bomb went off outside a federal office building, killing 168 people. A member of the _____ also died while trying to save the victims. The bomb destroyed most of the nine-story building and damaged many other buildings in the area.

e.

HIGH WINDS HIT THE YUCATAN

Cancun, October 22—_____ Wilma, the most powerful Atlantic storm ever recorded, struck the popular tourist resorts of Mexico's Yucatan Peninsula, leaving 8 dead and destroying many beach hotels. Winds of 150 miles per hour broke windows and caused trees to fall.

f.

THE _____ OF '93

Boston, March 22—Described as a "hurricane with snow," the giant storm hit the eastern third of the United States. The winds created snowdrifts as high as 14 feet in New England.

g.

A LONG DRY WINTER

Santa Barbara, March 23—As a result of 73% less rain than usual over the last year, California is experiencing its worst _____ since the 1930s. The state is going to stop water deliveries to farms in an effort to save water.

h.

MAN RESCUED FROM _____

Banff, Canada, March 27—An employee at Sunshine Village ski resort was buried when a 200-meter-wide wall of snow hit him and caused him to fall. A rescue team reached him in less than four minutes. The employee is fine.

CHALLENGE   Write a paragraph about an emergency or a natural disaster.

Emergency Procedures

1. **Look at page 150 in your dictionary. Complete the sentences.**

   a. The Rivera family ___is planning for an emergency___.

   b. Their _____ is Aunt Maria in California.

   c. If there is a flood, they have two _____ out of their house.

   d. Their _____ is Rt. 102, a road near their house.

   e. Their _____ is at the corner of Oak and Elm.

   f. The _____ is in their basement.

2. **Complete the disaster kit checklist. Use the words in the box.**

batteries	blankets	bottled water	can opener	canned food
coins	important papers	packaged food	towelettes	~~warm clothes~~

EMERGENCY CHECKLIST

Clothing and Bedding

☐ ___warm clothes___ (hat, gloves, etc.)
     a.

☐ _____ or sleeping bags
     b.

Tools and Supplies

☐ flashlight and extra _____
             c.

☐ non-electric _____
        d.

☐ _____ (1 gallon per person per day)
   e.

Food

☐ ready-to-eat _____ (cereal, bread)
        f.

☐ _____ (soup, juice)
    g.

Sanitation

☐ toilet paper   ☐ moist _____
                              h.

Special Items

☐ medication   ☐ extra eyeglasses

☐ cash and _____   ☐ copies of _____
       i.   j.

3. **Look at page 151 in your dictionary. What are people doing? Write sentences.**

   a. Carlos is looking out at the sky. _____ *He's watching the weather.* _____

   b. Rosa is packing her suitcase. _____

   c. The Riveras are listening to the radio and watching TV. _____

   d. Carlos is carrying a woman's suitcase to the shelter. _____

   e. The family is leaving their home. _____

   f. They are entering a hurricane shelter. _____

   g. Kenji and his son are under the table. _____

   h. They are not looking outside at the weather. _____

   i. Kenji and his family are in their car. _____

   j. Rosa is on the phone with Aunt Maria. _____

   k. Kenji and Rosa are in their basements. _____

   l. Kenji is in his front yard. _____

4. **What about you? Are you ready? Look at the checklist in Exercise 2. Complete the chart.**

Things I have	Things I don't have	Things I'm going to get
Other:	Other:	Other:

CHALLENGE What things should you have in a first aid kit? Make a list.

Go to page 254 for Another Look (Unit 7).

Community Cleanup

1. **Look at the top row of pictures on pages 152 and 153 in your dictionary. Complete the chart. Check (✓) the columns.**

	Donuts	Hammers & More	Pharmacy	Flowers
a. This store has broken windows.	✓	✓	✓	✓
b. There is a streetlight in front.				
c. There is litter in front.				
d. There is graffiti on the store.				
e. It is next to the hardware store.				
f. It is across the street from the pharmacy.				

2. **Complete the conversation. Use the words in the box.**

> streetlights   hardware store   litter   graffiti
> change   give a speech   ~~petition~~

Marta: Excuse me. Would you please sign this ___petition___?
a.

We really need to _____ things here.
b.

Main Street is a mess. There's a lot of _____
c.

painted on the stores.

Customer: Yes, there is. And there's a lot of _____
d.

in the street. Is that what the petition is for?

Marta: No. I am going to talk about those things when I _____ to the city council,
e.

but the petition is to repair the _____. They don't work.
f.

Customer: Oh, of course, I'll sign it. This street is a mess.

Marta: Thanks. And can you give some of your time?

We need volunteers to do the rest of the work.

Customer: Sure. I can help plant some flowers. And I work right next door

at the _____. I can ask the manager to give some free paint.
g.

Marta: Oh, great! Thank you.

3. **Look at pages 152 and 153 in your dictionary. How many . . . do you see?**

a. stores on the street _4_

b. signatures on the petition ___

c. broken streetlights ___

d. city council members who are applauding ___

e. people who are giving a speech ___

4. **Read Amar's web post. Circle the words to complete the sentences.**

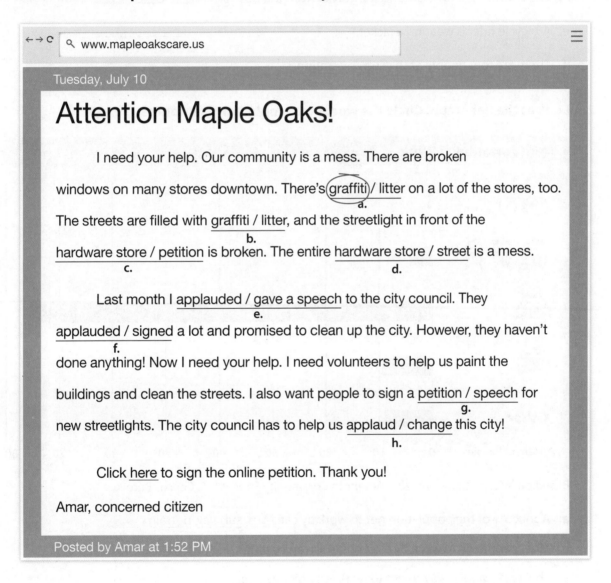

← → C   🔍 www.mapleoakscare.us   ≡

Tuesday, July 10

Attention Maple Oaks!

I need your help. Our community is a mess. There are broken

windows on many stores downtown. There's (graffiti) / litter on a lot of the stores, too.
                                         a.

The streets are filled with graffiti / litter, and the streetlight in front of the
                                  b.

hardware store / petition is broken. The entire hardware store / street is a mess.
        c.   d.

Last month I applauded / gave a speech to the city council. They
              e.

applauded / signed a lot and promised to clean up the city. However, they haven't
        f.

done anything! Now I need your help. I need volunteers to help us paint the

buildings and clean the streets. I also want people to sign a petition / speech for
                                                                  g.

new streetlights. The city council has to help us applaud / change this city!
                                                          h.

Click here to sign the online petition. Thank you!

Amar, concerned citizen

Posted by Amar at 1:52 PM

CHALLENGE Imagine there are problems in your community. Write a web post. Tell people about the problems and ask for help. Use Exercise 4 as a model.

Basic Transportation

1. **Look at pages 154 and 155 in your dictionary. *True* or *False*? Correct the <u>underlined</u> words in the false sentences.**

   a. A passenger is getting into the ~~truck~~. *taxi*   <u>   false   </u>

   b. There is one <u>motorcycle</u> on the street.   <u>   </u>

   c. The <u>helicopter</u> is flying over the airport.   <u>   </u>

   d. The subway station is around the corner from the <u>bus stop</u>.   <u>   </u>

   e. A <u>bicycle</u> rider is wearing a jacket.   <u>   </u>

   f. There are four people at the <u>subway station</u>.   <u>   </u>

2. **Look at the bar graph. Circle the words to complete the sentences.**

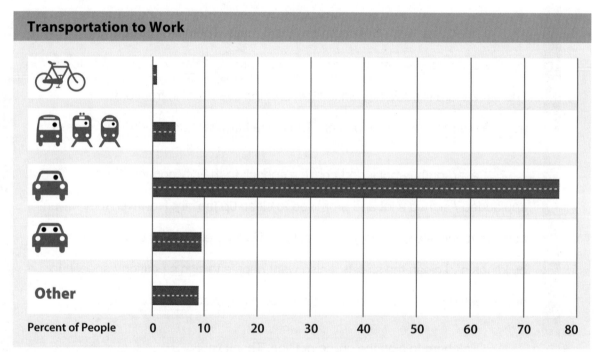

   Transportation to Work

   Percent of People   0   10   20   30   40   50   60   70   80

   Based on information from: 2013 American Community Survey, U.S. Census Bureau.

   a. About 5% of the population get to work by <u>car /</u> <u>bus, subway, or train</u>.

   b. Most people go to work by <u>car / bus, subway, or train</u>.

   c. The least popular way to get to work is by <u>bicycle / car</u>.

   d. More people go to work by <u>bicycle / car</u> than by subway, bus, or train.

   e. More than 75% of people ride to work <u>alone / as a passenger</u> in a car.

3. **What about you? How do you get to work? school? the market? the airport? Use your own paper.**

4. **Compare these types of transportation. Write sentences with *than* and the words in parentheses ( ).**

a. ___The plane is safer than the car.___
(plane / car / safer)

b. _____
(bus / subway / faster)

c. _____
(plane / bus / more expensive)

d. _____
(bicycle / motorcycle / more dangerous)

e. _____
(bus / taxi / cheaper)

f. _____
(car / truck / more comfortable)

5. **Look at the chart. Complete the sentences.**

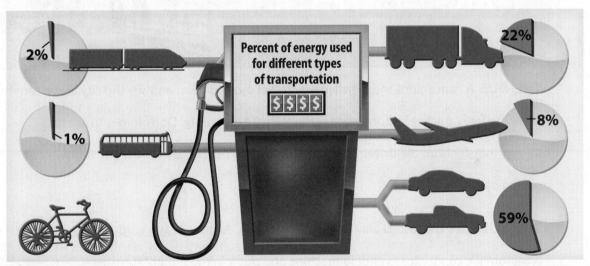

Based on information from: Center for Climate and Energy Solutions, 2012.

a. Small ___trucks___ and _____ use 59% of the total energy for all types of transportation.

b. At 22%, large _____ use more energy than planes, buses, and trains combined.

c. At 1%, _____ use less energy than trains.

d. _____ use only 8% of the total energy for transportation.

e. _____ and _____ together use just 3% of the total energy for transportation.

f. And, of course, _____ use no energy at all!

CHALLENGE   What are the advantages (positive points) and disadvantages (negative points)
of different types of transportation? Compare your answers with a classmate's list.
Example: *A bicycle is good exercise. It doesn't use gas, but it isn't very fast.*

155

1. **Look at page 156 in your dictionary. What are the people talking about? Where are they?**

		What?	Where?
a.	"<u>It</u> goes in this way."	_fare card_	_subway station_
b.	"<u>This</u> says there's one at 6:30."	_____	_____
c.	"Use <u>this</u>, Miss, to change at Avenue A."	_____	_____
d.	"<u>It</u> says $22.00, so I'll tip $3.30."	_____	_____
e.	"Is <u>it</u> for a one-way trip or a round trip?"	_____	_____

2. **Circle the words to complete the pamphlet.**

PUBLIC TRANSPORTATION OPTIONS

THE BUS A convenient, inexpensive way to get around town and see the city at the same

time. The (fare) / track is just one price—for one mile or twenty! Don't forget to ask for a
      a.

token / transfer from the driver, so you can change to other buses or the subway without
    b.
paying again.

THE SUBWAY The fastest way to get around town. Just buy a <u>fare card / schedule</u> from
          c.

an automatic <u>conductor / vending machine</u> and put it in the <u>meter / turnstile</u>.
      d.   **e.**

TAXIS Convenient, but expensive. Watch the <u>meter / shuttle</u> as your <u>driver / rider</u> takes you
      f.   **g.**

to your destination. The faster you go, the faster it changes (and the more you pay)!

TRAINS For longer distances, a good form of public transportation. A round-trip ticket is

sometimes less expensive than two <u>one-way / round-trip</u> tickets, so plan ahead! Buy one at
      h.

the <u>subway car / ticket window</u> and then wait on the <u>platform / track</u> for your train.
  i.   **j.**

⌐**CHALLENGE**⌐ Describe the advantages and disadvantages of different types of public transportation.
        Example: *The subway is fast, but you can't see the street from it.*

1. **Look at page 157 in your dictionary.** *True* or *False*? **Correct the** <u>underlined</u> **words in the false sentences.**

   a. A woman is walking ~~down~~ the steps.   <u>_false_</u>
      (up above "down")

   b. A man is running <u>across the street</u>.   _____

   c. The yellow truck is going to <u>drive through the tunnel</u>. _____

   d. The blue car is <u>getting off</u> the highway.   _____

2. **Look at the map of Toronto. Circle the words to complete the directions.**

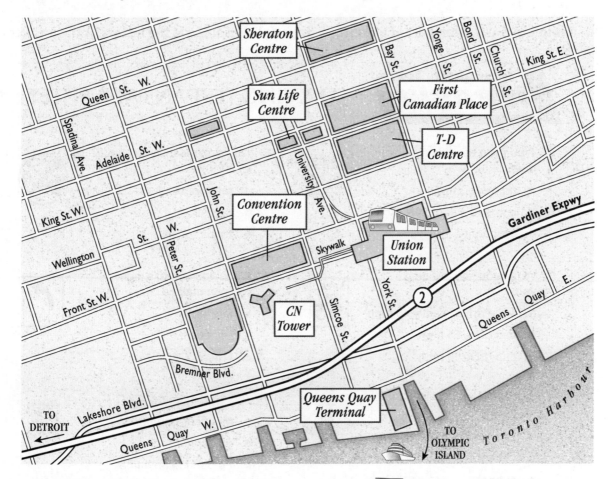

   a. To go from Union Station to Toronto Harbour, <u>get off</u> / ⟨go under⟩ the Expressway on York St.

   b. To go from the Convention Centre to the Sun Life Centre, get <u>into / out of</u> the taxi on King St.

   c. To go from Queen's Quay Terminal to Olympic Island, go <u>across / around</u> Toronto Harbour.

   d. To go from Union Station to Detroit, get <u>on / off</u> the Expressway at York Street.

   e. To go from CN Tower to Union Station on foot, go <u>over / under</u> the Skywalk.

   [CHALLENGE] Write directions from your home to:
               school   the bus station   Other: _____

1. **Look at page 158 in your dictionary. Which signs have . . . ?**

   a. numbers   _____*speed limit*_____ and _____

   b. letters, not words   _____ and _____

   c. pictures of people   _____, _____, _____,

            and _____

   d. arrows (→)   _____, _____, _____,

            _____, and _____

2. **Complete the written part of a test for a driver's license. Circle the letters of the answers.**

   ## Transport Texas Licensing — DRIVING TEST ANSWER SHEET

   1. When you see this sign, you must ____.

       a. go more slowly

       (b.) come to a complete stop

       c. turn right

   2. When you see this sign, you ____.

       a. must drive exactly 45 mph

       b. can drive 55 mph

       c. can drive 60 mph

   3. This sign means ____ crossing.

       a. pedestrian

       b. railroad

       c. school

   4. This sign means ____.

       a. you can't enter the street

       b. the street is very dangerous

       c. the street ends

   5. This sign means you should look for ____.

       a. restrooms

       b. rivers

       c. trains

   6. When you see this sign, you can make a ____.

       a. left turn

       b. right turn

       c. U-turn

   7. This sign means ____.

       a. handicapped parking

       b. a hospital

       c. no parking any time

   8. This sign means ____.

       a. do not enter

       b. the street ends

       c. there's a cemetery nearby

CHALLENGE Draw some other traffic signs. Explain their meanings.

1. **Look at page 159 in your dictionary. *True* or *False*? Correct the underlined words in the false sentences.**

   east
   a. The car went ~~west~~ on Elm Street.   ___false___

   b. It <u>didn't stop at the corner</u> of Elm and Main.   _____

   c. It turned <u>right</u> on Pine.   _____

   d. It continued to drive <u>south</u> on Oak.   _____

2. **Look at the Internet map. Circle the words to complete the sentences.**

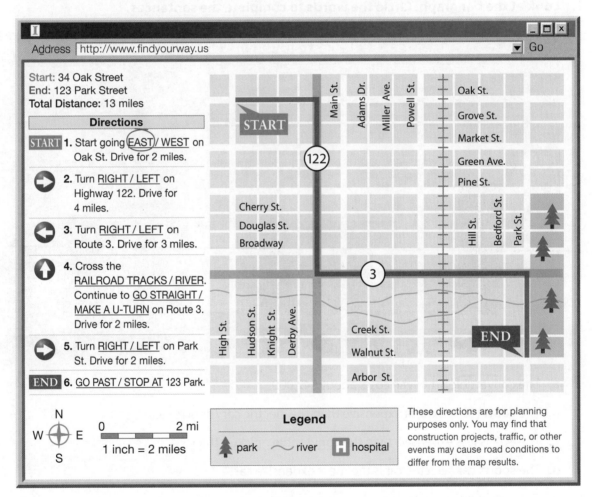

3. **Look at the map in Exercise 2. Circle the words to complete the sentences.**

   a. The <u>Internet map</u> / (river) is blue.   c. The map has a <u>symbol</u> / <u>key</u> for parks.

   b. According to the <u>scale</u> / <u>GPS</u>, one inch is 2 miles.   d. The <u>streets</u> / <u>highways</u> are orange.

   [CHALLENGE] Look at the map in Exercise 2. Give directions from 123 Park Street to 34 Oak Street.

1. Look at page 160 in your dictionary. Which car or truck . . . ?

a. takes furniture from one place to another   *moving van*

b. takes children to school   _____

c. helps move your car if it's in an accident   _____

d. uses both gas and electricity   _____

e. transports oil from one place to another   _____

f. can pour sand on the ground   _____

2. Look at the bar graph. Circle the words to complete the sentences.

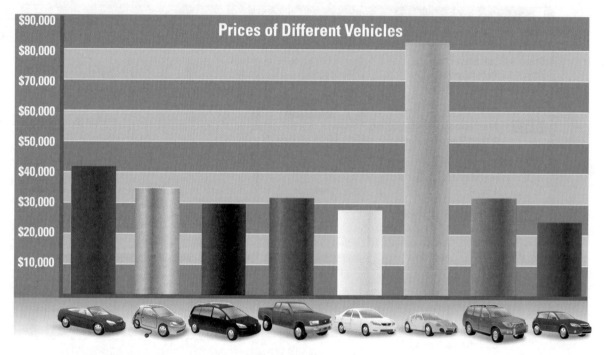

Prices of Different Vehicles

a. The (convertible) / minivan costs about $42,000.

b. The convertible is more expensive than the <u>electric car / sports car</u>.

c. The SUV is less expensive than the <u>convertible / pickup truck</u>.

d. The <u>sports car / electric car</u> is the most expensive car.

e. The <u>pickup truck / hatchback</u> is the least expensive vehicle.

f. The <u>sedan / SUV</u> costs about $28,000.

3. What about you? Look in your dictionary. Which car would you choose? Why?
Example: *I would choose a pickup truck. I carry a lot of things, but not many passengers.*

CHALLENGE   Look at newspaper or online ads. Find the price range of the car you chose in Exercise 3.

1. **Look at page 161 in your dictionary. Complete the sentences.**

   a. Juan wanted to buy _a used car_____.

   b. He _____ in the newspaper and online.

   c. When he _____, he learned how many miles were on the car.

   d. When he _____, he learned that it was in good condition.

   e. He _____ of $8,000.

   f. After he got the title from the seller, he _____.

2. **Look at the checklist. What did Juan do? What didn't he do? Write sentences.**

Car Maintenance
- ☑ Fill the tank with gas.
- ☑ Check the oil.
- ☐ Put in coolant.
- ☐ Go for a smog check.
- ☐ Replace the windshield wipers.
- ☑ Fill the tires with air.

   a. _He filled the tank with gas._____

   b. _____

   c. _He didn't_____

   d. _____

   e. _____

   f. _____

[CHALLENGE] List other things people do to maintain their cars. **Example:** *They check the spare tire and add air if necessary.*

Parts of a Car

1. **Look at pages 162 and 163 in your dictionary. How many . . . does the car have?**

   a. hubcaps _4_

   b. license plates ___

   c. gauges ___

   d. power outlets ___

   e. side-view mirrors ___

   f. tailpipes ___

   g. rearview mirrors ___

   h. spare tires ___

2. **Complete the conversations. Use the words in the box.**

   | air conditioning button | front seat | ~~gas gauge~~ | gas pedal | glove compartment |
   | license plate | radio | rearview mirror | stick shift | temperature gauge |

   a. **Passenger:** Look, the _____ *gas gauge* _____ is almost on empty.
      Driver: There's a gas station. I'll stop there.

   b. **Driver:** Where would you like to sit?
      Passenger: In the _____, next to you.

   c. **Driver:** It would be good to hear a traffic report.
      Passenger: I'll turn on the _____.

   d. **Passenger:** It's getting hot in here.
      Driver: Push the _____.

   e. **Passenger:** Do we have a map?
      Driver: There should be one in the _____.

   f. **Passenger:** That truck is getting very close!
      Driver: Don't worry. I'm watching it in the _____.

   g. **Passenger:** Step on the _____! You're going much too slow.
      Driver: OK.

   h. **Passenger:** Look at the _____.
      Driver: Oh. The radiator needs coolant. It's much too hot.

   i. **Passenger:** That car is leaving the accident scene!
      Driver: Quick! Let's call the police. Write down the _____ number!

   j. **Passenger:** Do you like using a _____?
      Driver: Yes. I've always driven a car with a manual transmission.

162

3. **Circle the words to complete the information from a driver's manual.**

BASIC DRIVING

a. The bumper / (steering wheel) gives you control over your car.

b. Always have the correct amount of air in your hubcaps / tires. Check the air pressure.

c. When you step on your brake pedal / clutch, your car should stop quickly and smoothly.

d. Jumper cables / Turn signals tell other drivers which direction you are going to go.

e. Brake lights / Taillights tell other drivers that you are slowing or stopping.

f. Your hood / horn lets other drivers and pedestrians hear that you are there.

g. Lug wrenches / Headlights are important in night driving, rainy weather, and fog.

h. The defroster / windshield should be free of cracks and breaks. Use your gearshift / windshield wipers to clean it.

PREVENTING INJURIES

i. Check your fan speed / speedometer to see how fast you are going.

j. All new cars come with airbags / spare tires that open in case of an accident. They keep you from hitting your head against the dashboard / trunk or steering wheel.

k. Back seats / Seat belts help prevent injury or death in case of an accident. Always use them.

l. Use your jacks / door locks to keep your doors from opening in an accident.

m. Buy child safety seats / hazard lights for small children and always use them. It's the law!

AIR AND NOISE POLLUTION CONTROL

n. Make sure there is enough coolant in the battery / radiator.

o. If your car is making a lot of noise, you may need to replace your ignition / muffler.

CHALLENGE Look in your dictionary. Choose five parts of the car that are not described in Exercise 3. What are they for? **Example:** *audio display—to listen to the radio or music.*

An Airport

1. **Look at pages 164 and 165 in your dictionary. Who's speaking? About what?**

		Who?	About what?
a.	"My other bag isn't on <u>it</u>! "	*passenger*	*baggage carousel*
b.	"Put your keys in <u>it</u>, too, with your briefcase."		
c.	"You didn't fill <u>it</u> out."		
d.	"Put <u>it</u> over your face."		

2. **Circle the words to complete the travel trips.**

ESL INTERNATIONAL TRAVEL TIPS

BEFORE YOUR FLIGHT

- Arrive at customs / <u>(the airline terminal)</u> three hours before your flight.
  a.
- Check the <u>departure monitor</u> / tray table for information about your flight.
  b.
- If you don't have a <u>boarding pass</u> / life vest, check in electronically at the
  c.
  <u>screening area / check-in kiosk</u> or show your e-ticket to the pilot / <u>ticket agent</u>.
  d.   e.
- After going through the cockpit / <u>screening area</u>, go to your bin / <u>gate</u>.
  f.   g.
- Wait in the cockpit / <u>boarding area</u>.
  h.

ON THE PLANE

- After you find your emergency card / <u>seat</u>, find / <u>stow</u> your carry-on bag in the
  i.   j.
  <u>overhead compartment</u> / upright seat near your seat.
  k.
- Pay attention as your <u>flight attendant</u> / TSA agent shows you how to put on your
  l.
  <u>oxygen mask</u> / reclined seat and gives you other important safety information.
  m.
- <u>Fasten</u> / Stow your seat belt and keep it on in case of turbulence.
  n.
- Put your cell phone in check-in / <u>airplane</u> mode.
  o.
- Fill out <u>a declaration form</u> / an arrival monitor before you land.
  p.

AFTER YOU LAND

- Go to the check-in kiosk / <u>baggage carousel</u> to check in / <u>claim your baggage</u>.
  q.   r.
- Take your bags through <u>customs</u> / the emergency exit.
  s.

164

3. **Look at Taking a Flight on page 164 in your dictionary.** *Before* **or** *After*? **Circle the words to complete the sentences.**

   a. The passenger checked his bags <u>before /(after)</u> he checked in electronically.

   b. He stowed his carry-on bag <u>before / after</u> he found his seat.

   c. He put his cell phone in airplane mode <u>before / after</u> the plane took off.

4. **Look at the flight information.** *True* **or** *False*? **Write a question mark (?) if the information isn't there.**

HAPPY *Travel*	MERLIN, JARED PAGE 1 OF 1 FILE #142-34-02-54-2	

Reconfirm reservations 72 hours prior to each flight. Failure to do so may result in missing your flight or having the space canceled by the airline.

AIRWAY AIRLINES	FLIGHT 613	10 MAR SUN
DEPART 0755A	NEW YORK LGA	CHECK-IN REQUIRED
ARRIVE 1048A	MIAMI INTERNATIONAL	MEALS: SNACK
AIRWAY AIRLINES	FLIGHT 695	10 MAR SUN
DEPART 1115A	MIAMI INTERNATIONAL	SEAT 23D NON-SMOKING
ARRIVE 1215P	SAN JUAN	MEALS: SPECIAL LOW-SALT

a. The passenger bought his ticket from Happy Travel.   _____*true*_____

b. This is a mobile boarding pass.   _____

c. The arrival time in Miami is 11:15 a.m.   _____

d. The departure time from New York is 7:55 a.m.   _____

e. Passengers will board Flight 613 at 7:35 a.m.   _____

f. Passengers can have two carry-on bags.   _____

g. Flight 613 takes off on Sunday morning.   _____

h. It lands on Sunday afternoon.   _____

i. The passenger doesn't have to check in for Flight 613.   _____

j. He is in seat 23D on Flight 695.   _____

k. The seat is next to an emergency exit.   _____

l. The passenger requested a special meal.   _____

m. Passengers will claim their baggage at Carousel 4.   _____

CHALLENGE   Write a paragraph about a plane trip you or someone you know took.

Go to page 255 for Another Look (Unit 8).

1. **Look at pages 166 and 167 in your dictionary. Number the sentences in the correct order. (Number 1 = the first thing that happened)**

   ___ **a.** They have a flat tire.

   ___ **b.** They are lost.

   ___ **c.** They run out of gas.

   ___ **d.** They look at scenery.

   ___ **e.** They reach their destination.

   ___ **f.** They get a speeding ticket.

   _1_ **g.** Joe and Rob leave Seattle, their starting point.

   ___ **h.** Their car breaks down.

   ___ **i.** They meet a ranger at Yellowstone National Park.

2. **What's happening? Match.**

   _2_ **a.** "Where are we? Was that our turn?"   1. They're calling a tow truck.

   ___ **b.** "There are many eagles and bears in the park."   2. They're lost.

   ___ **c.** "The car is stopping. We forgot to buy gas!"   3. They're running out of gas.

   ___ **d.** "You were way over the speed limit."   4. They're getting a speeding ticket.

   ___ **e.** "Our bags are in the car. Let's go to New York!"   5. They're packing.

   ___ **f.** "The mountains are beautiful!"   6. They're talking with a ranger.

   ___ **g.** "There's smoke coming out of the engine!"   7. They're leaving their starting point.

   ___ **h.** "Please send a truck. We're five miles   8. They're looking at scenery.
   from New York City."

   ___ **i.** "I'm going to bring my bathing suit and   9. Their car is breaking down.
   suntan lotion."

   ___ **j.** "I'll take the flat tire off. Would you get the   10. They're changing a flat tire.
   spare tire?"

3. **What about you? Check (✓) the things that have happened to you. Tell a classmate about your experiences.**

   ☐ I forgot to pack something important.   ☐ I ran out of gas.

   ☐ I got a speeding ticket.   ☐ I had a flat tire.

   ☐ My car broke down.   ☐ I was lost.

   ☐ I saw some wildlife.   ☐ I saw beautiful scenery.

4. Complete the story. Use the words in the box.

pack	scenery	mechanic
road trip	run out of gas	tow truck
get a ticket	breaks down	~~destination~~

Destination
_____ : **CHICAGO**
a.

"I'm tired of San Diego," Jane says. "Let's take a _____
b.

on spring break and visit Lia in Chicago." "Let's _____
c.

our bags!" says Tonya. "I can't wait." A week later, Jane and Tonya are driving through the

beautiful _____ in Utah. But problems are still in front of them.
d.

They _____ in Colorado because they are driving too fast. In Kansas,
e.

they _____. Jane walks to a gas station and buys some. Finally,
f.

their car _____ only fifty miles from Chicago. Tonya calls
g.

a _____, and the truck takes the car to a mechanic. "Your car will be ready
h.

in two days," says the _____. The friends rent a car. Two hours later,
i.

they're at Lia's door.

5. Complete the sentences about Jane and Tonya's trip home. Use the words in the box.

get a ticket	~~have any problems~~	run out of gas
break down	get lost	have a flat tire

a. Jane and Tonya had a great trip home because they didn't _have any problems_____.

b. They always obeyed the speed limit, so they didn't _____.

c. A mechanic checked their car, so their car didn't _____.

d. They remembered to buy gas, so they didn't _____.

e. They bought some new tires, so they didn't _____.

f. They got good directions on the Internet, so they didn't _____.

CHALLENGE Write a story about a road trip. Use your own experience or your imagination.

167

Job Search

1. **Look at pages 168 and 169 in your dictionary.** *Before* or *After*? **Circle the words to complete the sentences.**

   a. Dan set a goal (before)/ after he started looking for a job.

   b. He networked with friends before / after he wrote his resume.

   c. He contacted references before / after he researched local companies.

   d. He checked employment websites before / after he went to an employment agency.

   e. He wrote a cover letter before / after he submitted his application.

   f. He completed an application before / after he went on a job interview.

2. **Look at Chin's plan for the day. Put his activities in order.**

   1. Look at employee reviews of R&P Company.
   2. Email Professor Marks about being a personal reference.
   3. Look for new ads on SuperJobs.com and FindWork.com.
   4. Call Teresa & Matt to see if they know anyone who's hiring.
   5. Check the store windows along Broad St.
   6. Drop by ABC Employment.

   _2_ **a.** contact references

   ___ **b.** go to an employment agency

   ___ **c.** talk to friends

   ___ **d.** research local companies

   ___ **e.** look for help wanted signs

   ___ **f.** check employment websites

3. Complete the information. Use the words in the box.

set up an interview	check employment websites	apply for a job
write a resume	~~talk to friends~~	go on the interview
complete an application	~~get a job~~	go to an employment agency
research local companies	look for help wanted signs	

← → C   🔍 www.jobtips/default.us   ☰

Looking for a Job
It can take a lot of time—and work—to find a job. Here are some tips.

Tell everyone that you are looking for work. Begin close to home. _____*Talk to friends*_____,
a.

relatives, teachers, and classmates. Keep your eyes open. When you're walking down the street,

_____ in store windows. _____ to find out where
b.   c.

you would like to work. Go online to _____. If you want someone to help you
d.

with the process, _____. They can even help you _____
e.   f.

by listing all your work experience and education.

Applying for a job: When you _____, send in your resume and a cover letter.
g.

Interested employers will call you to _____. Then, you will probably have to
h.

_____. This gives the employer basic information about your skills and experience.
i.

When you _____, you will have the chance to talk about your experience in more
j.

detail. It's a long process. Remember: Be patient and don't give up. You may have to try many different

approaches before you finally _____ and get that first paycheck!
k.

4. What about you? What do you think are the best ways to find a job? Rank the ways. (Number 1 = the best) Add to the list. Explain your choices to your classmates.

Ways to find a job

____ networking   ____ going to employment agencies

____ looking for help wanted signs   ____ checking employment websites

____ sending out resumes and cover letters   ____ Other: _____

____ researching local companies   ____ Other: _____

1. **Look at page 170 in your dictionary. Write the job titles.**

JOBS *A3*

a. _Baker_ to make bread, pies, and cakes at our midtown restaurant. $9.67/hr. 555-2343

b. _____ to prepare and sell meat at our busy counter. S & W Supermarket. $28,000/yr. Call 555-4345

c. _____ to receive payment, give change and receipts to customers. Amy's Foods. Mineral Springs Road. 555-2243

d. _____ to plan and design public buildings at our growing firm. MCKAY, BROWN, & PETRILLO. 555-3451

e. _____ to watch our two preschoolers. Good storytelling skills a must! Excellent references required. $15/hr. 555-3406

f. _____ to put together parts in radio factory. On-the-job-training. $450/wk. Call Frank Collins. 555-9922.

g. _____ to repair and maintain cars at small garage. Part-time, weekends. 555-7396

h. _____ to help build shelves and doors in new building. $525/wk., 555-4345. Ask for Mr. Heller.

i. _____ to perform in plays for a small theater company. TV, stage, or movie experience. 555-8299

j. _____ to plan and organize appointments for busy business executive. H. Thomas & Sons. 555-8787

2. **Circle the words to complete the sentences.**

   a. A carpenter / (childcare worker) works with children.

   b. An auto mechanic / accountant needs to be good with numbers.

   c. An appliance repairperson / assembler can fix refrigerators.

   d. An architect / artist enjoys painting.

   e. Many business owners / businesspeople have their own stores.

3. **What about you? Look at the ads in Exercise 1. Which job would you like? Which job wouldn't you like? Why?**

CHALLENGE Look at page 264 in this book. Follow the instructions.

1. **Look at page 171 in your dictionary. *True* or *False*? Correct the underlined words in the false sentences.**

    a. The home healthcare aide and the ~~customer service representative~~ work with patients.
    dental assistant
                false

    b. The graphic designer uses a computer.
                _____

    c. The delivery person works for a gardener.
                _____

    d. The firefighter and the dock worker wear hard hats.
                _____

2. **Look at the bar graph. Circle the words to complete the sentences.**

How Stressful* Is the Job?

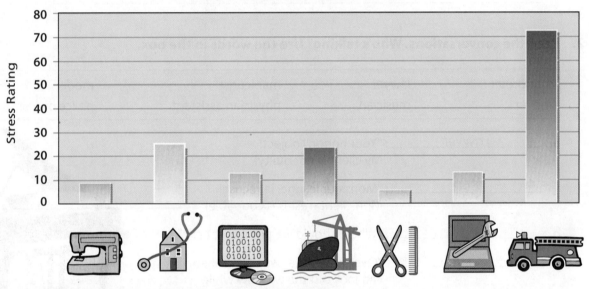

* A *stressful* job can make you feel nervous and not relaxed.
Based on information from: The 2015 Jobs Rated Report.

    a. A computer technician /(firefighter) has the job with the most stress.

    b. A hairdresser / computer software engineer has the job with the least stress.

    c. A computer technician's job is less stressful than a garment worker's / home healthcare aide's job.

    d. A computer technician / dock worker and a computer software engineer have about the same amount of job stress.

    e. After hairdressers, computer technicians / garment workers have the least stress.

3. **What about you? Look in your dictionary. Which job do you think is the most stressful? the least stressful? Why?**

CHALLENGE Look at pages 170–173 in your dictionary. Find five other stressful jobs. Tell a classmate. Do you and your classmate agree?

Jobs and Occupations H–P

1. Look at page 172 in your dictionary. Cross out the word that doesn't belong. Give a reason.

a. homemaker   ~~musician~~   housekeeper

     A musician doesn't work in the home.

b. machine operator   nurse   occupational therapist

_____

c. (house) painter   medical records technician   manicurist

_____

d. police officer   messenger   homemaker

_____

e. physician assistant   nurse   model

_____

2. Read the conversations. Who's talking? Use the words in the box.

interpreter	~~lawyer~~	manicurist	model
mover	musician	physician assistant	police officer

a. _____Lawyer_____: "Your honor, I object! My client is not guilty!"

_____: "Monsieur le juge, je récuse! Mon client n'est pas coupable!"

b. _____: "Where should we put this couch?"

_____: "Over there. That way our patients can look out the window while they're waiting."

c. _____: "I'll be wearing a red dress at the fashion show."

_____: "Well, this color nail polish will look great with it."

d. _____: "Where were you yesterday between 11:00 and 11:30 p.m.?"

_____: "I was at the Blue Note Club, detective. I was playing the piano."

CHALLENGE   Write three short conversations between a police officer and a house painter, a homemaker and a mover, and a messenger and a physician assistant. Use the conversations in Exercise 2 as an example.

1. **Look at page 173 in your dictionary. Who said . . . ?**

    a. "These shoes are very comfortable. Would you like to try them on?"   *retail clerk*

    b. "It can be difficult being a single mom, but we can help you." _____

    c. ". . . 18, 19, 20 . . . . That's 20 boxes of desk lamps." _____

    d. "You can get a very special offer, but you must order today!" _____

    e. "Ms. Davidson's office is through the glass doors to your left." _____

2. **Look at the chart. *True* or *False*?**

Occupation	🎤	🚛	👮	🚚	☕	🐕	🧴	📘
$ a year	37,200	33,660	24,470	39,520	18,730	87,590	37,420	58,850

    Based on information from: Bureau of Labor Statistics, U.S. Department of Labor, *Occupational Outlook Handbook, 2016–17 Edition.*

    a. A truck driver makes more money than a sanitation worker.   *true*

    b. A server makes the least money. _____

    c. A security guard makes more money than a sanitation worker. _____

    d. Welders and reporters make almost the same amount of money. _____

    e. Writers make more than twice as much as security guards. _____

    f. A veterinarian makes over $60,000 more than a reporter. _____

3. **What about you? Look at the occupations in Exercise 2. Write answers to the questions.**

    a. Which of these jobs do you think is the most exciting? Why?

    b. Which of these jobs do you think is the most boring? Why?

    c. Which of these jobs do you think is the most difficult? Why?

CHALLENGE Look at job ads online or in the newspaper. Find four jobs. Make a chart like the one in Exercise 2. Then write four sentences comparing the jobs.

1. **Look at pages 174 and 175 in your dictionary. Complete the sentences.**

   a. A woman is visiting a _____career planning center_____.

   b. She wants to _____ her career options.

   c. The first step on the career path is _____.

   d. Another woman is taking an _____ in medical transcription.

   e. A man is doing an _____ as an electrician.

2. **Look at Carol's career plan. Complete the sentences. Use the words in the box.**

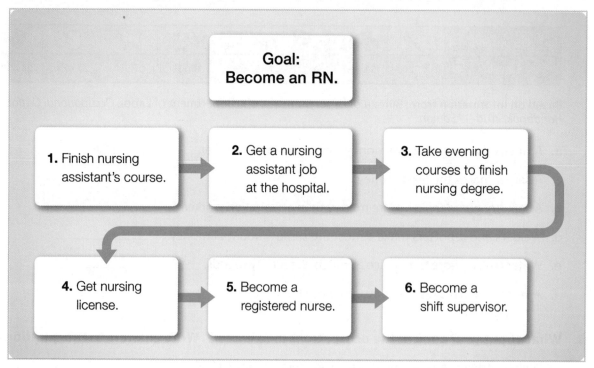

**Goal:
Become an RN.**

1. Finish nursing assistant's course.

2. Get a nursing assistant job at the hospital.

3. Take evening courses to finish nursing degree.

4. Get nursing license.

5. Become a registered nurse.

6. Become a shift supervisor.

entry-level job	promotion	professional development
~~long-term goal~~	college degree	short-term goals

   a. Carol's _____long-term goal_____ is to become an RN.

   b. One of her _____ is to finish her nursing assistant course.

   c. Then she will get an _____ at a hospital.

   d. She wants to continue her _____ while she is working as a nursing assistant.

   e. Before she can become a licensed RN, she needs to get a _____.

   f. After she begins working as an RN, she wants to get a _____.

3. **Complete the FAQs (Frequently Asked Questions) from a website. Use the words in the box.**

> career ~~counselors~~   vocational training   soft skills   technical skills
> on-the-job training   internship   interest inventory

← → C   ☰

⊙⊙⊙ Career Counseling Center

Q. I'm not really sure about the kind of job I want. Can you help me?

A. Yes! Come in and consult with one of our _career counselors_ . Take an
a.

_____ to help you find out what kinds of jobs you will enjoy.
b.

Q. I'm worried because I don't have any specific _____ yet. Will I be too
c.

unqualified to get a job?

A. Many jobs offer _____ . You learn the skills after you are hired. Try listing your
d.

_____ . For example, are you good at problem solving? Do you get along well
e.

with others?

Q. How can I learn skills before I'm hired?

A. There are several possibilities. _____ teaches practical skills for a special job,
f.

for example a car mechanic or a computer programmer. But you can also get an

_____ with a company before you graduate from school.
g.

---

4. **What about you? Write your answers.**

What is your long-term goal?   _____

What is one of your short-term goals?   _____

What kind of training do you need to achieve your goals? _____

CHALLENGE   When is it good to have vocational training? List four jobs. Tell a classmate.

1. Look at page 176 in your dictionary. Complete the job descriptions.

a. A cashier _____ *uses a cash register* _____.

b. A childcare worker _____.

c. A garment worker _____.

d. A carpenter _____.

e. A server _____.

f. An interpreter _____.

2. What about you? Complete the questionnaire. Check (✓) the job skills you have.

Can you...?	Kim	Alexis	Carlos	Diana	Your name: _____
solve math problems	✓				
program computers	✓			✓	
type	✓		✓	✓	
sell cars		✓		✓	
repair appliances				✓	
operate heavy machinery			✓		
drive a truck		✓			
teach	✓				
do manual labor	✓		✓		
assemble components		✓	✓		

3. Look at the chart in Exercise 2. *True* or *False*?

a. Kim could apply for a job as a teacher. _____ *true* _____

b. Carlos could get a job as a truck driver. _____

c. Only Diana could apply for a job as a repairperson. _____

d. Both Kim and Alexis could get jobs as assemblers. _____

e. Alexis could apply for a job as a salesperson, but not as a repairperson. _____

f. Kim, Carlos, and Diana could be administrative assistants. _____

g. You and Kim could work as accountants. _____

h. You and Carlos can both work with your hands. _____

CHALLENGE Look at page 264 in this book. Follow the instructions.

1. **Look at page 177 in your dictionary. What does the administrative assistant need to do to follow the boss's instructions?**

   a. "Please put these files in alphabetical order." ___*organize materials*___

   b. "I'd like to meet with Mr. Lorenzo next Friday, if possible." _____

   c. "Could you send this report to Amy Ma at 555-3523?" _____

   d. "We need enough copies for thirty people." _____

2. **Read the conversations. Circle the words to complete the sentences.**

   Ana

   a. **Ana:** J & R Associates. Good morning.
      Caller 1: Hello. Can I speak to John Smith, please?

      Ana is putting the caller on hold /(greeting the caller.)

   b. **Caller 2:** Is Marta Rodriguez there?
      Ana: Yes. I'll connect you.

      Ana is checking messages / transferring the call.

   c. **Caller 3:** Can I speak to Tom Chen, please?
      Ana: I'm sorry. Mr. Chen isn't in.
      Caller 3: OK. Please tell him that I called.
      Ana: Sure. What is your name and number, please?

      Ana is leaving a message / taking a message.

3. **Look at the pictures. Write what the office assistant can do.**

   a. ___*He can transcribe notes.*___   c. _____

   b. _____   d. _____

CHALLENGE Look in your dictionary. Make a list of the office and telephone skills you have.

1. **Look at page 178 in your dictionary. Complete the sentences.**

    a. I'm an ___honest___ person. I've never taken company property home.

    b. I'm very organized and can _____ my time well.

    c. I like to work in groups and always _____ with my _____.

    d. I can think _____ and _____ problems.

2. **Complete the employee evaluation. Use the words in the box.**

clarify instructions	communicate clearly	make decisions	patient
~~positive~~	responded well to feedback	solve problems	willing to learn

EMPLOYEE EVALUATION

Employee Name: Rafael Garza

Strengths:

Rafael is an excellent employee. His co-workers like him. He is a very ___positive___

a.

person and always has something good to say. He is friendly and _____ with

b.

new co-workers while they are learning the job.

Rafael is also smart. He doesn't ask the managers for help with every difficulty. Instead, he

tries to _____ by himself before he asks for help. In his job, he needs to make

c.

many choices, and Rafael is not afraid to _____.

d.

I often ask Rafael to meet with customers because he speaks well and can _____.

e.

When we put in the new software recently, Rafael didn't know how to use it, but he was very

_____. He made mistakes, but he always _____.

f. **g.**

Needs to Improve:

Sometimes Rafael forgets to _____. He goes ahead with his work even though

h.

he doesn't understand exactly what to do.

CHALLENGE What are your main strengths? What areas do you need to improve? Explain your answers to a partner. Give examples.

1. **Look at page 179 in your dictionary. Write the interview skill.**

   a. "I worked there for four years."   *talk about your experience*

   b. "Is there health insurance?"   _____

   c. "Nice to meet you."   _____

   d. "Hmm. This website says GBG has 100 employees."   _____

2. **Look at the pictures. Circle the words to complete the interviewer's notes.**

CHALLENGE   Look at Exercise 2. Would you give Amy Cho a job? Why or why not?

1. **Look at pages 180 and 181 in your dictionary. Complete the sentences.**

   a. An elderly man _____yells_____ at Leo when he adjusts the bed.

   b. A woman _____ about him because he's new.

   c. There are men and women on the _____ at the nursing home.

   d. The nursing home _____ has private rooms and common areas for the residents.

   e. One elderly _____ used to be an actor.

   f. The morning _____ ends at 3:30 p.m.

   g. A co-worker _____ Leo to Room 10D.

2. **Look at pages 180 and 181 in your dictionary. How does Leo show that he is a team player?**

   _____

3. **Circle the words to complete the conversations.**

   A: I seem to be lost. Could you (direct)/ distribute me to Room 24?
                                        a.
   B: It's straight ahead on the right. You can't miss it.

   A: Nice to meet you. Do you work here?

   B: No. Actually I'm one of the staff / residents. I volunteer to help out when I can.
                                        b.

   A: Are you going to work now?

   B: No. I'm going to bed! I work the night shift / staff.
                                                c.

   A: Do you think we should hire Martina full-time?

   B: Yes, I do. She's a real co-worker / team player.
                                          d.

   A: Wow! This place looks beautiful.

   B: Yes, it's a brand-new resident / facility.
                                          e.

   A: Please don't yell / direct at the residents. You always need to remain calm.
                               f.
   B: You're right. I'm sorry.

   A: How many people work here?

   B: We have 35 people on our staff / facility.
                                            g.

4. **Look at the pictures. Write a sentence about each picture. Use the words in the box.**

facility	co-workers	distribute	team players	staff	complain

a. ___The co-workers are very friendly.___

b. _____

c. _____

d. _____

e. _____

f. _____

I don't like it!

5. **What about you? Discuss the questions with a partner.**

a. Are you a team player? Give an example. _____
_____

b. Do you get along with your co-workers? Why or why not? _____
_____

c. What shift do you prefer to work? Why? _____
_____

d. What's the best way to deal with a complaining customer? _____
_____

The Workplace

1. **Look at pages 182 and 183 in your dictionary. Who . . . ? Check (✓) the columns.**

	The Employer	The Receptionist	The Payroll Clerk	The Supervisor	All Employees
a. uses a time clock					✓
b. greets customers					
c. signs paychecks					
d. receives paychecks					
e. hands out paychecks					
f. gives instructions					

2. **Complete the conversations. Use the words in the box.**

customer	~~deductions~~	employee	entrance
payroll clerk	~~receptionist~~	time clock	pay stub

Receptionist :   Irina's Computer Service. How can I help you?
a.

_____: I need to bring in my computer. Could you tell me your address?
b.

_____: This is my first day. I need to clock in, but I can't find the
c.

           _____ .
            d.

Supervisor: It's over there. To the right of the _____ where you
                                            e.

come in.

Employee: I don't understand my _____ . Why are there so
                                          f.

many _____ ?
           g.

_____: Well, this one is for federal. This is for state. This is for Social Security.
h.

3. **What about you? Look at pages 182 and 183 in your dictionary. Answer the questions. Discuss your answers with a classmate.**

     a. Would you like to work at Irina's Computer Service? Why or why not?

     _____

     b. Would you prefer to work in the office or the room with the time clock? Why?

     _____

4. Look at pages 182 and 183 in your dictionary. *True* or *False*? Correct the underlined words in the false sentences.

A customer
a. ~~An employee~~ is standing in the entrance.   _____false_____

b. Employees can find the safety regulations near the door   _____
that says *Employees Only*.

c. Irina Sarkov is in the office.   _____

d. The payroll clerk is giving Kate Babic a paycheck.   _____

e. The supervisor is talking to the employer.   _____

5. Look at the pay stub and paycheck. Answer the questions.

a. What is the employee's name?

_____Enrique Gutierrez_____

b. What is the employer's name?

_____

c. What is the pay stub amount?

_____

d. What are the wages before deductions?

_____

e. How many deductions are there?

_____

f. Which is more, the state deduction or
the Social Security deduction?

_____

g. What is the amount of the paycheck?

_____

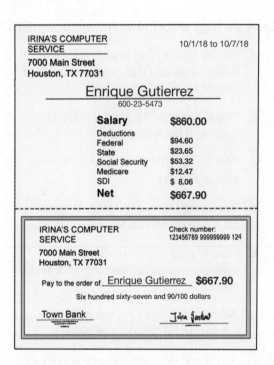

CHALLENGE Look at the pay stub in Exercise 5. What is *SDI*? Does the state you live in have this type
of deduction? Look up *SDI* online or ask someone you know.

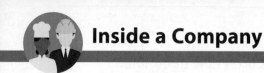

Inside a Company

1. **Look at page 184 in your dictionary. Write the name of the department.**

   a. A woman has someone on hold on the phone. _____logistics_____

   b. A woman is making a presentation with a graph. _____

   c. A woman is helping a new employee. _____

   d. A man is pointing at a slogan on a whiteboard. _____

   e. The employees are wearing blue uniforms. _____

   f. An employee is moving a large box. _____

   g. A woman is using a calculator. _____

2. **Where do they work? Match the quote with the department.**

   _3_ a. "We've just begun testing the new flavors. I should have some results for you next week."

   ___ b. "Have you tried turning it off and turning it back on again?"

   ___ c. "We'll have that wall repaired by the end of the day."

   ___ d. "Good morning. My name is Anna. How can I help you today?"

   ___ e. "You'll need to complete the insurance forms before the end of the month."

   ___ f. "We need to work on the advertising campaign for the new cereal."

   ___ g. "I'm sorry, sir, you'll have to leave this area. Only employees are allowed here."

   ___ h. "I'm very busy right now because it's tax season."

   ___ i. "The new cereal is doing great! We're selling more than ever."

   ___ j. "We need to clear out Warehouse 23 to make room for the new products."

   1. information technology
   2. customer service
   3. research and development
   4. security
   5. accounting
   6. human resources
   7. logistics
   8. sales
   9. marketing
   10. building maintenance

CHALLENGE Look online. Find out which large companies have corporate offices in your state. Find a company that has branches in all fifty states.

1. **Look at page 185 in your dictionary. Complete the factory newsletter.**

THE LAMPLIGHTER

"WE LIGHT UP YOUR LIFE"   Vol. 25, no. 2   June 7, 2019

T. J. Rolf, President
and ___*factory owner*___
a.

"As we enter our 25th year of business, I want to thank the following people for their dedication and hard work."

WELCOME TO LAMPLIGHTER

Jan Larson,
_____
d.

Jan has been hired to
_____
e.
a new desk lamp. We will begin to _____
f.
this new product in September.

WELCOME JAN!

20 YEARS

Pete Johnson,
Shipping Clerk

Pete has been with us for more than 20 years. He has stood on the _____ carefully
b.
checking the orders that we _____ to over
c.
32 states. Congratulations, Pete!

Employee of the Month!

15 YEARS

Ivonne Campis,
Assembler

For 15 years, Ivonne has assembled the _____
g.
that make our lamps. Her skills and care have contributed to the high quality of our product.

10 YEARS

Doug Wilson,
_____
h.
For 10 years, Doug has watched over the assembly line, assuring the highest product quality. He helps create a friendly and productive work environment.

5 YEARS

Alice Carver,
_____
i.
Alice Carver has worked in the _____ for 5 years,
j.
taking finished lamps off the conveyor belt and putting them in boxes ready for shipment.

CHALLENGE Look in your dictionary. Write short paragraphs about the shipping clerk and the order puller for the factory newsletter in Exercise 1. Use your imagination.

Landscaping and Gardening

1. Look at page 186 in your dictionary. Complete the sentences.

a. The _____*trowel*_____ is to the left of the hedge clippers.

b. The gardening crew leader is talking to the _____.

c. You can use a _____ or a _____
to remove leaves from your lawn.

d. You can use a _____ to remove weeds.

e. You need a _____ to plant a tree.

f. You can cut the grass with a _____.

g. You can use a _____ to move dirt or plants.

h. You can water the lawn by hand, or you can install a _____.

2. Look at the picture. Complete the note to the gardening crew.

Carlos,

I ___*fertilized*___ the plants and
    a.

_____ the hedges, but please:
    b.

_____
    c.

_____
    d.

_____
    e.

_____
    f.

_____
    g.

                   Thanks!!

CHALLENGE Compare a shovel to a trowel and hedge clippers to pruning sheers. How are they the
same? How are they different? What can you use them for?

186

1. Look at page 187 in your dictionary. **Cross out the word that doesn't belong. Write the category.**

a. _Places for animals_	barn	corral	~~vegetable garden~~
b. _____	hired hand	field	orchard
c. _____	vineyard	soybeans	wheat
d. _____	grower	tractor	farmworker
e. _____	hay	livestock	cattle

2. Circle the words to complete the blog.

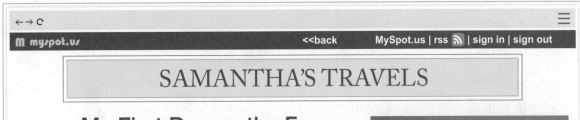

← → C   m myspot.us   <<back   MySpot.us | rss 🔊 | sign in | sign out

SAMANTHA'S TRAVELS

JULY 10: **My First Day on the Farm**

When I got up, it was still dark. John Johnson, the

(farmer) / hired hand who owns the place, was already
    a.

in the corral / barn. He was harvesting / milking the
    b.   **c.**

cows. My job was to feed / plant the chickens and
      d.

other cattle / livestock.
    e.

Breakfast here is great! We have fresh eggs and ham along with tomatoes from

the vegetable garden / vineyard and fruit from the barn / orchard. After breakfast, it
    f.   **g.**

is time to work in the fence / field. John says that in the old days horses pulled most
    h.

of the farm equipment / livestock. Today, a hired hand / tractor does the job. John and
    i.   **j.**

his farmworkers / ranchers planted rows of corn and other crops / wheat. They also
    k.   **l.**

grow alfalfa / cotton for animal feed. I'd like to come back when they harvest / milk
    m.   **n.**

the corn in the summer. I like life on the farm.

POSTED BY <u>SAMANTHA</u> AT 1:52 PM   [REPLY TO THIS]

CHALLENGE Would you like to spend some time on a farm or a ranch? Write a paragraph explaining your opinion.

1. **Look at page 188 in your dictionary. Answer the questions.**

    a. Who is in the reception area?   ___the receptionist___

    b. Who is working in the cubicle next to the conference room?   _____

    c. Who is walking to the supply cabinet?   _____

    d. Who is cleaning the floor?   _____

    e. Where is the presentation?   _____

    f. Who is standing at the file cabinet?   _____

2. **Match the word parts.**

    _5_ a. paper   1. bands

    ___ b. correction   2. book

    ___ c. postal   3. scale

    ___ d. rubber   4. pad

    ___ e. appointment   5. shredder

    ___ f. legal   6. fluid

3. **Read the notes. What do you need to do the job? Use the words from Exercise 2.**

    Please collate these pages, but don't staple them.

    Thanks.
    L.

    There are some mistakes in this report. Please correct them before you make copies.

    * This is for your eyes only!

    Please read and destroy.

    a. ___rubber bands___   b. _____   c. _____

    Please let me know when my next meeting with L. J. Inc. is.

    I'll be out of the office on Friday. Please take notes at the staff meeting.
    Thanks.
    R.F.

    Mail two packages to Anne Miles.

    d. _____   e. _____   f. _____

4. **Look at pages 188 and 189 in your dictionary. Cross out the word that doesn't belong. Give a reason.**

a. janitor   file clerk   ~~mailer~~   receptionist   _A mailer isn't a person._

b. scanner   desk   file cabinet   supply cabinet   _____

c. envelope   ink pad   letterhead   sticky note   _____

d. rubber band   paper clip   paper cutter   staples   _____

e. calculator   computer   fax machine   stapler   _____

5. **Circle the words to complete the instructions.**

MEMO

To: Alice Rader

From: Marta Lopez _ML_

---

* The electric pencil sharpener / (photocopier) is broken again. Please call the repairperson.
     a.
You'll find the phone number in the laser printer / rotary card file under "p."
                                   b.

* The book on my desk goes to A. Olinski at 354 Main Street. The mailing label / stamp
                                                                 c.
is already filled out. Please use glue / clear tape so you can read the address through it.
                                  d.

* The Thompson report is more than 500 pages. Use the stapler / laser printer so it prints
                                                       e.
out faster. Before you file it, use the paper cutter / shredder to make it 8 × 10 inches.
                                                   f.
The paper in the printer now is too long.

* Please stamp all letters to Japan "airmail." (The legal / ink pad is in the top
                                                      g.
left drawer.)

* Please order more rubber bands / clear tape. (I like the ones that come in different colors
                                    h.
and sizes.)

Thanks.

CHALLENGE Look at the office supplies in your dictionary. Which items can you use for the same
job? **Example:** _You can use an inkjet printer or a laser printer to print out computer files._

Information Technology (IT)

1. **Look at pages 190 and 191 in your dictionary. Complete the sentences.**

   a. The computer operations specialist is working on a _____*mainframe computer*_____.

   b. A _____ drive is plugged into a _____ port on the laptop.

   c. An _____ is connected to the laptop through a _____.

   d. The power cord is plugged into a _____.

   e. The desktop computer has a mouse, but the laptop has a _____.

   f. A cable connects the tower to a _____.

   g. A man is using a _____ because his computer has a virus alert.

   h. The microprocessor, the _____, and the

      _____ are inside a tower.

   i. A _____ program is good for keeping track of things.

   j. A _____ program is good for showing pictures and text.

2. **Look at the desktop and the laptop computers in your dictionary. *True* or *False*?**

   a. A laptop is smaller than a desktop computer.   _____*true*_____

   b. A laptop has a tower.   _____

   c. Both types of computers have keyboards.   _____

   d. Both computers use spreadsheet programs.   _____

   e. You can use a printer with both computers.   _____

3. **What about you? Check (✓) the items that are in your classroom. Explain the purpose of each item to a partner.**

   ☐ laptop computer   ☐ speaker

   ☐ tablet   ☐ router

   ☐ desktop computer   ☐ webcam

   ☐ headset   ☐ tower

   ☐ keyboard   ☐ microphone

4. **Read the statements from callers to the IT help line. Match the problems with the statements.**

_5_ **a.** "I keep clicking, but nothing on the screen is moving."

___ **b.** "The paper comes out, but there's nothing on it."

___ **c.** "The website doesn't recognize my password."

___ **d.** "The movie won't play."

___ **e.** "I can't get the new version of the software."

___ **f.** "Nothing happens when I push the 'on' button."

1. He can't stream video.

2. She can't log on.

3. She can't install the update.

4. The computer won't start.

5. His screen froze.

6. It won't print.

5. **Complete the notes. Use the words in the box.**

| data | headsets | presentation program | printers | router | speakers | webcams | ~~Wi-Fi~~ |

IT DEPARTMENT

Recent issues

a. Jill Adams wasn't able to get online because there was a problem with the ___Wi-Fi___ connection on the third floor. The _____ that distributes the Wi-Fi signal was not working, so we replaced it.

b. Amin Jarrar called to ask for _____ for the conference room so that meeting participants could listen, speak, and type without bothering others. He will return them on Friday.

c. Two people at the meeting were not able to share video because the _____ on computers 12 and 13 aren't working.

d. Kenneth Gale has asked for a new _____ to replace the old one. He says that a newer program will allow him to create better slide shows.

e. Kara Molina says we need to replace the _____ in the Accounting Office. They won't print.

f. Jon Kim wants external _____ . He says the volume on his computer is too low.

g. HyunJa Park's computer had a virus that destroyed several files. We are trying to recover her _____ .

CHALLENGE Give two examples of a word processing program, a spreadsheet program, and a presentation program. Do an Internet search or ask your classmates.

A Hotel

1. Look at page 192 in your dictionary. Read these job descriptions. Write the job.

   a. Register and check out guests: *desk clerk*

   b. Carry the guests' luggage on a luggage cart: _____

   c. Take care of the guests' cars: _____

   d. Clean the guests' rooms: _____

   e. Repair and service hotel equipment: _____

2. Circle the words to complete the hotel website.

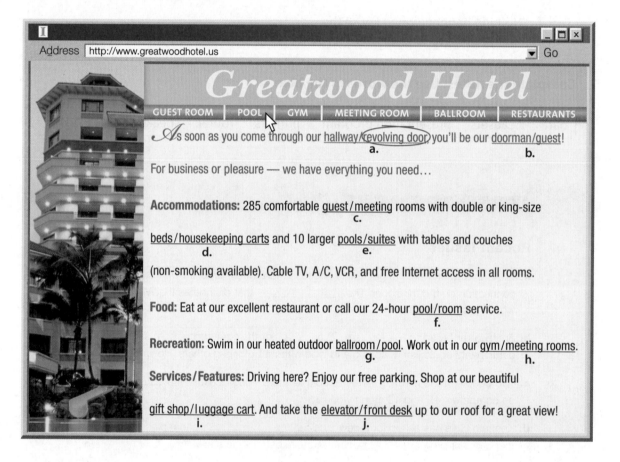

Address http://www.greatwoodhotel.us   Go

Greatwood Hotel

| GUEST ROOM | POOL | GYM | MEETING ROOM | BALLROOM | RESTAURANTS |

As soon as you come through our hallway/**revolving door** you'll be our doorman/guest!
          a.   **b.**

For business or pleasure — we have everything you need...

Accommodations: 285 comfortable guest/meeting rooms with double or king-size
                                       c.

beds/housekeeping carts and 10 larger pools/suites with tables and couches
     d.   **e.**

(non-smoking available). Cable TV, A/C, VCR, and free Internet access in all rooms.

Food: Eat at our excellent restaurant or call our 24-hour pool/room service.
                                                  f.

Recreation: Swim in our heated outdoor ballroom/pool. Work out in our gym/meeting rooms.
                                              g.   **h.**

Services/Features: Driving here? Enjoy our free parking. Shop at our beautiful

gift shop/luggage cart. And take the elevator/front desk up to our roof for a great view!
      i.   **j.**

CHALLENGE   Imagine you are staying at the hotel in your dictionary. Write a postcard.
                    Describe the hotel.

1. **Look at page 193 in your dictionary. Read these job descriptions. Write the job.**

www.restaurantopening.us

Large Hotel Restaurant Now Hiring for the Following Positions:

a. <u>caterer</u> : to prepare and serve food for large banquet room events

b. _____ : to plan menus

c. _____ : to help the head chef

d. _____ : to bring food and drinks to the diners

e. _____ : to clear the tables

f. _____ : to prepare hamburgers and other fast food

g. _____ : to supervise servers

h. _____ : to carry food from the walk-in freezer and storeroom into the kitchen

i. _____ : to greet guests and show them to their tables

j. _____ : to wash dirty glasses and plates

To apply, please visit our website at www.hotelgrand.us

2. **What about you? Would you like to be a . . . ? Check (✓) Yes or No. Give a reason.**

		Yes	No	
a.	short-order cook	☐	☐	_____
b.	dishwasher	☐	☐	_____
c.	food preparation worker	☐	☐	_____
d.	sous-chef	☐	☐	_____
e.	server	☐	☐	_____
f.	headwaiter	☐	☐	_____
g.	bus person	☐	☐	_____
h.	caterer	☐	☐	_____
i.	runner	☐	☐	_____

CHALLENGE Write a job ad for a restaurant worker. Use the job descriptions in Exercise 1 as an example.

Tools and Building Supplies

1. **Look at pages 194 and 195 in your dictionary. Cross out the word that doesn't belong. Then write the section of the hardware store.**

   a. _____Hardware_____   nail   bolt   ~~C-clamp~~   wood screw

   b. _____   ax   plunger   pipe   fittings

   c. _____   circular saw 2 × 4   router   electric drill

   d. _____   paintbrush   paint roller spray gun   chisel

   e. _____   wire stripper drill bit   extension cord   wire

   f. _____   hacksaw   chain   adjustable wrench   mallet

2. **Complete the conversations. Use the words on the toolbox.**

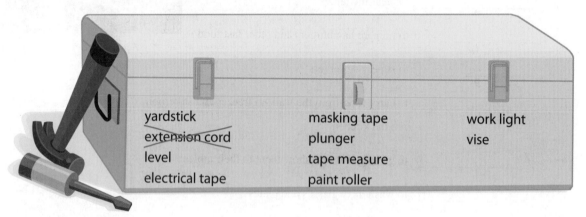

yardstick
~~extension cord~~
level
electrical tape

masking tape
plunger
tape measure
paint roller

work light
vise

   a. **Ty:**   I want to use this electric drill over there, but the cord is too short.
      Jade: No problem. Use this _____extension cord_____.

   b. **Ian:** I've been painting for hours, and I still have three more walls to do.
      Tina: Why don't you use this _____? It's faster than a paintbrush.

   c. **Lily:** Oh, no. The toilet is stopped up again.
      Dan: Here. Use this _____. It always works.

   d. **Kim:** Do you know how long the shelf in the dining room is?
      Lian: No. Use the _____ or _____ to find out.

   e. **Eva:** Help! I could use a third hand here!
      Jana: Use the _____ to hold the wood in place.

   f. **Jules:** Don't get paint on the glass!
      Lyle: I won't. I always put _____ around the panes before I start.

   g. **Nico:** That wire doesn't look very safe.
      Iris: Don't worry. I'll put some of this _____ on before using it.

   h. **Olga:** Does this shelf look straight?
      Boris: Hmm. I'm not sure. Let's use the _____. Then we'll know for certain.

   i. **Enzo:** It's so dark behind here. I can't see what I'm doing!
      Pia: Here. Use the _____.

3. **Look at the pictures. Each situation shows a mistake. Describe the mistake and tell the people what they need to do the job right.**

a.

You can't paint on that wall.
You need to use a scraper first.

b.

_____
_____

c.

_____
_____

d.

_____
_____

e.

_____
_____

f.

_____
_____

4. **What about you? Check (✓) the tools you or someone you know has used. What did you use them for?**

☐ hammer _____ ☐ plane _____

☐ ax _____ ☐ wrench _____

☐ handsaw _____ ☐ vise _____

☐ screwdriver _____ ☐ electric drill _____

☐ pliers _____ ☐ Other: _____

CHALLENGE Imagine you can have only three tools from the ones in Exercise 4. Which would you choose? Explain your choices.

Construction

1. **Look at page 196 in your dictionary.** *True or False*? **Correct the underlined words in the false sentences.**

   thirteen
   a. There are ~~eight~~ construction workers on the site. ___false___

   b. One worker is climbing a <u>ladder</u>. _____

   c. Two construction workers are helping move the <u>plywood</u>. _____

   d. The worker in the <u>cherry picker</u> is not hammering. _____

   e. One worker is using a <u>sledgehammer</u>. _____

2. **Complete the sentences. Use the words on the bricks.**

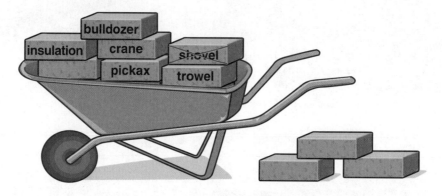

bulldozer · insulation · crane · shovel · pickax · trowel

   a. You can use a _____*shovel*_____ to dig a small hole in the ground.

   b. A _____ moves earth or large rocks from one place to another.

   c. _____ keeps a house warm.

   d. A _____ can lift and place beams on high floors.

   e. A _____ is used to lay bricks.

   f. A _____ is used to dig in very hard ground.

3. **What about you? Check (✓) the materials that your school and home are made of.**

	School	Home
bricks		
shingles		
stucco		
wood		
Other:		

CHALLENGE Look for pictures of buildings in your dictionary, a newspaper, or a magazine. What building materials are used? **Example:** *The condominium on page 52 is made of brick.*

1. Look at page 197 in your dictionary. *True* or *False*?

a. The man listening to music is a careful worker.   _____false_____

b. The frayed cord is near the slippery floor.   _____

c. There's a fire extinguisher near the flammable liquids.   _____

d. Poisonous fumes are coming from the radioactive materials. _____

2. Circle the words to complete the safety poster.

⚠ **WARNING**

PROTECT YOURSELF
from Head to Toe!

Protect your head: A (hard hat) / respirator can protect you from falling objects. Don't forget
a.
your hair. If it's long, wear your hair back so it won't get caught in machinery.

Protect your eyes: Always wear safety glasses / work gloves or earmuffs / safety goggles.
b.   c.

Protect your ears: Noise can cause hearing loss. Wear earplugs / safety goggles or
d.

earmuffs / particle masks if you work near loud machinery.
e.

Protect your hands: Always wear work gloves / back support belts when handling
f.

knee pads / radioactive materials.
g.

Protect your feet: Knee pads / Safety boots protect you from falling objects.
h.

Avoid dangerous situations: Don't use power tools in wet locations or near

radioactive / flammable liquids or gases. Keep a fire extinguisher / respirator on the wall
i.   j.

in case of fire. And have a frayed cord / two-way radio so you can communicate with
k.

other workers. Remember: Better safe than sorry!

3. What about you? What safety equipment do you use? When do you use it?

Example: *I wear earplugs when I go to a loud concert.*

[CHALLENGE] Look at page 264 in this book. Follow the instructions.

A Bad Day at Work

1. **Look at pages 198 and 199 in your dictionary. How many . . . do you see?**

    a. accidents that have happened or will happen   _7_

    b. bricklayers   ___

    c. dates on the schedule   ___

    d. electrical hazards   ___

    e. budgets   ___

    f. notes about people who called in sick   ___

    g. floor plans   ___

2. **Look at page 198 in your dictionary. Answer the questions.**

    a. How much will the drywall cost?   _$200,000_

    b. When did construction start?   _____

    c. Who called in sick?   _____ and _____

    d. How much will the wiring cost?   _____

    e. When will the walls be put up?   _____

    f. Who is the contractor?   _____

3. **Circle the words to complete the conversation.**

    Sam: Hello. Lopez Contracting.

    Pat: Hello, Mr. Lopez. It's Pat. I'm (calling in sick)/ worried today.
    　　　　　　　　　　　　　　　　　　　　　　　a.

    Sam: Oh, no. I need you to help me with the budget / floor plan. We're over by $50,000.
    　　　　　　　　　　　　　　　　　　　　　　　　　　　b.

    Pat: Could you email the budget? I can look at it at home. I think it would be

    　　　　an electrical hazard / dangerous for me to come to work today. I'm really sick.
    　　　　　　　　　　c.

    Sam: OK. I'll send it right now. See if we can cut costs with the wiring / bricklayer.
    　　　　　　　　　　　　　　　　　　　　　　　　　　　　　d.

    Pat: Hmm . . . Well, I don't think so. That could be a contractor / an electrical hazard.
    　　　　　　　　　　　　　　　　　　　　　　　　　　e.
    　　　　I'll look at the budget. Maybe we can pay the bricklayers / clinics less.
    　　　　　　　　　　　　　　　　　　　　　　　　f.

    Sam: No, we can't do that! They're the best.

    Pat: Maybe we could pay the floor plan / contractor less.
    　　　　　　　　　　　　　　　　g.

    Sam: You know what, you're sick and need to rest. I'll ask Sue to help me.

4. **Complete the notes. Use the words in the box.**

> called in sick   budget   wiring   electrical hazard
> floor plan   ~~bricklayer~~   clinic

Mr. Lopez:

A ___bricklayer___ got hurt on
        a.
the job. I took him to

the _____.
        b.
I'll be back after lunch to finish

the plumbing.

Daniel

Mr. Lopez:

Mrs. Simone called.

The _____ is an
        c.
_____. Her
        d.
company will charge $40,000

to repair it in the building.

Mark

Mr. Lopez:

The steel will cost $840,000.

That makes us $30,000 over

_____.
        e.

Lilia

Mr. Lopez:

Todd _____.
        f.
He'll be back tomorrow. He

said the _____
        g.
is on his desk if you need it.

Pat

5. **What about you? Look in your dictionary. Which job do you think would be the hardest? the easiest? the most dangerous? Why?**

CHALLENGE   Write a report about the construction site in your dictionary. Write about the problems that happened that day.

Schools and Subjects

1. **Look at page 200 in your dictionary. Where are the students learning . . . ?**

   a. to teach preschool _____in community college_____

   b. to multiply numbers _____

   c. to repair a car _____

   d. to count to four _____

   e. about biology _____

   f. about history _____ and _____

2. **Look at page 200 in your dictionary. Which school do students of these ages usually attend?**

Age	Type of School
a. 11–14 years old	_____middle school_____
b. 18–22 years old	_____, _____,
	_____, or vocational school
c. under 5 years old	_____
d. 14–18 years old	_____ or vocational school
e. 22 years old and older	_____, _____,
	_____, or vocational school
f. 5–11 years old	_____

3. **Complete this journal entry. Use Exercise 2 for help.**

   It's the end of Tommy's first week in __elementary school__ ! It seems like yesterday that I

            a.

   took him to _____ . His first grade class went to a farmers' market this week

    b.

   and brought home things beginning with the letters A and B—apples, beans, bananas. He's

   learning to read! In just six years, he'll be in _____ studying geography and history.

                            c.

   After that, he'll be a teenager in _____ , and we'll really have to think about his

           d.

   future. After graduation, will he go to _____ like his Dad? Or go to

           e.

   _____ and study computers, like I did? Wait a minute. He's just starting his second

  f.

   week of first grade now. Let's just enjoy this year.

4. **Look at page 201 in your dictionary. In which class are students . . . ?**

   a. painting   _arts_

   b. exercising   _____

   c. singing   _____

   d. learning about the Civil War   _____

   e. doing experiments   _____

   f. studying the novel *Moby Dick*   _____

   g. speaking Spanish and Chinese   _____

   h. learning words in English   _____

5. **Look at the things Katia needs for school. Complete her schedule.**

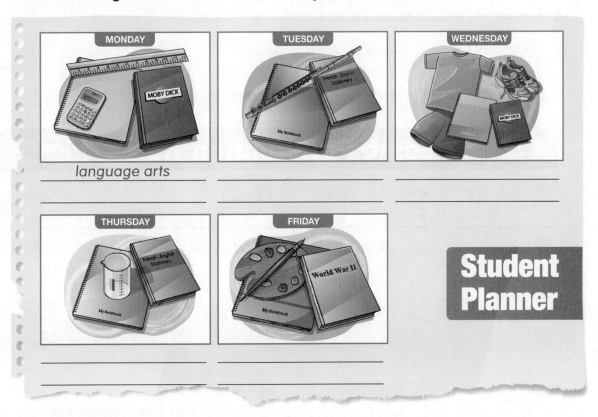

6. **What about you? Check (✓) the classes you would like to take.**

   ☐ math   ☐ music

   ☐ science   ☐ world languages   If *yes*, which? _____

   ☐ history   ☐ arts   If *yes*, which type? _____

   ☐ physical education   ☐ Other: _____

   [CHALLENGE] Explain your choices in Exercise 6.
   Example: *I would like to take history because I like to learn about the world.*

201

English Composition

1. **Look at page 202 in your dictionary.** *True* or *False*? **Correct the <u>underlined</u> words in the false sentences.**

   body
   a. The ~~conclusion~~ of the essay has two paragraphs.   _____false_____

   b. The <u>title</u> of the essay has four words.   _____

   c. The student indented the first <u>sentence</u> in each paragraph.   _____

   d. There's a quotation in the <u>introduction</u>.   _____

   e. There's a <u>comma</u> after the citation.   _____

   f. The student capitalized <u>names</u>.   _____

   g. The <u>footnote</u> tells us where the student got his information.   _____

   h. The student used parentheses in the first <u>sentence</u>.   _____

2. **Look at the punctuation rules. Complete the sentences.**

Some Punctuation Rules

a Use a __question mark__ at the end of a question. *Where do you come from?*

b Use a _____ at the end of a statement. *I come from Ecuador.*

c Use an _____ to show a strong feeling. *I love Quito!*

d Use an _____ in a contraction. *It's a beautiful city.*

e Use a _____ before a list. *I miss a lot of things: my home, my friends, my school.*

f Use a _____ between items in a list. *I email Ana, Enrique, and Tomas every week.*

g Use _____ around additional information. *I like Los Angeles (especially the beach), and I'm beginning to feel more at home here.*

h Use a _____ between parts of a word. *We live in a three-year-old building.*

i Use _____ around a person's exact words. My mother says, *"There's no place like home."*

3. **What about you? Write three sentences about your experience in this country. Use . . .**

   a. a period   _____

   b. quotation marks   _____

   c. an exclamation point   _____

4. **Look at page 203 in your dictionary. What is Carlos doing?**

   a. "For this draft, I'll just use my notebook." _writing a first draft_

   b. "Oh, it should be *came*, not *come*!" _____

   c. "Here it is, Mr. Wilson." _____

   d. "I'll write *work* in this circle." _____

   e. "What do you think of the title, Mindy?" _____

   f. "Hmmm . . . Maybe I could write about my first day at work." _____

   g. "For this draft, I'll use my computer." _____

   h. "Paragraph 3 will be about success." _____

5. **Read the student's essay. Answer the questions.**

Things Get Better

The Greek philosopher Heraclitus said, "There is nothing permanent except change," and my life has been proof of that. My family has moved six times, to four different cities and two countries. The biggest change was when we came to Chicago in 2010. At first I was very unhappy. I didn't know anyone besides my family, and I missed hearing my native language and eating my country's food. But I wasn't alone. According to the U.S. Census Bureau, more than 20% of the people in Chicago are foreign-born.* I soon learned that seeking support from others and having a good attitude could make this change the best thing that ever happened to me.

My life began to improve when I started school. The other students were also from other

*U.S. Census Bureau Quick Facts, Chicago Illinois, 2015

   a. What is the title of the essay? _Things Get Better_

   b. Who is the source of the quotation? _____

   c. The writer says, "I wasn't alone." What evidence does he cite?

   _____

   d. What source does the writer cite in the footnote?

   _____

   e. Which part of the essay is the first paragraph?_____

   f. Which parts of the essay are missing? _____

CHALLENGE   Write an essay about how you felt when you came to this country or started this school. Write a first draft, edit it, get feedback, rewrite it, and turn it in to your teacher.

Mathematics

1. **Look at pages 204 and 205 in your dictionary. Cross out the word that doesn't belong. Write the category.**

   a. <u> Types of Math </u>   algebra   calculus   geometry   ~~solution~~

   b. _____ even   negative   numerator   odd

   c. _____ add   divide   equation   subtract

   d. _____ circle   curved   perpendicular   straight

   e. _____ acute   diagonal   obtuse   right

   f. _____ cone   cylinder   parallelogram   sphere

   g. _____ cube   rectangle   square   triangle

2. **Complete the test. Circle the letter of the correct answer.**

Mathematics test

Name: _____

Date: _____

School: _____

1. The number 12 is ___.
   a. even
   b. odd
   c. negative

2. The ___ of 8 × 3 = 24.
   a. sum
   b. difference
   c. product

3. An equation always has ___.
   a. an equal (=) sign
   b. a fraction
   c. pi

4. In an equation, x is called ___.
   a. an endpoint
   b. a graph
   c. a variable

5. The first odd number after 7 is ___.
   a. 5
   b. 8
   c. 9

6. The number -20 is ___.
   a. positive
   b. negative
   c. odd

7. You can use ___ to solve a word problem.
   a. a dictionary
   b. an equation
   c. a ruler

8. In the fraction 2/3, 3 is the ___.
   a. denominator
   b. numerator
   c. quotient

3. **What about you? Which operations or types of math do you use? When do you use them?**

   Example: *I multiply to change dollars to Mexican pesos.*

4. **Look at page 205 in your dictionary. Complete the sentences.**

   a. A _____*triangle*_____ has three straight lines.

   b. Perpendicular lines have two _____ angles.

   c. An _____ angle is bigger than a right angle.

   d. A square is a _____ with four equal sides.

   e. A cube has six _____.

   f. The diameter of a circle is two times longer than the _____.

   g. The distance between two _____ lines is always equal.

   h. _____ lines look like the letter *T*.

5. **Complete the analogies.**

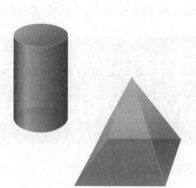

   a. circle : sphere = square : _____*cube*_____

   b. triangle : three = rectangle : _____

   c. add : subtract = multiply : _____

   d. triangle : shape = pyramid : _____

   e. divide : quotient = subtract : _____

   f. circle : circumference = rectangle : _____

   g. straight line : square = curved line : _____

6. **Follow the instructions.**

   a. Draw a circle inside the square.

   b. Draw the diameter.

   c. Draw a diagonal line from the top left corner of the square to the bottom right corner.

   d. Draw a line parallel to the left side of the square.

   e. Draw a line parallel to the right side of the square.

   f. Draw a line perpendicular to the top line of the square. Begin your line at the middle point of the top line of the square, and end your line at the bottom line of the square.

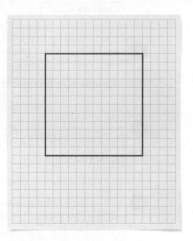

   Compare your drawing with a classmate's. Are they the same?

CHALLENGE Look at page 101 in your dictionary. Find examples of lines, shapes, and solid forms.
Example: *The dryer door is a circle.*

Science

1. **Look at pages 206 and 207 in your dictionary. Complete each sentence.**

   a. The _____*biologist*_____ is using a microscope to examine a leaf.

   b. The nucleus is in the center of the _____.

   c. Plants make oxygen through the process of _____.

   d. Many _____ live in the desert.

   e. Many _____ live in the ocean.

   f. The ocean is the _____ of many invertebrates.

2. **Look at the science book. Complete the definitions.**

THE PARTS OF A MICROSCOPE

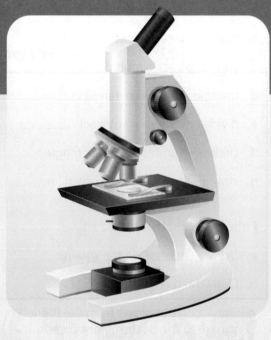

a _____*eyepiece*_____: the part you look through

b _____: the large piece on the side that you turn to make the image clear

c _____: the small piece on the side that you turn (after b.) to make the image clearer

d _____: the large flat area under the objectives where you place the slide

e _____: a lens that makes the image larger—there are usually 3 or 4 different sizes

f _____: the part that holds the objectives—it turns so you can change the power

g _____: the parts that hold the slide on the stage

h _____: the bottom of the microscope

i _____: the part that sends light through the diaphragm

j _____: the round part under the stage—it has different sized holes that control the amount of light

k _____: the part you hold when you carry the microscope

206

3. Look at page 207 in your dictionary. *True* or *False*? Correct the underlined words in the false sentences.

       chemist

a. The ~~physicist~~ is discussing a molecule.   _____*false*_____

b. A molecule has different <u>atoms</u> in it.   _____

c. <u>An electron</u> is positive.   _____

d. The <u>neutron</u> is in the center of the atom.   _____

e. The physicist is using <u>the periodic table</u> to show that c = the speed of light.   _____

f. The physicist drew a picture of a prism and a <u>molecule</u> on the board.   _____

4. Look at the lab experiment. Complete the student's notes.

Chemistry Experiment

Equipment:

ring stand, tubing, rubber stopper,
   Bunsen burner
_____ , _____ ,
       a.   b.
_____ , _____ ,
       c.   d.
_____
       e.

Procedure:

Boil a solution of salt and water
in a _____ . Collect the
            f.
condensed liquid in a _____ .
                 g.
Allow a drop of the liquid to dry on a
_____ .
       h.

Is there any salt in the water?
No!

condensed liquid

rubber stopper

salt solution

tubing

condensed liquid

ring stand

5. Look at the student's notes in Exercise 4. Check (✓) the things the student did.

✓ use a Bunsen burner   ☐ observe

☐ state a hypothesis   ☐ record the results

☐ do an experiment   ☐ draw a conclusion

CHALLENGE Describe the use of crucible tongs, forceps, a graduated cylinder, a balance, and a funnel. **Example:** *You use crucible tongs to pick up hot objects.*

U.S. History

1. Look at page 208 in your dictionary. Complete the information.

DID YOU KNOW...?

★ Thomas Jefferson wrote the <u>Declaration of Independence</u>, and on July 4, 1776, the
a.
_____ adopted it. The thirteen colonies were a free country—the
b.
United States of America!

★ The _____ consisted of New Hampshire, Massachusetts,
c.
Rhode Island, Connecticut, New York, Pennsylvania, New Jersey, Maryland, Delaware,
Virginia, North Carolina, South Carolina, and Georgia. The _____
d.
who lived there came from Spain, France, Sweden, Holland, and England, but they were all
under British control.

★ George Washington was elected _____ of the United States.
e.
He stopped going to school when he was only 15 years old!

★ The first amendment (or changes) to the U.S. Constitution is called the
_____ . These rights guarantee freedom of religion, speech,
f.
and the press.

★ When Europeans first came to North America, there were around 10 million
_____ living there. By the year 2000, there were only 4.1 million.
g.

★ The _____ between the thirteen colonies and Great Britain
h.
lasted for 8 years.

★ A British soldier was called a _____ because of the color of
i.
his uniform.

★ A _____ was an American soldier. He got this name because
j.
he had to be ready in a minute in order to be among the first to arrive at a battle.

★ The U.S. _____ was written in 1787 in fewer than 100 days! It
k.
was signed by 55 _____ , also called the "Fathers of our Country."
l.

CHALLENGE Look at page 265 in this book. Follow the instructions.

208

1. **Look at page 209 in your dictionary. Circle the words to complete the sentences.**

   a. The Egyptian pyramids are a product of (an ancient) / a modern civilization.

   b. <u>An emperor</u> / A president is the ruler of a group of countries.

   c. A <u>dictator</u> / prime minister is the leader of a country who controls everything and has all the power.

   d. A dictator / <u>monarch</u> is a king or a queen.

   e. An activist / <u>army</u> fights during a war.

   f. Invention / <u>Immigration</u> is moving from one country to another.

2. **Complete the chart.**

Category	Person		Country	Famous for...
composition	J. S. Bach (1685–1750) <u>composer</u> **a.**		Germany	He is considered the greatest writer of Baroque music.
invention	Alessandro Volta (1745–1827) ———— **b.**		Italy	In 1800, he invented the first electric battery.
———— **c.**	Vasco da Gama (1469?–1524) explorer		Portugal	In the late 1400s, he was the first to sail from Europe around the Cape of Good Hope in Africa to India.
———— **d.**	Rosa Parks (1913–2005) ———— **e.**		U.S.A.	Known as the "mother of the Civil Rights Movement," in 1955 she refused to give up her seat on a bus to a white passenger.
architecture	I. M. Pei (1917–) architect		U.S.A. ———— **f.** (from China)	He is famous for his modern skyscrapers, museums, and government buildings.

[CHALLENGE] Do an Internet search or use an encyclopedia or history book. Find another example of an explorer, an inventor, a composer, an immigrant, or an activist. Give information like the information in the chart in Exercise 2.

Digital Literacy

1. **Look at page 210 in your dictionary. Put the sentences in order.**

   _2_ **a.** She chooses "New Blank Document" in the file menu to create a new document.

   ___ **b.** She saves the document.

   ___ **c.** Michelle clicks on the icon to open the program.

   ___ **d.** She quits the program.

   ___ **e.** She closes the document.

   ___ **f.** She types the beginning of her vocabulary notebook.

2. **Complete the instructions. Use the words in the box.**

~~click on the screen~~	delete	copy	drag to select the text	paste	double-click

   a. In order to ___*click on the screen*___, you need to quickly tap your mouse button or your track pad.

   b. If you want to _____ a word, first you need to select it. Then you can erase it easily.

   c. You can usually _____ to select a word.

   d. Sometimes you want to select more than a word or just part of a word. Then you can

   _____.

   e. If you want to _____ text, first you need to select it.

   f. Once you have copied the text, you can _____ it in a new location.

3. **Look at Ana's note. Write instructions for her.**

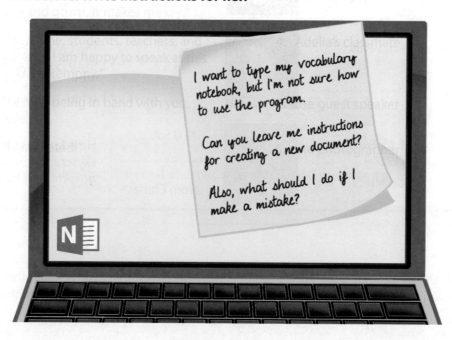

I want to type my vocabulary notebook, but I'm not sure how to use the program.

Can you leave me instructions for creating a new document?

Also, what should I do if I make a mistake?

4. Look at page 211 in your dictionary. Circle the words to complete the sentences.

a. You can (scroll) / drag up and down the screen by using the account / arrow keys.

b. When you register on a website, the first thing you need to do is <u>click submit /</u> <u>create a username</u>.

c. When you <u>create a password / copy text</u>, the website will ask you to <u>create / reenter</u> it to make sure it's right.

d. Many sites ask you to <u>attach a file / type a verification code</u> because this shows that you are a real person and not a "robot" program.

e. Once you have all of the information entered correctly, you need to <u>create a username /</u> <u>click submit</u>.

f. With a username and password, you can <u>attach a file / log in to your account</u> whenever you need to.

5. Look at Jason's email. What did he do right (☺) ? What did he do wrong (☹) ? Use the words in the box.

address the email	attach a file	~~log in to his account~~
check his spelling	compose the message	type the subject

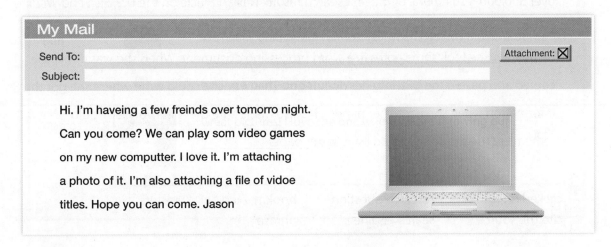

My Mail

Send To: _____   Attachment: ☒

Subject: _____

Hi. I'm haveing a few freinds over tomorro night.
Can you come? We can play som video games
on my new computter. I love it. I'm attaching
a photo of it. I'm also attaching a file of vidoe
titles. Hope you can come. Jason

a. *He logged in to his account.*   d. _____

b. _____   e. _____

c. _____   f. _____

CHALLENGE Do you think it's important to check your spelling in an email? Why or why not? Write a paragraph about your opinion.

211

Internet Research

1. **Look at page 212 in your dictionary. Complete the sentences.**

   a. She typed "top jobs U.S." into the _____search box_____.

   b. The _____ include different links to articles about jobs.

   c. Her _____ was, "What are the top jobs in the U.S. right now?"

   d. "Top," "jobs," and "U.S." are the _____ from her research question.

   e. One of the _____ is to an article called "The Top 10 Jobs You Need to Explore."

   f. The name of the _____ is Search!

2. **Read the story and answer the questions. Use the words in the box.**

   Lindsey was writing a paper about elephants, and she needed to know if African elephants are endangered. She decided to try a new website called *Search!* to look for the answer to her question. She typed "African elephants endangered" into the search box. This search had over 500,000 results. One of the first search results was an article on the U.S. Fish and Wildlife Service website. She went to that article and learned several interesting facts about elephants. She took some notes in a word processing document. When she was done, she copied and pasted the URL into her document. That way she could write where she got the information when she wrote her paper. She also made sure that her browser would remember the site so she could list it in her paper.

clicked on a link	research question	bookmarked	results
cite the source	~~search engine~~	phrase	

   a. Lindsey selected a new ____search engine____ called *Search!*

   b. Her _____ was, "Are African elephants endangered?"

   c. She didn't type the whole question into the search box. Instead, she typed in a

      _____.

   d. When she looked at the _____, she was surprised by how many there were.

   e. She _____ to an article on the U.S. Fish and Wildlife website.

   f. She _____ the site so that she could find it again later.

   g. She copied the link into her document so that it would be easy to _____ when she wrote her paper.

3. **Look at page 213 in your dictionary. Complete the sentences.**

   a. The _____URL_____ is www.money.wwnews.org.

   b. The _____ is to the left of the website address.

   c. The _____ button is to the right of the address.

   d. The _____ is above the browser window.

   e. There's a _____ under "Career."

   f. The _____ are at the bottom left of the browser window.

   g. This website has a _____ at the bottom right.

4. **Read the search advice. Circle the words to complete the sentences.**

Search Tips!

a. There are millions of <u>tabs</u> / <u>web pages</u> on the Internet, and many of them do not have reliable information.

b. If you want to use a site as a <u>source</u> / <u>content</u>, check it carefully!

c. Sometimes the <u>URL</u> / <u>menu bar</u> can tell you something about where the information comes from. For example, if it ends in .gov, it's a government web page.

d. If it isn't clear who created the <u>content</u> / <u>links</u> for the website, check some other sources to make sure the information is good.

e. If there are a lot of <u>drop-down menus</u> / <u>pop-up ads</u>, it's a sign that the purpose of the site is to make money, not to provide information.

f. It's easy to compare websites by opening several <u>tabs</u> / <u>video players</u>. That way you can click back and forth to compare the information.

g. Many articles have been on the Internet for years, and sometimes it's hard to find a <u>date</u> / <u>refresh button</u>. Make sure you aren't citing old information!

h. Don't forget to keep a <u>browser</u> / <u>record</u> of ALL of your sources. If you change computers or your browser history gets erased, it can be hard to find them again.

5. **What about you? Write answers to the questions.**

   a. Which search engine do you use the most? Why?

   _____

   b. Do you ever use the social media links on a web page? What do you use them for?

   _____

   c. How do you decide if you can trust an online source?

   _____

Geography and Habitats

1. **Look at page 214 in your dictionary.** *True* or *False*? **Correct the underlined words in the false sentences.**

   rain forest
   a. There's a waterfall in the ~~forest~~.   _____*false*_____

   b. An ocean is larger than <u>a pond or a bay</u>.   _____

   c. There's a <u>beach</u> around the lake.   _____

   d. There's a canyon between the <u>mountain ranges</u>.   _____

   e. There are flowers in the <u>valley</u>.   _____

   f. Hills are lower than <u>mountain ranges</u>.   _____

2. **Complete the descriptions. Use the words in the box.**

   | desert | island | lake | mountain peak | ocean | river | ~~waterfall~~ |

   # WORLD FACTS

   a **Angel Falls** (3,212 feet) is the highest _____*waterfall*_____ in the world. It is located on the Churun River in southeast Venezuela.

   b The **Pacific** is the largest (64,186,300 square miles) and the deepest (12,925 feet) _____ in the world. It covers almost one third of the earth's surface.

   c Located in the Himalaya range, **Everest** (29,028 feet) is the highest _____ in the world. In 1953, Hillary and Norgay were the first to reach the top.

   d At 4,160 miles, the **Nile**, in Africa, is the longest _____ in the world. Its water supplies electricity and helps agriculture in Egypt and Sudan.

   e The **Sahara** in Africa is the biggest _____ in the world. At 3,500,000 square miles, it is almost as large as the United States. It gets only five to ten inches of rain a year and sometimes has dry periods that last for years.

   f Surrounded by water, **Greenland** (840,000 square miles) is the largest _____ in the world. It lies in the Arctic Circle and is a part of Denmark, although it is 1,300 miles away.

   g The **Caspian Sea** (144,000 square miles) is the largest _____ in the world. It's called a sea because its water is salty.

CHALLENGE   Look online, in an encyclopedia, or in an almanac. Write some facts about a rain forest, a canyon, and plains.

214

1. **Look at page 215 in your dictionary. Complete the chart.**

PLANET NAME	DISTANCE FROM THE SUN (IN MILES)	SYMBOL	DIAMETER (IN MILES)
a. *Mars*	142 million	♂	4,220
b.	67 million	♀	7,521
c.	93 million	⊕	7,926
d.	888 million	♄	74,975
e.	484 million	♃	88,732
f.	1.8 billion	♅	31,763
g.	2.8 billion	♀	30,755
h.	36 million	♄	3,031

2. **Circle the words to complete the sentences. You can use your dictionary for help.**

   a. There are eight moons / (planets) / stars in the solar system.

   b. Uranus was the first planet discovered using a comet / solar system / telescope.

   c. The astronaut / astronomer / space station William Herschel first observed Uranus in 1781.

   d. Constellations / Observatories / Comets look like pictures in the sky.

   e. The Earth's galaxy / orbit / space (a group of billions of stars) is called the Milky Way.

   f. It takes 27 days for the moon to go from a new moon to a full moon and then back to a crescent moon / new moon / quarter moon again.

3. **What about you? Describe what you can see when you look at the night sky. Use your own paper.**

   Example: *I can see the constellation called the Big Dipper ...*

CHALLENGE   Look online or in an encyclopedia, an almanac, or a science book. Find out more about three planets. How long does a day last? How long does it take to orbit the sun?

Trees and Plants

1. **Look at page 216 in your dictionary. What has...? You will use some answers more than once.**

Flowers	Berries	Needles	Leaves That Can Give You a Rash
dogwood	_____	_____	_poison ivy_
_____	_____	_____	_____
_____	_____		_____

2. **Circle the words to complete the article. You can use your dictionary for help.**

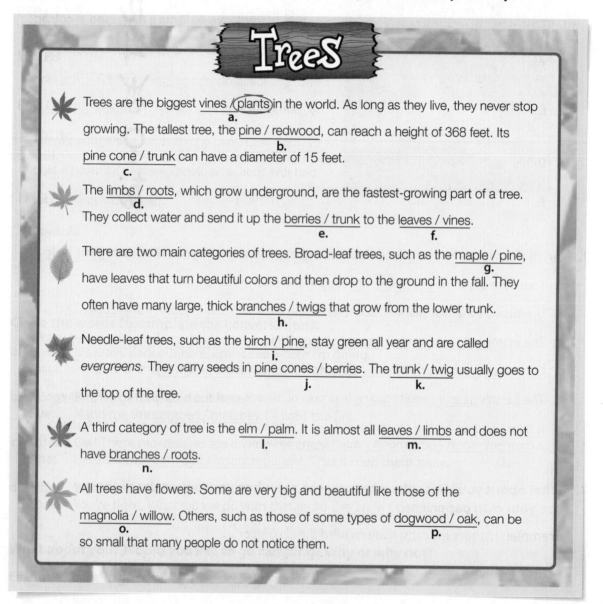

Trees are the biggest vines /(plants) in the world. As long as they live, they never stop
a.
growing. The tallest tree, the pine / redwood, can reach a height of 368 feet. Its
b.
pine cone / trunk can have a diameter of 15 feet.
c.

The limbs / roots, which grow underground, are the fastest-growing part of a tree.
d.
They collect water and send it up the berries / trunk to the leaves / vines.
e. **f.**

There are two main categories of trees. Broad-leaf trees, such as the maple / pine,
g.
have leaves that turn beautiful colors and then drop to the ground in the fall. They
often have many large, thick branches / twigs that grow from the lower trunk.
h.

Needle-leaf trees, such as the birch / pine, stay green all year and are called
i.
evergreens. They carry seeds in pine cones / berries. The trunk / twig usually goes to
j. **k.**
the top of the tree.

A third category of tree is the elm / palm. It is almost all leaves / limbs and does not
l. **m.**
have branches / roots.
n.

All trees have flowers. Some are very big and beautiful like those of the
magnolia / willow. Others, such as those of some types of dogwood / oak, can be
o. **p.**
so small that many people do not notice them.

CHALLENGE Make a list of five tree products. **Example:** *apples*

216

1. Look at page 217 in your dictionary. Complete the order form for this bouquet.

WESTSIDE Florist   **ORDER FORM**

1 mixed bouquet:

a. _4 red tulips_
b. _____ pink _____
c. _3_
d. _1 yellow_
e. _purple_
f. _red_
g. _1_

2. Look in your dictionary. Complete the sentences with information from the chart.

Flower	Grown from	Season	Comments
		spring–fall	remove thorns for bouquets
		late spring–late summer	water often
		summer–early winter	plant seedlings in June
		early spring	very short stems
	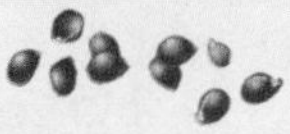	winter–spring	good houseplant
		spring–summer	lovely perfume

a. _____ _Lilies_ _____ and _____ grow from bulbs.

b. _____, _____, and _____
grow from seeds.

c. _____ have thick white petals and smell very nice.

d. Don't hurt your finger when you make a bouquet of _____!

CHALLENGE Write about flower traditions in your country. **Example:** *In the United States, men often give red roses to their wives or girlfriends on Valentine's Day.*

Marine Life, Amphibians, and Reptiles

1. **Look at pages 218 and 219 in your dictionary. Match the animals that look similar.**

   _3_ **a.** frog   **1.** garter snake

   ___ **b.** salamander   **2.** porpoise

   ___ **c.** dolphin   **3.** toad

   ___ **d.** tortoise   **4.** crocodile

   ___ **e.** alligator   **5.** lizard

   ___ **f.** eel   **6.** sea lion

   ___ **g.** walrus   **7.** turtle

2. **Complete the conversations. Use the words in the box. Use your dictionary for help.**

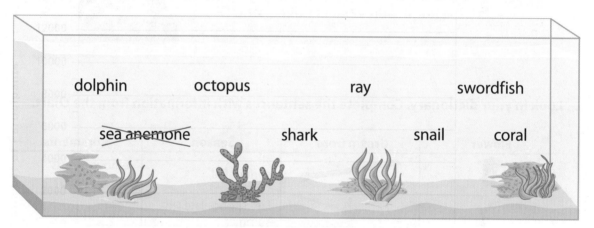

dolphin   octopus   ray   swordfish

~~sea anemone~~   shark   snail   coral

a. Kim: Wow! This aquarium is great. Is that a flower?
    Teacher: No, it's an animal. It's called a ____ *sea anemone* ____.

b. Silvia: What's that flat, blue and gray fish with the long tail?
    Viktor: I think it's a _____.

c. Yi-Wen: What a long nose! Is it sharp?
    Teacher: Sure. That's why that fish is called a _____.

d. Teacher: Look, Josette. That animal doesn't have any gills. Is it a fish?
    Josette: No, it's a _____. That's a kind of mammal.

e. Teacher: How many legs does the _____ have?
    Ho-Jin: Eight.

f. Omar: What's that large fish with the fin on the middle of its back?
    Teacher: It's a _____.

g. Roman: Is that sea animal with the black shell dead?
    Teacher: No, it just moves very slowly. That's why people sometimes say
    "as slow as a _____."

h. Runa: Is that orange thing a rock?
    Teacher: No. That's _____. It's made by small, soft-bodied animals that
    live together in large colonies.

3. Circle the words to complete the article.

Animal Defenses

Animals have many ways of protecting themselves. One fish, the cobra /(flounder) can
a.
change its color. Two sea animals, the squid / starfish and the sea otter / octopus, squirt ink into
b.   c.
the water / rock and hide in its dark cloud.
d.

Some poisonous amphibians / seals and reptiles warn enemies to keep away. The bright
e.
colors of some cod / frogs tell other animals they are not safe to eat. The garter snake / rattlesnake
f.   g.
makes a loud sound with its tail before it bites. The turtle's / tuna's hard shell and the sharp needles
h.
of the sea urchin / scallop are another kind of protection.
i.

Sea mammals like dolphins / newts use language to warn each other of danger. Scientists
j.
have recorded the songs that whales / worms sing to each other. Other members of this group,
k.
such as walruses and sea lions / seahorses, live in large groups to protect their babies.
l.

4. Circle the correct letter for each sentence. Write the letters in the circles below.

	True	False
a. Mussels are sea mammals.	A	(O)
b. Whales can sing.	L	Z
c. All sea mammals have gills.	J	O
d. Some mammals have fins.	R	L
e. Rattlesnakes are poisonous.	E	B
f. Crabs don't have legs.	G	C
g. Bass have scales.	D	P
h. Scallops and shrimp are black.	E	I
i. Jellyfish look like fish.	T	C

O ___ ___ ___ ___ ___ ___ ___ ___

Now unscramble the letters to find the name of an animal: _____

CHALLENGE Find out more information about at least two animals in Exercise 4. Look online, in an
encyclopedia, or in a science book.

219

Birds, Insects, and Arachnids

1. **Look at page 220 in your dictionary. Write the name of the bird, insect, or arachnid.**

    a. It makes honey from flowers. Unlike the wasp, it dies after it stings. _____honeybee_____

    b. It looks like a big duck and is raised for food and feathers. _____

    c. It's very small. It eats blood and often lives in the fur or skin
       of mammals. It can make people sick. _____

    d. It's brown with an orange breast. _____

    e. It's very small and red, and it has black polka dots. _____

    f. It has sharp claws and big eyes in the front of its head. _____

    g. It begins its life as a caterpillar. _____

    h. It has a long bill for eating nectar from flowers.
       It moves its wings 1,000 times a second. _____

    i. It catches insects by making holes in trees with its beak. _____

    j. It doesn't fly, but swims in icy water to catch fish. _____

    k. It lives near water. It flies and bites people for blood. _____

    l. It looks like a small grasshopper and eats cloth like a moth.
       It makes music by rubbing its wings together. _____

    m. It has beautiful blue feathers and eats insects and fruit. _____

    n. It likes human food and causes many diseases. A spider often
       catches it in its web. _____

    o. It's very big with long, colorful feathers. _____

2. **Write comparisons with *than*.**

    a. fly / tick (small) _____A tick is smaller than a fly._____

    b. peacock / sparrow (colorful) _____

    c. beetle / scorpion (dangerous) _____

    d. pigeon / eagle (large) _____

    e. butterfly / moth (beautiful) _____

3. **What about you? Make a list of some common birds, insects, and arachnids where you live. Use your own paper.**

CHALLENGE   Look up information about a bird, an insect, or an arachnid in your list from Exercise 3.
            Where does it live? What does it eat? How does it help or hurt people?

1. **Look at page 221 in your dictionary. Which animals . . . ?**

   a. eat nuts ____chipmunks____ and _____

   b. are babies _____ and _____

   c. have wings _____, _____, and _____

   d. live in holes _____ and _____

   e. give us milk _____, _____, and _____

   f. carry people _____ and _____

2. **Look at the magazine article. Complete the sentences.**

Care and Cost of Common Pets

✓ a lot of care	$ very expensive
✓ moderate care	$ moderately expensive
✓ not much care	$ not expensive

a. _____Dogs_____ need the most care. In addition to giving them food and water, you need to train them and play with them. They are also the most expensive.

b. _____ need less care than dogs. With enough water and food, they can be alone during the day. They are less expensive than dogs, but more expensive than other pets.

c. If you like birds, think about getting one or more _____. They aren't expensive and don't need much care. They like to climb, so give them a tall cage with a ladder.

d. Perhaps the easiest and cheapest pets are _____. They can live long and healthy lives in a big bowl of fresh water with plants and room to swim.

e. Don't be afraid of these rodents. Mice and white _____ (not the ones that live in the city!) make nice pets. They don't cost much, and they don't need a lot of care.

f. Bushy-tailed and long-eared, _____ aren't expensive, but they do need moderate care and special food. No carrots!

CHALLENGE Look at the farm animals in the dictionary. Make a list of the products humans get from each animal.

1. **Look at pages 222 and 223 in your dictionary. Circle the words to complete the sentences.**

   a. The lion has a pouch / mane and hooves / paws.

   b. The opossum / raccoon has a striped tail / trunk.

   c. The moose / mountain lion has antlers / quills and hooves / whiskers.

   d. The coyote / koala has a gray coat / hump.

   e. The baboon / buffalo has horns / tusks.

   f. The chimpanzee and the orangutan / platypus are in the same animal family.

   g. The beaver / hyena, the panther / skunk, and the antelope / deer live in North America.

2. **Look at the bar graph. Complete the sentences.**

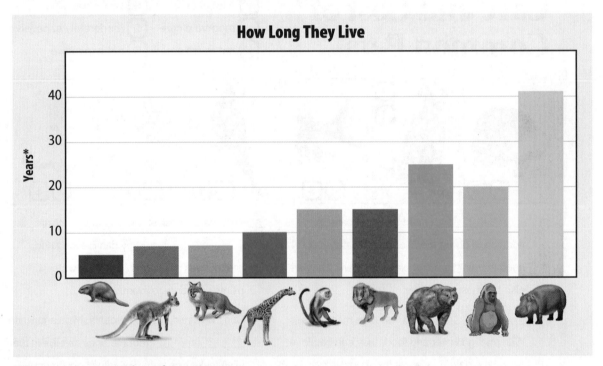

How Long They Live

*Years = average number of years in a zoo
Based on information from: *The World Almanac and Book of Facts, 2016* (Simon and Schuster, 2015).

   a. The grizzly _____bear_____ lives 25 years.

   b. The red fox lives as long as the _____.

   c. The _____ lives as long as the lion.

   d. The gorilla lives 10 years longer than the _____.

   e. The _____ lives the longest life.

   f. The _____ lives the shortest life.

   g. The _____ lives twice as long as the beaver.

3. **Look at the maps. Make a list of endangered* animals and the continents where they live.**

*Endangered = There are very few of these animals and they may not continue to live.
Based on information from: U.S. Fish and Wildlife Service.

_____wolf, North America_____   _____

_____   _____

_____   _____

_____   _____

_____   _____

CHALLENGE List reasons why some animals are endangered. Search online or in an encyclopedia for "endangered species." **Example**: _People kill elephants for their tusks._

Energy and the Environment

1. **Look at page 224 in your dictionary. Circle the words to complete the sentences.**

   a. Nuclear / (Solar) energy comes directly from the sun.

   b. Coal, oil, and natural gas / radiation are sources of energy.

   c. Another source of energy is acid rain / wind power.

   d. Hydroelectric power / Geothermal energy comes from water.

   e. A danger of nuclear energy is air pollution / radiation.

   f. Old batteries are examples of biomass / hazardous waste.

   g. Acid rain / Fusion kills trees.

   h. Water pollution and oil spills / smog hurt the oceans.

2. **Look at the pie chart.** *True* or *False*?

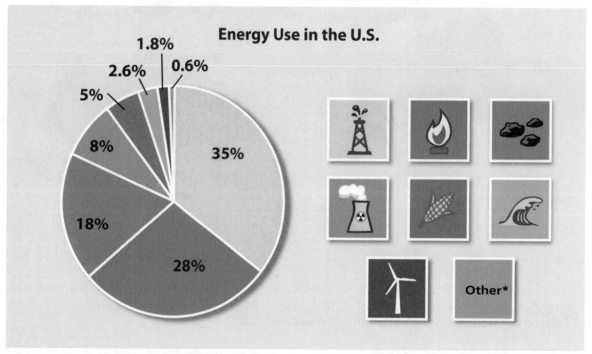

*Other sources include geothermal and solar.
Based on information from: U.S. Energy Information Administration, Monthly Energy Review (2015).

   a. More than 30% of energy used in the United States is from oil.   _____true_____

   b. Almost 30% of energy produced is from coal.   _____

   c. The United States uses more energy from oil than from natural gas.   _____

   d. Less than 10% of its energy use is from nuclear energy.   _____

   e. It uses more energy from hydroelectric power than from biomass sources.   _____

   f. It doesn't use much energy from geothermal or solar power.   _____

3. **Look at page 225 in your dictionary. Complete the sentences.**

   a. The streets will look better if people ___don't litter___.

   b. You can _____ by using a "regular" coffee cup instead of a paper one.

   c. You can _____ by turning off the faucet when you brush your teeth.

   d. If you _____ bottles and cans, you help reduce garbage and improve
   the environment at the same time!

4. **Look at the chart. Check (✓) the correct column(s).**

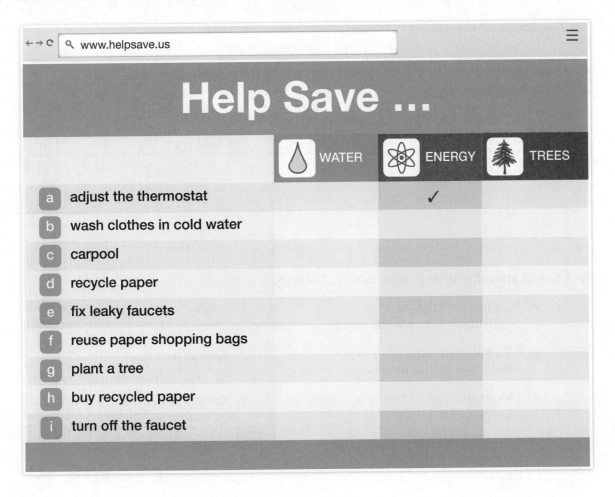

		WATER	ENERGY	TREES
a	adjust the thermostat		✓	
b	wash clothes in cold water			
c	carpool			
d	recycle paper			
e	fix leaky faucets			
f	reuse paper shopping bags			
g	plant a tree			
h	buy recycled paper			
i	turn off the faucet			

5. **What about you? List the things in Exercise 4 you do.**

   Example: *I carpool to work to save energy.*

CHALLENGE   List other things people can do to help conserve energy and resources.
   Example: *They can recycle batteries or use rechargeable batteries.*

Go to page 258 for Another Look (Unit 11).   225

A Graduation

1. **Look at pages 226 and 227 in your dictionary.** *True* **or** *False***?**

   a. Adelia is wearing a cap and gown in six photos.   _____false_____

   b. Adelia's <u>mother</u> is taking pictures.   _____

   c. The guest speaker is <u>the mayor</u>.   _____

   d. The photographer is taking a picture of <u>ten</u> people.   _____

   e. <u>The photographer</u> is crying.   _____

   f. <u>Adelia</u> is speaking at the podium.   _____

2. **Look in your dictionary. Write the letters of the false sentences in Exercise 1. Make them true.**

   _a._   _Adelia is wearing a cap in five photos._ _____

   ___   _____

   ___   _____

   ___   _____

   ___   _____

3. **Look in your dictionary. Who said . . . ? Match.**

   _3_ **a.** "Adelia, I want to take a photo of you with your diploma."   **1.** Adelia

   ___ **b.** "OK, everyone. I want this one to be a serious photo."   **2.** Adelia's mother

   ___ **c.** "Adelia, you look so beautiful in your cap and gown. It makes me cry."   **3.** Adelia's father

   ___ **d.** "Welcome, students, teachers, and parents. I am happy to speak at this year's ceremony."   **4.** Adelia's classmate

   ___ **e.** "I'll miss being in band with you, Adelia!"   **5.** the guest speaker

   ___ **f.** "I graduated!"   **6.** the photographer

4. Complete the comments on Adelia's web page. Use the words in the box.

celebrate	funny	caps	guest speaker	~~takes~~
cry	gown	photographer	podium	

People	Comments
Tamara	Congratulations! Your Dad _____*takes*_____ great pictures. **a.** You look great in your cap and _____! **b.**
Jeff	Hey, Adelia. What a great day. I like the _____ photo. **c.** The _____ was so upset, but it's a great memory! **d.**
Wendy	I thought the _____ gave a great speech. **e.** Of course, she's my mother. She didn't _____ until **f.** after her speech!
Dan	We finally graduated! I almost fell when I got my diploma at the _____ . Now it's time to _____ ! I'm **g.** **h.** having a party on Saturday.
Marcos	Great pictures! I love the one where we are throwing our _____ in the air! **i.**

5. What about you? Imagine you were at the graduation. Tell a partner about it. Answer these questions:

a. Were you a graduate or a friend or relative of a graduate?

b. How did you feel? Did you cry?

c. What photos did you take?

d. Who did you talk to?

e. How did you celebrate?

CHALLENGE Write comments to Adelia. Tell her what you think of the photos on her web page on pages 226 and 227 of the dictionary. Write at least six sentences.

227

1. **Look at pages 228 and 229 in your dictionary. Where can you go to . . . ?**

   a. hear music _____*rock concert*_____, _____,

   or _____

   b. see sharks and starfish _____

   c. see flowers, trees, and plants _____

   d. hear people sing _____ or _____

   e. see paintings _____

   f. go on rides _____

   g. dance _____

   h. buy old clothes _____

   i. see a movie _____

   j. see elephants _____

   k. play alone or on a team _____

2. **Look in your dictionary. Recommend places to go for these people.**

   a. David wants to be a gardener. _____*botanical garden*_____

   b. Julia needs some things for her home. _____

   c. Tina likes looking at quilts and farm animals. _____

   d. Amy enjoys seeing a "live" performance in a theater. _____

   e. Karl wants to be an artist. He likes paintings. _____

3. **What about you? Look at the places in your dictionary. Where do you go? Why? Complete the chart.**

	Places I go . . .	Why?
Often		
Sometimes		
Never		
Never, but I'd like to go.		

4. Look at pages 228 and 229 in your dictionary. Complete the newspaper listings below.

WHAT'S HAPPENING

ART

NEWPORT _Art Museum_
a.
Special exhibit of sculpture and paintings by local artists. Through August 25. **Tickets $5**.

MUSIC

CITY CENTER

Adriana Domingo sings the leading role in Antonio Rivera's new _____,
b.
Starry Night. 8:00 p.m., August 14 and 15.

Tickets $10–$30.

PLM HALL

Oakland Chamber Orchestra, with Lily Marksen at the piano, performs a _____
c.
featuring works by Beethoven, Bach, and Brahms. 8:00 p.m., August 15.

Tickets $20-$30.

THEATER

CURTAINS UP

The Downtown Players perform _The Argument_, a new _____ by J.L. Mason, starring
d.
Vanessa Thompson and Tyrone Williams as a married couple. Through August 20. **Tickets $20**.

CHILDREN

CROWN_____
e.
Roller coaster, merry-go-round, and other rides provide fun for kids and adults. Open daily 10:00 a.m. to 5:00 p.m. **Free admission**.

GENERAL INTEREST

Newport _____ Food, exhibitions,
f.
and prizes for best cow, quilt, and more. August 14–15, 10:00 a.m. to 7:00 p.m. **Free**.

SAL'S _____
g.
Dance to the music of rock band, Jumpin' Lizards. 8:00 p.m. to midnight. Must be 18 or older (ID required). **$10.00 (includes 1 beverage)**.

5. Look at the events in Exercise 4. _True_ or _False_?

a. The play is free. _____false_____

b. You can see an opera at City Center. _____

c. The county fair is open until 10:00 p.m. _____

d. A seventeen-year-old can go to Sal's. _____

e. There's an evening concert at PLM Hall on August 15. _____

f. Tickets to the amusement park are expensive. _____

g. You can see the special art exhibit on August 24. _____

[CHALLENGE] Look at a local newspaper, an online website of weekend events, or the listings in Exercise 4. Talk to two classmates and agree on a place to go. Write your decision and give a reason.

The Park and Playground

1. **Look at page 230 in your dictionary. Where can you hear . . . ?**

   a. "I love playing in the sand."   _____sandbox_____

   b. "OK. Now try to hit this to left field."   _____

   c. "Here. Have some more chicken."   _____

   d. "We're the only cyclists here today."   _____

   e. "Push me higher, Mommy!"   _____

   f. "Bring your racket all the way back when you serve the ball."   _____

2. **Read about the children. What should they use?**

   a. Toby likes to jump.   _____jump rope_____

   b. Jennifer is a little too young to ride a bicycle.   _____

   c. Jason is thirsty.   _____

   d. Cindi likes to climb bars.   _____

   e. Shao-fen likes to climb up and go down quickly.   _____

   f. Carlos is tired and just wants to sit down and rest.   _____

3. **What about you? Look at the park in your dictionary. What would you like to do there . . . ?**

   a. alone

      I'd like to ride my skateboard.

   b. with three of your classmates

      _____

   c. with a three-year-old child

      _____

   d. with a ten-year-old child

      _____

   e. with a seventy-five-year-old relative

      _____

CHALLENGE   Design the ideal park. What does it have? Write a description.

230

1. **Look at page 231 in your dictionary. Complete the sentences.**

    a. The boy with the diving mask has _____*fins*_____ on his feet.

    b. There's a pink _____ hanging from the lifeguard station.

    c. The little girl in the red bathing suit is listening to a _____.

    d. A _____ is "catching" a wave on his surfboard.

2. **Circle the words to complete the hotel ad.**

The (Sandcastle) / Seashell Inn
a.

Your number one choice for fun in the sun

Relax under a beach blanket / an umbrella on our 1-mile white-sand
b.

beach / pier. Swim among the gentle sky / waves of our beautiful
c.   d.

blue-green ocean / scuba tank. There's a private lifeguard / wetsuit
e.   f.

on duty for your safety. Eat inside our fine restaurant or buy a fresh

fish sandwich to put in your kite / cooler. Surfers / Surfboards and
g.   h.

sand / scuba equipment available.
i.

For more information or for reservations call 1-800-000-SAND or visit our website at www.sandcastle.us.

3. **What about you? What would you take to the beach? What would you buy or rent?
   Check (✓) the columns.**

	Take	Buy / Rent
surfboard		
beach chair		
beach umbrella		
blanket		

	Take	Buy / Rent
sunscreen		
cooler		
fins		
Other:		

CHALLENGE   Imagine you are at the beach in your dictionary. Write a postcard describing it.
Example: *I'm sitting . . .*

1. **Look at page 232 in your dictionary. Find and correct five more mistakes in the email.**

My Mail

Send To: robin@eol.us

Subject: Hi

Our first camping trip. That's Jose and me setting the picnic table while Tomas and Luz put

up our ~~lantern~~ *tent*. See the woman fishing? She just caught dinner with her rope and fishing

net. On the lake, two people are canoeing, one

person is boating in a small blue motorboat, and

one person is rafting. Back on land, people are

horseback riding, hiking, and mountain biking. One

man is backpacking. His life vest sure looks heavy!

There's something for everyone here. Last night we

built a beautiful canteen (photo attached). Not bad

for our first! More later.

Love, A.

2. **Circle the words to complete the conversations.**

    a. **Luke:** It's really dark out here. I can't see where I'm going.
        Mike: Here. Take this camping stove /(lantern) with you.

    b. **Ming:** *Brrr.* It's getting cold out here.
        Sue: Hand me the canteen / matches. I'll light the fire.

    c. **Jose:** Ow! These mosquitoes are driving me crazy.
        Ana: Here's some foam pad / insect repellent. That'll keep them away.

    d. **Mia:** This rope is too long.
        Tom: You're right. What did we do with that multi-use knife / sleeping bag?

3. **What about you? Would you like to go camping? Why or why not?**

    Example: *I'd like to go camping. I like sleeping outside.*

CHALLENGE Look in your dictionary. Imagine you are on a camping trip. List the five most important items to have. Give reasons.

1. **Look at page 233 in your dictionary. For which sports do you need . . . ?**

    a. a motorboat _____waterskiing_____

    b. waves _____

    c. wind _____ and _____

    d. a mask and fins _____ and _____

2. **Look at the chart. Complete the sentences.**

2014 WINTER OLYMPICS IN SOCHI

		GOLD (First Place)	SILVER (Second Place)	BRONZE (Third Place)
	MEN	Matthias Mayer Austria 2:06:23	Christof Innerhofer Italy 2:06:29	Kjetil Jansrud Norway 2:06:33
	WOMEN	Tina Maze Slovenia 1:41:57 Dominique Gisin Switzerland 1:41:57		Lara Gut Switzerland 1:41.67
	MEN (15 km)	Dario Cologna Switzerland 1:08:15.4	Marcus Hellner Sweden 1:08:15.8	Martin Johnsrud Sundby Norway 1:08:16.8
	WOMEN (10 km)	Justyna Kowalczyk Poland 28:17.8	Charlotte Kalla Sweden 28:36.2	Therese Johaug Norway 28:46.1
	MEN	Yuzuru Hanyu Japan	Patrick Chan Canada	Denis Ten Kazakhstan
	WOMEN	Adelina Sotnikova Russia	Kim Yu-na Korea	Carolina Kostner Italy
	MEN (500 m)	Michel Mulder Netherlands 69.312	Jan Smeekens Netherlands 69.324	Ronald Mulder Netherlands 69.46
	WOMEN (500 m)	Lee Sang Hwa Korea 74.70	Olga Fatkulina Russia 75.06	Margot Boer Netherlands 75.48

    a. Netherlands won four medals in _____speed skating_____.

    b. Switzerland won a gold and a bronze medal in _____.

    c. Japan won one gold medal in _____.

    d. Poland won a gold medal in women's _____.

    e. Tina Maze and Dominique Gisin had exactly the same time in _____.

    f. _____ is not a timed event.

CHALLENGE Which winter sports or water sports are best for where you live? Why?

Individual Sports

1. **Look at page 234 in your dictionary. Cross out the word that doesn't belong. Give a reason.**

   a. billiards   ~~martial arts~~   table tennis   _It doesn't use a ball._

   b. fencing   gymnastics   wrestling   _____

   c. boxing   inline skating   skateboarding   _____

   d. cycling   horse racing   badminton   _____

2. **Look at the line graph. Circle the words to complete the sentences.**

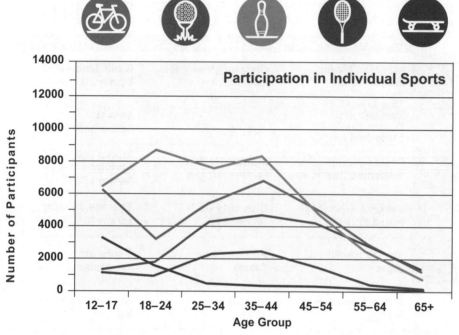

Based on information from: a survey of homes by the National Sporting Goods Association (2009) as reported by U.S. Census Bureau, *Statistical Abstract of the United States: 2012.*

   a. (Bowling)/ Cycling is the most popular sport for people 18 to 24 years old.

   b. Skateboarding / Tennis is the least popular sport for people over 25.

   c. Golf / Cycling is the most popular sport for people over 65.

   d. Participation in tennis / skateboarding goes down after the age of 24.

   e. Between the ages of 34 and 44, participation in cycling / skateboarding goes up.

   f. Participation in cycling / bowling goes down after the age of 12, but then it goes up again.

3. **What about you? How has your participation in sports changed? Write sentences.**

   Example: *I started to play more soccer in high school.*

   CHALLENGE Write five more sentences using information from the line graph in Exercise 2.

234

1. **Look at page 235 in your dictionary. Circle the words to complete the sentences.**

   a. There are two goalies / (teams) on the basketball court.

   b. The coach / official is on the court, too.

   c. The home fan / score is 83.

2. **Look at the bar graph.** *True* or *False*? **Correct the** underlined **words in the false sentences.**

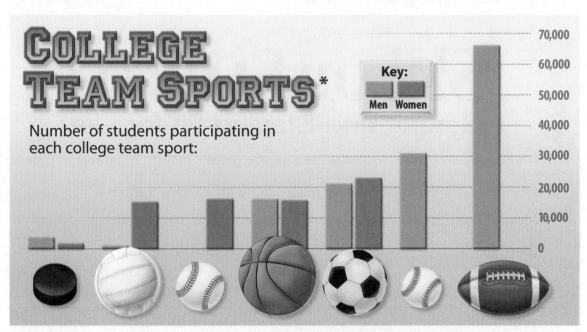

COLLEGE TEAM SPORTS*

Number of students participating in each college team sport:

Key: Men Women

70,000
60,000
50,000
40,000
30,000
20,000
10,000
0

*Note: These teams are in colleges which are members of the National Collegiate Athletic Association, an organization that governs college sports competitions in the United States.

   Based on information from: U.S. Census Bureau, *Statistical Abstract of the United States: 2012.*

   Football
   a. ~~Baseball~~ is the most popular team sport among college men.   *false*

   b. More women than men play soccer.   _____

   c. College men don't play on volleyball teams.   _____

   d. Women don't play on college baseball and football teams.   _____

   e. About 24,000 women play college basketball.   _____

   f. Not many men or women participate in college ice hockey.   _____

   g. More college students play baseball than softball.   _____

CHALLENGE   Interview five or more people. Which sports do they like to play? Which sports do they like to watch?

1. **Look at page 236 in your dictionary. Cross out the word that doesn't belong.**

   a. with your feet   ~~catch~~   kick   jump

   b. with a ball   hit   serve   bend

   c. in water   swim   skate   dive

   d. with other people   serve   tackle   pass

2. **Circle the words to complete the article.**

Ski or Swim?
Getting and Staying Fit for Life

There are many choices for people who want to get and stay fit. Some sports require very little special equipment. All you really need is a good pair of shoes to walk your way to good health. But you can also (dive) / dribble into a pool and ski / swim your
a.   b.
way to fitness.

Want to exercise / serve with other people? Many communities have gyms that you
c.
can join. There you can tackle / work out alone or with others. Bending / Pitching and
d.   e.
hitting / stretching help firm muscles and keep your body flexible.
f.

For those people who enjoy competing, there are many opportunities to race / pass in
g.
city marathons. But remember: Winning isn't everything. Even if you don't finish / start
h.
the race, you should feel good that you participated.

It's not really important which sport you choose. You can throw / shoot a baseball
i.
or kick / swing a golf club. Just start slowly and be careful. Most of all, enjoy what you
j.
do and do it regularly. In order to get and stay fit, sports should be a part of your
everyday life.

CHALLENGE   Look in your dictionary. Where else can a person swim, work out, ski, or race?
Write two sentences for each verb. **Example:** *You can swim in the ocean. You can swim in . . .*

1. **Look at page 237 in your dictionary. Which pieces of equipment are customers talking about?**

   a. "These are a little too heavy for me." _____ *weights* _____

   b. "Oh, I see them now. They're under the target and next to the bow." _____

   c. "There's one. Under the volleyball." _____

   d. "They look like ice skates with wheels!" _____

   e. "Great! It's blue and white—the same as my team's colors." _____

   f. "I'd love to throw one of those around. I'd like red, maybe pink." _____

   g. "Well, this will really protect my head." _____

   h. "Wow! These will make me look really big!" _____

   i. "Oh, there they are. Between the snowboard and the ski poles." _____

   j. "Do you have one for left-handed pitchers?" _____

   k. "I have to wear them to protect my legs during soccer games." _____

2. **Make comparisons with *than*. Use the words in parentheses.**

   a. volleyball / basketball (big)

   A basketball is bigger than a volleyball.

   b. golf club / hockey stick (long)

   _____

   c. ice skates / ski boots (warm)

   _____

   d. baseball / football (small)

   _____

   e. bowling ball / soccer ball (heavy)

   _____

3. **What about you? Look in your dictionary. What sports equipment would you buy from the store? Why?**

   Example: *I'd buy a bat for my niece because she wants to play baseball.*

   CHALLENGE Look online or at a newspaper ad. Find the prices of these pieces of sports equipment.

   a baseball glove _____   a tennis racket _____

   Other: _____

1. **Look at pages 238 and 239 in your dictionary. Complete the crossword puzzle.**

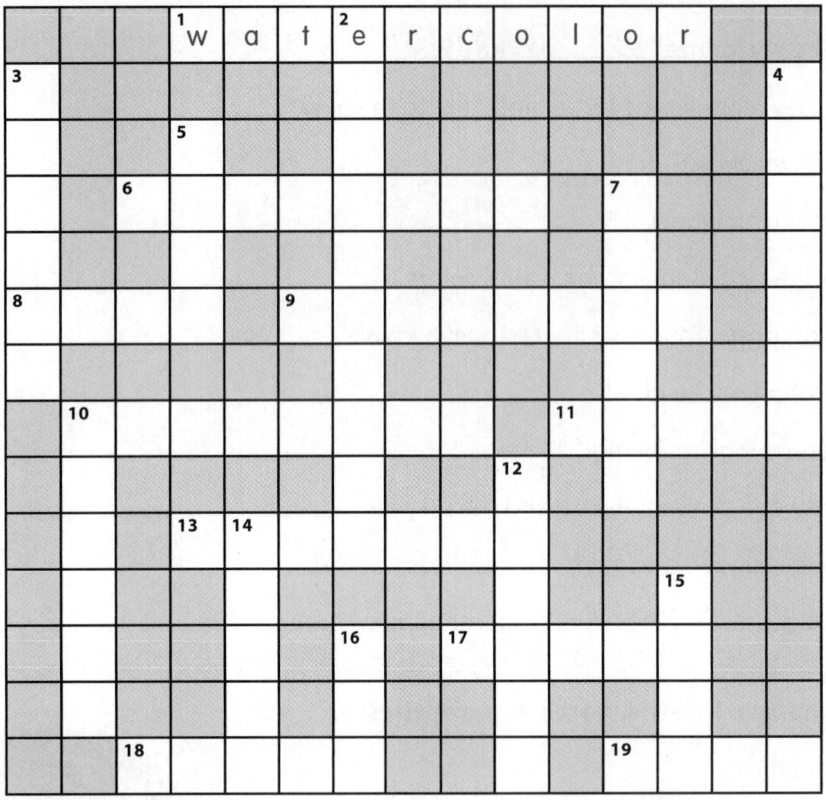

The crossword grid shows 1 Across filled in: w a t e r c o l o r

Grid numbers: 1, 2 (top row); 3, 4; 5; 6, 7; 8, 9; 10, 11; 12; 13, 14; 15; 16, 17; 18, 19

ACROSS

1. It's not oil paint
6. This one looks like a kitten
8. It comes in a stick
9. Red, but not hearts
10. A board game
11. Black, but not spades
13. Type of paint
17. Type of game
18. It holds a canvas
19. I like to _____ games

DOWN

2. It has a flower on it
3. Collect _____
4. You use them to knit
5. These are cubes
7. You can build these with a kit
10. It's on the easel
12. Type of figure
14. A board game
15. This toy looks like a person
16. Type of paint

2. **Cross out the word that doesn't belong. Give a reason.**

a. checkers	chess	~~crocheting~~	*It's not a board game.*
b. dolls	diamonds	clubs	_____
c. watercolor	acrylic	glue gun	_____

3. Look at the bar graph. Circle the words to complete the sentences.

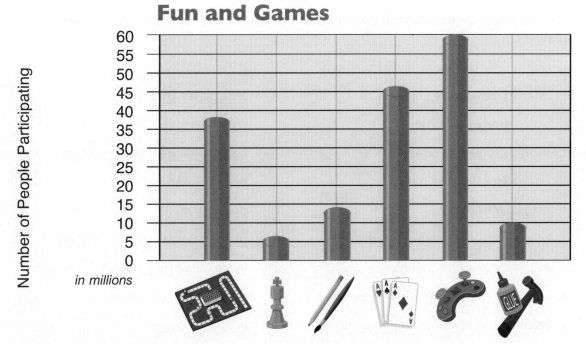

Fun and Games

Number of People Participating

in millions

Based on information from: U.S. Census Bureau, *Statistical Abstract of the United States: 2012* (information is for 2010).

a. Playing cards /(video games) was the most popular of the six activities.

b. About 14 million people drew or painted / played board games.

c. More than 40 million people played cards / did woodworking.

d. The least popular of the six activities was chess / woodworking.

e. Drawing and painting was about two times as popular as playing chess / board games.

4. What about you? How often do you . . . ? Check (✓) the columns.

	Every Week	Every Month	Never
play cards			
play board games			
use a video game console			
do crafts			
play with model trains			
paint			
quilt			
Other:			

CHALLENGE   Make a list of things to collect. Compare your list with your classmates' lists.

Electronics and Photography

1. **Look at pages 240 and 241 in your dictionary. What can you use to . . . ? Circle the answers.**

   a. charge your cell phone away from home   battery pack / (portable charger)

   b. listen to music while you run   MP3 player / turntable

   c. watch a movie at home   DVD / personal CD player

   d. show pictures on a screen   battery charger / LCD projector

   e. listen to music in the park   boom box / tuner

   f. hold an MP3 player   dock / plug

   g. keep photos on a memory card   digital camera / charging station

   h. watch a movie on a train   video MP3 player / universal remote

   i. keep your paper photos in one place   photo / digital photo album

   j. listen to music without headphones   adapter / speakers

   k. record your own voice   battery pack / microphone

2. **Look at the chart. Complete the sentences.**

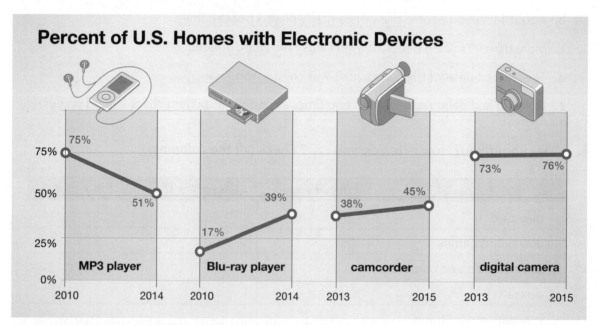

Based on information from: The Pew Research Center (2015), IGN Entertainment Games (2010), and The Consumer Electronics Association (2014).

   a. The number of homes with _____MP3 players_____ dropped sharply from 2010 to 2014.

   b. In 2015, 45% of U.S. homes had _____.

   c. The number of homes with _____ went up only 3% from 2013 to 2015.

   d. Just over half of all homes had _____ in 2014.

   e. A lot of people bought _____ between 2010 and 2014.

3. **Complete the instructions for a universal remote control.**

Operation Buttons

INSTRUCTIONS

a. _____play_____ : to watch a DVD

b. _____ : to go back

c. _____ : to stop the DVD for a short time during playing or recording

d. _____ : to record a program (You must press PLAY at the same time.)

e. _____ : to go to the end quickly

4. **Look at the pictures. Circle the words to complete the sentences.**

a. The (photo)/ screen is out of focus.

b. She didn't use a <u>camera case / tripod</u>.

c. The photo is <u>overexposed / underexposed</u>.

d. He didn't use a <u>memory card / zoom lens</u>.

5. **What about you? Look at the electronic devices in Exercise 2. Which is the most important to you? Why?**

CHALLENGE | Write instructions for using a personal CD player, a boom box, an MP3 player, or another electronic device.

1. **Look at pages 242 and 243 in your dictionary. Where can you hear . . . ?**

   a. "And now a look at what's happening today in Europe." _news program_

   b. "Goodbye, girls. Goodbye, boys. See you tomorrow." _____

   c. "And now, for $50,000 . . ." _____

   d. "Don't be afraid. I come from a friendly planet." _____

   e. "This beautiful dress can be yours for just $55.99!" _____

   f. "I love you and only you! Not your sister!" _____

   g. "Pandas live in the forest of central China." _____

   h. "Lopez is trying to get the ball from Jackson!" _____

   i. "I'm almost finished brushing my teeth." _____

2. **Circle the words to complete the TV movie listings.**

Movie Listings
This Week's Highlights

Titanic*** (1997)	Rich girl (Kate Winslet) meets poor boy (Leonardo DiCaprio) on the historic sinking ship, and it's love at first sight. Don't miss this beautiful mystery / (romance.) (194 minutes) a.	Fri 8:00 P.M. Ch 7
Jurassic Park III* (2001)	Dinosaurs attack (again) in this scary horror story / western with Sam Neill, William H. Macy, and Téa Leoni. b. You'll be scared out of your seat. (92 minutes)	Fri 9:00 P.M. Ch 4
Spider Man 3* (2007)	Tobey Maguire stars again as the superhero Spider Man in this exciting action story / comedy. Great special effects. (140 minutes) c.	Fri 10:00 P.M. SCI
Romeo and Juliet (1996)	Starring Leonardo DiCaprio as Romeo and Claire Danes as Juliet, this modern version of Shakespeare's mystery / tragedy will bring tears to your eyes. (120 minutes) d.	Sat 9:00 P.M. ENT
Mr. & Mrs. Smith*** (2005)	An "average" husband (Brad Pitt) and wife (Angelina Jolie) live secret and surprising lives in this very funny comedy / tragedy. (120 minutes) e.	Sat 10:00 P.M. Ch 7

3. Look at the pie chart. *True* or *False*?

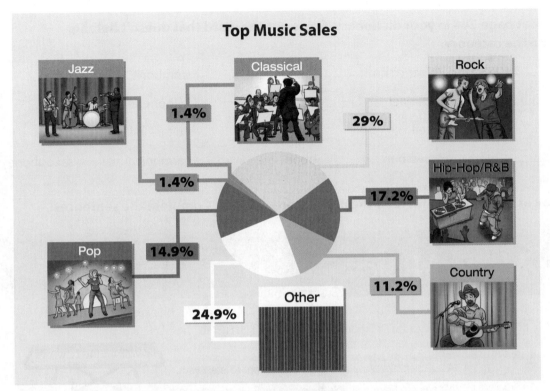

Based on information from: 2014 Nielsen Music U.S. Report.

a. At 29% of all sales, rock sold the most out of all types of music.   _____true_____

b. At just 1.4% of sales, pop and classical sold the least.   _____

c. Country music sold more than classical music.   _____

d. Jazz sold more than pop.   _____

e. 17.2% of sales came from hip-hop and R&B together.   _____

4. What about you? How often do you listen to . . . ? Check (✓) the columns.

	Often	Sometimes	Never
classical music			
jazz			
gospel			
reggae			
world music			

CHALLENGE   Write two short reviews of television programs or movies. Give them a one to six star (*) rating.

1. Look at page 244 in your dictionary. Cross out the word that doesn't belong. Write the category.

   a. ___Brass___   French horn   ~~bass~~   trombone   tuba

   b. _____   clarinet   tambourine   xylophone   drums

   c. _____   cello   violin   guitar   organ

   d. _____   bassoon   oboe   harmonica   saxophone

2. Look at the pictures and read the music store website. Complete the sentences.

Mary's Music

The Best Age to Start Playing an Instrument

6–8 YEARS OLD — A ___keyboard___ (a.) is a great instrument to start with. It's easy to learn a simple tune and make it sound good!

7–9 YEARS OLD — If your child wants to play a stringed instrument, start with the _____ (b.). Larger strings, like the cello and the bass, are too big for children's hands.

8–10 YEARS OLD — Many children like to play the _____ (c.) because it's easy to sing with. If they like rock music, they might want to play an electric one.

8–10 YEARS OLD — The _____ (d.) is the easiest to learn of the woodwinds. Some children might prefer the saxophone, which is a bit more difficult.

9–10 YEARS OLD — If your child wants to play a brass instrument, have them start with a _____ (e.). Save the trombone for when your child is a bit bigger!

10–12 YEARS OLD — _____ (f.) are better for older kids because they need to use their feet as well as their hands, and their legs need to be long enough!

Remember: These are just general guidelines. Every child is different, and the best instrument for *your* child to play is the one that he or she really wants to play!

1. Look at page 245 in your dictionary. Complete the holiday cards.

a.

I looked really hard to find this

_____card_____ *, just to say*
a.

on this special day—that you're

always a part of my _____ .
b.

Happy _____ .
c.

I think we're a great _____ !
d.

b.

Resolutions are made,

here comes the _____ .
e.

I'm more than ready,

so throw the _____ !
f.

The time is now near

to say Happy New _____ !
g.

c.

As _____
h.

light up the sky, the red, white,

and blue _____ will proudly
i.

fly! Happy _____ !
j.

d.

I hope that there will always

be _____ and
k.

candy _____ on your tree!
l.

Merry _____ .
m.

e.

It's late November — time to

remember to give thanks for the

good things this year and, not the

least, a delicious _____
n.

where _____ and stuffing
o.

appear. Happy _____ !
p.

f.

_____ burning bright, on a cool
q.

October night. In scary costumes and a

_____ , for _____ treats
r.   s.

the children ask. Happy _____ !
t.

2. What about you? Check (✓) the cards you send. Who do you send them to?

☐ New Year's _____

☐ Valentine's Day _____

☐ Christmas _____

☐ Other: _____

CHALLENGE   Make a card for one of the holidays in your dictionary or for any other event.

Go to page 259 for Another Look (Unit 12).   245

1. **Look at pages 246 and 247 in your dictionary. Match.**

   _5_ **a.** There are presents   **1.** wrapping Lou's gifts.

   ___ **b.** Lou is making a wish for   **2.** on a long table.

   ___ **c.** There are two cakes   **3.** from the deck.

   ___ **d.** A woman is videotaping the party   **4.** a new car.

   ___ **e.** Gani is   **5.** on a round table.

   ___ **f.** Amaka is   **6.** blowing out the candles.

2. **Lou's mom videotaped birthday messages for Lou and Gani. Circle the words to complete the messages.**

   a. "Hi, Lou. Happy 18th birthday! Did you ~~make a wish~~ / blow out the candles for a new car? I hope you get it. You can take me for a ride!"

   b. "Happy birthday, Gani. Eighty years old! Wow! You have a lot of candles to wrap / blow out!"

   c. "Hey, Lou. Have a great day. I hope you like the present I videotaped / brought."

   d. "Happy birthday, Gani. Open my present first! I sang / wrapped it in some pretty red paper."

   e. "Lou, happy birthday! I hid / brought your present in the yard. I hope you can find it!"

   f. "Enjoy the party, Lou! Your mom did a great job with the decorations / videotape. They look beautiful!"

3. **What about you? How do you celebrate birthdays in your family? Compare your list with a partner's.**

   ☐ have a party

   ☐ have a cake with candles

   ☐ put up decorations

   ☐ make a wish

   ☐ videotape the party

   ☐ bring gifts

   ☐ Other: _____

4. Look at the picture. *True* or *False*?

a. The present isn't for Lou.   *false*

b. The present is from Paul.   _____

c. He hid the present.   _____

d. The present is wrapped in
   blue and red paper.   _____

e. The present isn't a new car.   _____

5. What happened first? Number *1* and *2* for each pair.

a. _2_ I blew out the candles.   _1_ I made a wish.

b. ___ We videotaped the party.   ___ We watched the videotape.

c. ___ He gave me the present.   ___ He wrapped the present.

d. ___ I found my present on the deck.   ___ My mom hid my present.

e. ___ My dad cut the cake.   ___ We ate the cake.

6. Complete the card. Use the words in the box.

| hid | presents | ~~make~~ | blow | decorations | brought | wrapped |

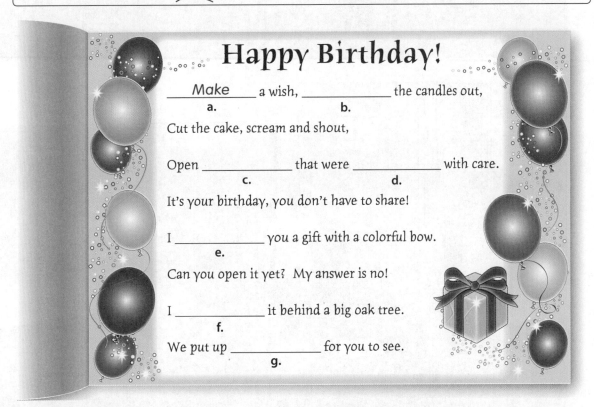

Happy Birthday!

_____Make_____ a wish, _____ the candles out,
   a.   **b.**

Cut the cake, scream and shout,

Open _____ that were _____ with care.
         c.   **d.**

It's your birthday, you don't have to share!

I _____ you a gift with a colorful bow.
   e.

Can you open it yet? My answer is no!

I _____ it behind a big oak tree.
   f.

We put up _____ for you to see.
            g.

CHALLENGE Write a birthday message for a greeting card. It can rhyme, but it doesn't have to.

Picture Comparison

Write about the two classrooms. How are they the same? How are they different?
Example: *Both classes are ESL classes. One class is ESL 101, and the other class is ESL 102. Both classes have six students. In class 101, half the students are women, but in 102…*

A Picture Is Worth a Thousand Words

Write about the people in the photographs.

Describe the people.

What is their relationship?

Where are they?

What are they doing?

How do they feel?

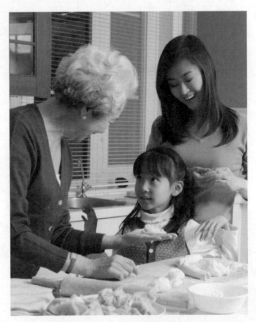

Another Look (Unit 3)

Word Map

Complete the diagram. Use the words in the box.

bathroom	bathtub	bed	bedroom	blanket
counter	dining area	dishes	drawer	dresser	end table
entertainment center	~~faucet~~	food processor	~~house~~	hutch
~~kids' bedroom~~	kitchen	lamp	living room	medicine cabinet
~~napkin~~	~~pillow~~	placemat	pot	rubber mat
~~stereo system~~	~~stove~~	~~stuffed animals~~	table	toothbrush	~~toy chest~~

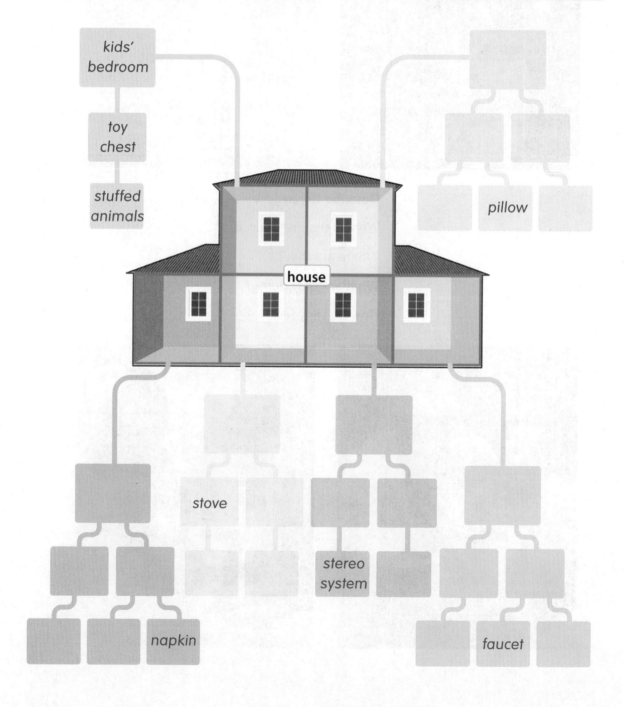

"C" Search

Look at the picture. There are more than 15 items that begin with the letter *c*. Find and circle them. Then write at least 8 sentences describing the picture. Use the circled words in your sentences.

Example: *One man is eating a cheeseburger.*

Pack It Up!

Imagine that you are going away for the weekend. What clothing and accessories will you take for each place? Put at least six items in each suitcase. Use your dictionary for help.

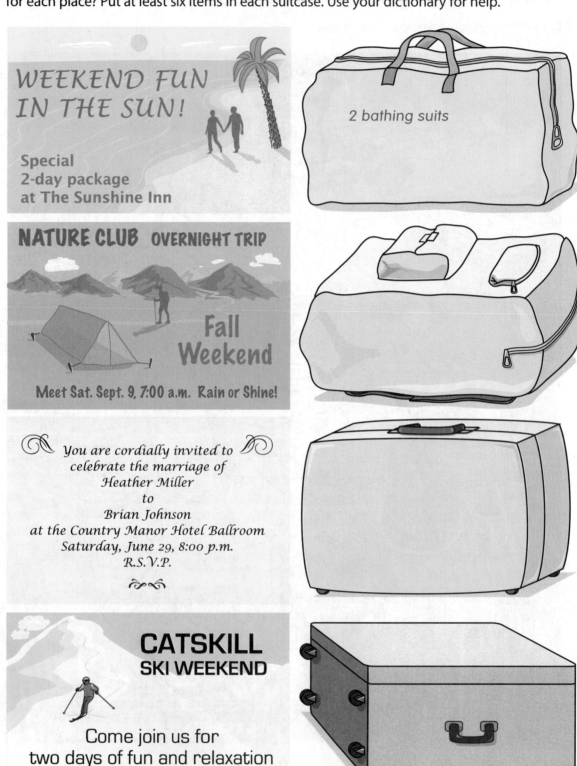

Crossword Puzzle

Complete the crossword puzzle.

ACROSS

1. Identification (short form)
3. _____ your teeth
6. A hole in a tooth
9. It holds your hair in place
10. She's _____ the hospital
13. Women wear it to smell good
14. Take with milk _____ food
15. _____ smoking!
17. Your brain is inside it
19. Your throat is inside it
20. It helps you walk
23. They operate on patients
26. Throw up
28. It's part of the foot
29. It's another part of the foot
32. _____-the-counter medication
34. High temperature
35. Your eye_____ covers your eye

DOWN

2. A serious disease
4. An eye specialist
5. You do this with your eyes
6. Cardiopulmonary resuscitation (short form)
7. Opposite of *arteries*
8. Listen _____ your heart
11. _____ not operate heavy machinery
12. One of the five senses
16. You put a bandage on this
18. Part of your face
21. *Break* (past form)
22. The dentist _____ a cavity yesterday
24. You shave with this
25. You do this with your nose
27. A doctor can look _____ your throat
30. Put _____ sunscreen
31. Intravenous (short form)
33. Registered nurse (short form)

Things Change

Look at the maps of Middletown 50 years ago and Middletown today. What's different? What's the same? Write sentences. Use your own paper.

Example: *There was a bakery on the southeast corner of Elm and Grove. Now there's a coffee shop. There's still a...*

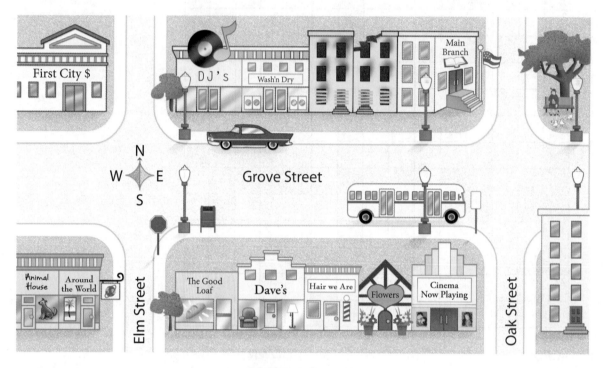

50 Years Ago

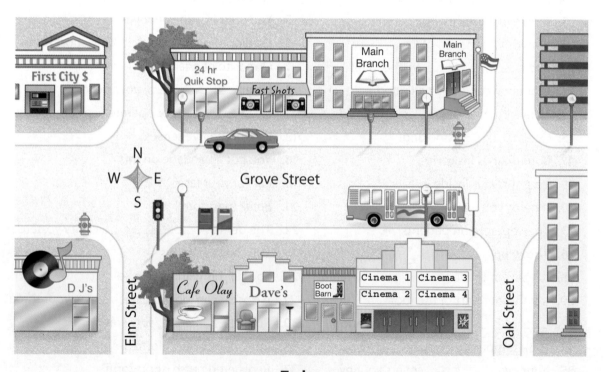

Today

What's Wrong with This Picture?

Look at the picture. Describe ten more problems.

Example: *A subway car is going over the bridge.*

Another Look (Unit 9)

Word Search

1. There are 25 words from Unit 9 in the box. The words go (→), (↓), and (↘). Find and circle them.

i	p	d	e	n	g	i	n	e	e	r	j	z	q	q
n	r	r	r	a	n	e	t	w	o	r	k	g	a	x
t	o	e	x	i	k	o	h	t	c	o	o	k	p	e
e	g	c	j	d	v	r	e	s	u	m	e	i	p	r
r	r	e	r	e	f	e	r	e	n	c	e	s	r	e
n	a	p	p	l	i	c	a	t	i	o	n	w	e	p
s	m	t	g	o	a	l	p	t	w	r	n	s	n	o
h	z	i	r	e	p	a	i	r	y	e	f	e	t	r
i	s	o	w	o	r	k	s	h	o	p	l	w	i	t
p	e	n	l	k	z	c	t	e	a	c	h	d	c	e
f	r	i	a	i	n	t	e	r	p	r	e	t	e	r
i	v	s	l	c	a	r	p	e	n	t	e	r	s	r
v	e	t	e	r	i	n	a	r	i	a	n	d	h	h
p	r	d	i	n	t	e	r	v	i	e	w	p	i	i
r	e	c	r	u	i	t	e	r	c	r	k	j	p	y

2. Put each circled word from Exercise 1 into the correct category.

Jobs	Job Training	Job Search	Job Skills

On the Job

Look at the pictures. Describe each photograph and answer the questions for each picture. Use your own paper.

1.

2.

3.

4.

a. Where are the people?

b. What are they doing?

c. What type of equipment are the people using?

d. Are they using safety equipment? If *yes*, what type?

e. What types of job skills do the people need to do these jobs?

f. How do you think the workers feel?

g. Compare the four jobs. How are they the same? How are they different?

h. Would you like to work in any of these places? Why or why not?

Another Look (Unit 11)

Word Map

Complete the diagram. Use the words in the box.

~~add~~	llama	chemistry	comma	computers
desert	~~DVD drive~~	English composition	~~essay~~	mammal
geography	~~high school~~	~~insect~~	wasp	magnet
~~math~~	mountain peak	mountain range	multiply	ocean
paragraph	~~physics~~	product	~~sand dune~~	science
sentence	~~sum~~	test tube	~~tower~~	biology

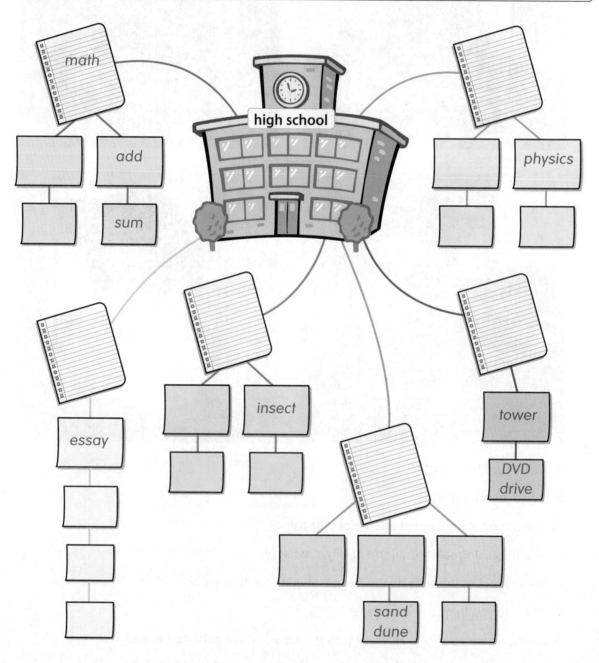

258

Crossword Puzzle

Complete the crossword puzzle.

1		2 s	u	r	f	i	3 n	g		4		5			
												6	7	
8									9					
				10		11	12					13	
	14		15									
16			17						18		
19			20		21			22			
	23								24	
		25				26				
27	28								
		29					30			

ACROSS

2. A water sport
4. A type of player for movies
6. A type of paint
8. _____ horn
11. You can use them to light a campfire
14. Personal _____ player
15. County _____
16. _____ and touch your toes
17. You see them in a theater
18. Type of block for your skin
19. Opposite of *yes*
23. A bike with three wheels
25. _____ & _____ music
26. It has three legs; you put your camera on it
27. _____ the ball with the bat
29. You can swim in it
30. String instrument

DOWN

1. _____ vest
2. A winter snow sport
3. _____ Year's Day
5. _____ crafts
7. _____ skating
9. New York 5, Los Angeles 3
10. Track and _____
12. Type of park
13. Downhill _____
16. You can sit on it in the park
20. You can tie up your boat to this
21. You can look at pictures and charts on it
22. You can see them in a theater
23. You can sleep in it
24. Billiards
28. This _____ the end of the Down clues!

Challenge Exercises

CHALLENGE for page 13

Use the formulas to convert the temperatures. Then describe the temperature. Use the Temperature words on page 13 of your dictionary.

To convert Fahrenheit to Celsius:	To convert Celsius to Fahrenheit:
Subtract (−) 32, multiply (×) by 5, divide (÷) by 9	Multiply (×) by 9, divide (÷) by 5, add (+) 32
Example: 50°F = _____?_____ °C	Example: 25°C = _____?_____ °F
$50 - 32 = 18$ $18 \times 5 = 90$ $90 \div 9 = 10$	$25 \times 9 = 225$ $225 \div 5 = 45$ $45 + 32 = 77$
Answer: 50°F = 10°C	Answer: 25°C = 77°F

a. 25°C = _77°_ F ___warm___

b. 41°F = ___ C _____

c. 59°F = ___ C _____

d. 95°F = ___ C _____

e. 30°C = ___ F _____

f. −20°C = ___ F _____

CHALLENGE for page 15

Look up the information in a phone book or online.

a. List one area code for each city.

Dallas, TX _____   Boston, MA _____

San Francisco, CA _____   Milwaukee, WI _____

b. List one city code and the country code for these locations.

	Country Code	City Code
Mexico City, Mexico		
Montreal, Canada		
Beijing, China		
Moscow, Russia		

CHALLENGE for page 19

Write six sentences comparing times in different cities. Use words, not numbers.

Example: *When it's five in the afternoon in Athens, it's eleven at night in Hong Kong.*

When it's noon Eastern Standard Time, it's ... in ... .

Athens	**7** P.M.	Hong Kong	**1** A.M.*	Riyadh	**8** P.M.
Baghdad	**8** P.M.	Mecca	**8** P.M.	St. Petersburg	**8** P.M.
Bangkok	**12** MIDNIGHT	Mexico City	**11** A.M.	San Juan	**12** NOON
Buenos Aires	**2** P.M.	Paris	**6** P.M.	Seoul	**2** A.M.*
Halifax	**1** P.M.	Rio de Janeiro	**2** P.M.	Tokyo	**2** A.M.*

* = morning of the next day

CHALLENGE for pages 34 and 35

Look at the pie chart. Discuss the questions with a partner.

How many children do American women have?

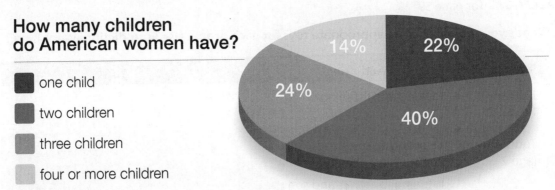

- one child
- two children
- three children
- four or more children

Based on information from: The Pew Research Center, Social and Demographic Trends, 2015.

a. What percentage of women have two children? _____

b. Are you surprised by any of these percentages? Why or why not?

c. What are some advantages and disadvantages to having only one child?

d. What are some advantages and disadvantages to not having any brothers or sisters?

CHALLENGE for pages 42 and 43

Imagine that you are the person in the far left of this picture. Complete the story.

When I went into the room, I felt

_____.
　　　　　　　　　a.

Everyone looked _____.
　　　　　　　　　　　　　　　b.

One person seemed _____.
　　　　　　　　　　　　　　　　　c.

The first thing I did was _____.
　　　　　　　　　　　　　　　　　　d.

That made me feel _____.
　　　　　　　　　　　　　　　　e.

Then I . . .

CHALLENGE for page 59

What's your opinion? Write appropriate toys for each group. Use your dictionary for help.

Age Group	Activities	Toys
Babies (under 2)	looking and listening holding things	*rattle,*
Toddlers (age 2–3)	throwing, rolling, and pushing objects listening to stories and songs	
Children over age 3	learning stories and songs drawing	

CHALLENGE for pages 72 and 73

Look at the receipts. Compare prices. Write six sentences.

Example: *Black beans are cheaper at Dave's.*

```
           DAVE'S
      54 CHURCH STREET
        CHICAGO, IL

1 CAN BLACK BEANS      $0.60
1 GAL APPLE JUICE      $4.99
2 LB FLOUR             $1.69
6 FROZEN BAGELS        $1.09
1 PINT ICE CREAM       $3.99
1 6-OZ FAT FREE
  BANANA YOGURT        $0.80


      THANK YOU FOR
    SHOPPING WITH US
```

```
        SHOPWELL

1 6-OZ FAT FREE
  BANANA YOGURT        $0.90
6 FROZEN BAGELS        $1.19
1 PINT ICE CREAM       $3.99
1 GAL APPLE JUICE      $4.39
2 LB FLOUR             $1.39
1 CAN BLACK BEANS      $0.80


      THANK YOU FOR
    SHOPPING WITH US
```

CHALLENGE for page 75

Check the labels on the containers of four of your favorite foods.
Make a chart like the one below.

Food	Serving Size	Calories	Calories from Fat	Protein	Carbohydrate
ice cream	1/2 cup	170	90	3g	17g

CHALLENGE for page 145

What type of punishment should crimes get? What do you think?
Check (✓) the columns to complete the chart.

Crimes	Prison	Hospitalization	Community Service*	Fines**
assault				
burglary				
drunk driving				
identity theft				
illegal drugs				
murder				
shoplifting				
vandalism				

* *Community service* is work that a person does without pay. An example is cleaning up the sidewalks.
**A *fine* is an amount of money a person has to pay for doing something wrong.

CHALLENGE for page 170

Look at the pairs of jobs. Compare them. What is the same for both jobs?
Use your own paper.

Example: *A childcare worker and a babysitter both work with children.*

a. a childcare worker and a babysitter

b. an accountant and a cashier

c. a butcher and a baker

d. an auto mechanic and an appliance repairperson

e. a businessperson and an administrative assistant

CHALLENGE for page 176

List three job skills. Check (✓) the ones you and a classmate have.

Job Skills	Your Name	Classmate's Name
_____	☐	☐
_____	☐	☐
_____	☐	☐

CHALLENGE for page 197

Look at the worker. Write about the safety hazards. What should the worker do
to protect herself?

Example: *She's wearing sandals. She should wear safety boots.*

Complete the quiz. Look up the information online.

Name: _____   Class: U.S. History 101

Circle the letter of the correct answer.

1. The slaves became free after _____.

   a. the Civil War   **b.** Progressivism   **c.** World War I

2. Armstrong walked on the moon during the _____ Age.

   a. Global   **b.** Space   **c.** Jazz

3. Millions of people died during the few years of _____.

   a. the Cold War   **b.** the Industrial Revolution   **c.** World War II

4. Many people moved to California in search of gold during _____.

   a. Western Expansion   **b.** Reconstruction   **c.** the Information Age

5. More than 25% of all workers couldn't find jobs during the _____.

   a. Global Age   **b.** Great Depression   **c.** Industrial Revolution